Yaddo

MAKING AMERICAN CULTURE

EDITED BY

MICKI MCGEE

The New York Public Library

Columbia University Press   New York

Columbia University Press
Publishers Since 1893
New York   Chichester, West Sussex

Copyright © 2008 The New York Public Library, Astor, Lenox and Tilden Foundations and The Corporation of Yaddo
All rights reserved

Published on the occasion of the exhibition "Yaddo: Making American Culture" presented at The New York Public Library, Humanities and Social Sciences Library, D. Samuel and Jeane H. Gottesman Exhibition Hall, October 24, 2008– February 15, 2009.

For their support of the exhibition, The New York Public Library is grateful to The Corporation of Yaddo and its donors: The Morris and Alma Schapiro Fund; Spencer Trask & Co.; Mary H. White and J. Christopher Flowers; the New York Council for the Humanities; public funds from the New York State Council on the Arts, a state agency; Gladys Krieble Delmas Foundation; George Rickey Foundation, Inc.; Harold Reed; Allan Gurganus; Peter C. Gould; Anthony and Margo Viscusi; Susan Brynteson; Nancy Sullivan; Bruce and Ellen Cohen; Rick Moody; Barbara Toll; Rackstraw Downes; Matthew Stover; Van der Veer Varner; Gardner McFall and Peter Olberg; Joseph Caldwell; John Ashbery; Geoffrey Movius; Patricia Volk; and two anonymous donors.

Support for The New York Public Library's Exhibitions Program has been provided by Celeste Bartos, Mahnaz Ispahani and Adam Bartos, Jonathan Altman, and Sue and Edgar Wachenheim III.

Support for this publication has been provided by Furthermore, a program of the J. M. Kaplan Fund.

Any views, findings, conclusions or recommendations expressed in this publication do not necessarily represent those of the National Endowment for the Humanities.

www.nypl.org

Library of Congress Cataloging-in-Publication Data

Yaddo : making American culture / edited by Micki McGee.
    p. cm.
  Published on the occasion of an exhibition presented at the New York Public Library, Oct. 24, 2008–Feb. 15, 2009.
  Includes bibliographical references and index.
  ISBN 978-0-231-14736-1 (cloth : alk. paper) — ISBN 978-0-231-14737-8 (pbk. : alk. paper)
  1. Yaddo (Artists' colony) 2. Arts, American—New York (State)—Saratoga Springs—20th century. I. McGee, Micki. II. New York Public Library. III. Title.

NX511.S39Y33 2008
700.9747'48—dc22   2008023729

Columbia University Press books are printed on permanent and durable acid-free paper.

This book is printed on paper with recycled content.

Printed in the United States of America

c 10 9 8 7 6 5 4 3 2 1
p 10 9 8 7 6 5 4 3 2 1

References to Internet Web sites (URLs) were accurate at the time of writing. Neither the editor nor Columbia University Press is responsible for URLs that may have expired or changed since the manuscript was prepared.

CONTENTS

FOREWORD

NINE YEARS AGO The New York Public Library acquired The Corporation of Yaddo's archives, making the letters, photographs, artworks, application files, and ephemera in Yaddo's records available to the public for the first time. The Yaddo Records, now catalogued and conserved by the library's Manuscripts and Archives Division, offer both a window into twentieth-century cultural history and an intimate view of one of the nation's most venerable creative communities. This volume and the exhibition that it accompanies celebrate this partnership and highlight the remarkable contribution of Yaddo and its artists to American arts and letters.

Spencer and Katrina Trask founded Yaddo in 1900 with a vision of nurturing the talents of writers, painters, composers, and other creative artists. When its first guests arrived in 1926, Yaddo was hailed by the *New York Times* as a "new and unique experiment, which has no exact parallel in the world of fine arts." When Yaddo opened its doors for its second season, a reporter for the *New York Herald Tribune* wrote, "It is a peculiar gratification to see in America such carefully conducted contributions as this to the nourishing of the spirit and its works in what we are told ad nau-

seam is a materialistic age. One sonnet would justify the whole experiment and render it immortal."

Since that time Yaddo has attained almost mythic status, quietly enduring a century of trials and triumphs, while hosting thousands of artists, including such luminaries as Hannah Arendt, Milton Avery, James Baldwin, Leonard Bernstein, Elizabeth Bishop, Truman Capote, Aaron Copland, Philip Guston, Patricia Highsmith, Langston Hughes, Ted Hughes, Sylvia Plath, Meyer Schapiro, Virgil Thomson, and William Carlos Williams.

The collection that forms the Yaddo Records is an important part of the library's rich and diverse Manuscripts and Archives Division and contributes significantly to its holdings of unique materials documenting twentieth-century literature and culture. The personal papers of many of Yaddo's illustrious visitors, including Truman Capote, Harold Clurman, Doris Grumbach, May

Sarton, Nora Sayre, and Robert Stone are owned by the library and are complemented by the Yaddo Records. The acquisition of the Yaddo Records was made possible by a grant from the Morris and Alma Schapiro Fund.

As it enters its second century, Yaddo continues to fulfill the vision of Katrina and Spencer Trask. The New York Public Library will receive further papers for the Yaddo Records at least through the year 2026, the centenary of the year Yaddo, in its present institutional form, received its first guests. Together our institutions support not only the making of American culture, but also the conservation of our cultural heritage.

David S. Ferriero,
Andrew W. Mellon Director,
The New York Public Libraries

Elaina Richardson, President,
The Corporation of Yaddo

[OPPOSITE] Group at Triuna, Yaddo's Lake George camp, 1928. *Standing*: Granville English, George Foster Peabody, Elizabeth Sparhawk-Jones, unidentified man, Marjorie Peabody Waite, Paul Reno, unidentified woman, unidentified man, unidentified woman, Edgar White Burrill. *Seated*: Elizabeth Ames, Alfred Kreymborg, unidentified man, Dorothy Kreymborg, Helen Pierce.

PREFACE

WHEN YADDO AND The New York Public Library determined that Yaddo's archive would have a permanent home at the library, scholars of American cultural history had cause to cheer. More than five hundred boxes of letters, journals, manuscripts, guest records, photographs, charts, and ephemera dating from 1870 to 1980, including fragile glass photographic negatives and rare wax cylinder sound recordings, would be made available for the first time to researchers and the general public.

Such a plan was not without risks. For Yaddo, in particular, there is more than a bit of boldness and daring in this decision. Unlike, for example, government files obtained under the Freedom of Information Act, Yaddo's papers were not redacted with broad strokes of black pen. Rather, the contents of the archive were (and are) unexpurgated records of an organization that navigated the roiled waters of the twentieth century while fostering some of the century's most distinguished talents. Yaddo's triumphs and tribulations, and those of its guests, members, and governing board, are available for any reader's review.

The guardians of Yaddo's archive before its placement at The New York Public Library—among them Susan Brynteson, Margo Viscusi, Linda Collins, Yaddo executive directors Curtis Harnack and Myra Sklarew, and Yaddo

presidents Michael Sundell and Elaina Richardson—imagined that the documents therein would serve as a rich resource for students of twentieth-century social and cultural history. In this volume a team of cultural critics, some associated with Yaddo as former guests, and some not, set out to take a first look into the Yaddo Records. They have returned with tales of refuge and resilience, community, conflict, and collaboration, and invention and forbearance in the face of daunting obstacles. In particular they have returned with a story of the power of human creativity to shape not only individual lives but also the cultural landscape against which those lives unfold. Other stories will no doubt emerge in the years to come as the Yaddo Records are further explored.

With this book and the exhibitions that accompany it, The Corporation of Yaddo, The New York Public Library, and a circle of libraries and archives across the country celebrate Yaddo and its artists. In addition to a major exhibition at The New York Public Library, a series of fourteen exhibitions will con-

tinue through 2009 at libraries and archives nationwide featuring the work of Yaddo artists and writers whose papers they hold.

The Hayden Library at Arizona State University will feature the work of Yaddo writer and activist Agnes Smedley. The Flannery O'Connor Collection at Georgia College and State University will explore O'Connor's 1948–1949 visit to Yaddo. The Harry Ransom Center at the University of Texas at Austin will look at the work of numerous Yaddo writers, including Elizabeth Hardwick, Carson McCullers, Evelyn Scott, Bernard Malamud, Celia Zukofsky, and Louis Zukofsky, for whom the center holds papers. The Houghton Library at Harvard University will feature the work of poet Robert Lowell, whose concerns about the political leanings of previous Yaddo guests led to Yaddo's notorious red scare. The Eudora Welty Education and Visitors Center of the Mississippi Department of Archives and History will examine Welty's formative summer at Yaddo, where she completed her first collection of short stories, *A Curtain of Green*. The University of

Maryland Libraries will mount an exhibition featuring their materials on Katherine Anne Porter, who was a guest at Yaddo and resident of Saratoga Springs in the 1940s and 1950s. Northwestern University Library will exhibit the papers of Harvey Breit, an early Yaddo guest who was responsible for introducing the poets Marcia Nardi and William Carlos Williams, thus changing the trajectory of Williams's famous poem *Paterson*. The Pennsylvania State University Libraries will present the work of Yaddo writers Kenneth Burke, Katherine Shattuck, and Janet Frame. Saratoga Springs Public Library will explore Yaddo's history, locale, and environs. The William Allan Neilson Library at Smith College will look at Newton Arvin's pivotal role in Yaddo's history, as well as at the work of Yaddo and Smith alumna Sylvia Plath. The Green Library at Stanford University will feature works by Yaddo writers Denise Levertov, Tillie Olsen, and Wallace Stegner. The Special Collections Research Center at Syracuse University will take a close look at the life and work of Granville Hicks, a longtime member of Yaddo's community. The Grolier Club of New York will feature rare books and ephemera related to Yaddo's history from the collection of Susan Brynteson. The University of Delaware Library will display works from the papers of John Malcolm Brinnin and Paul Bowles. And the University of North Carolina at Chapel Hill, which holds the papers of Yaddo writer Gail Godwin, will highlight that collection.

These distinguished partners join with The Corporation of Yaddo and The New York Public Library to celebrate the richness of our cultural history and the windows onto that history that libraries and archives make possible.

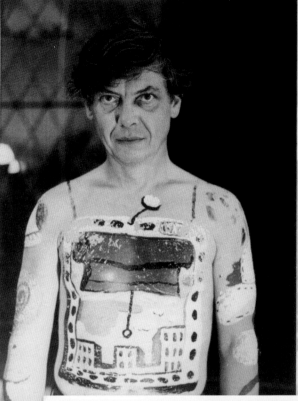
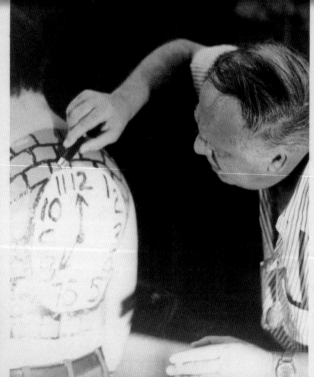
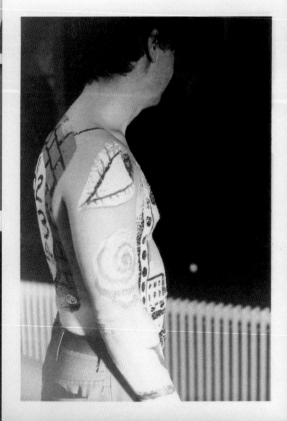
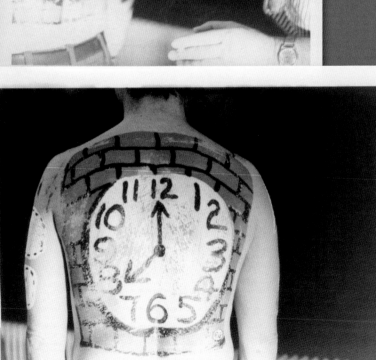

Painter Philip Guston and writer William Gass were guests in 1969. Here Guston uses Gass as an impromptu canvas for his characteristic cartoons.

1 / CREATIVE POWER

YADDO AND THE MAKING OF AMERICAN CULTURE

Micki McGee

Is it right for one person to own vast property whilst another has nowhere to lay his head? Should the fortunate few possess so much more than the unfortunate many who do the work? The wretched inequality of life staggers me. What right have I to an income that enables me to live a life of ease and luxury, whilst my fellow-men can wrest by their toil only the merest pittance. It is all wrong. The time will come when the distribution of wealth will be very different. In the meantime, however, no one alone can change the established order: we can only go on working and doing our best to make new laws and to help on a new order: and during the waiting for the coming of these economic changes great homes and great houses will still have their place; and our first individual duty is to make, in that waiting time, at least a new spiritual order.

—KATRINA TRASK, 1918

Yaddo we are glad to believe has come to be a source of fruitful help & inspiration to many, and especially to those Gifted with Creative power & who have had the impulse to use it for their fellow men.... We desire to found here a permanent Home to which shall come from time to time for Rest & Refreshment authors painters sculptors musicians and other artists both men & women few in number and chosen for their Creative Gifts & besides & not less for the power & the will & the purpose to make these Gifts useful to the World.

—SPENCER TRASK, 1900

FINANCIER AND philanthropist Spencer Trask and his wife, the poet and playwright Katrina Trask, conceived of Yaddo as a gift to those "gifted with Creative power"—as a place of respite for creative workers whose labors were not likely to be supported by the mechanisms of an expanding market economy that had so generously rewarded the Trasks' own undertakings.[1] The 400-acre artists' retreat in upstate New York was incorporated in 1900 at a moment in America's history when a division between popular and high culture had only recently taken hold. With this new cultural stratification came the idea that an elite culture, one that would uplift rather than pander to popular tastes, would require new, nonmarket-driven forms of patronage.[2] The ideal of culture as a gift to be protected from the exchanges of the marketplace emerged.[3] Yet despite these origins in a late-nineteenth-century moment when economic and cultural elites were concerned with supporting a particular sort of "pure" high art with a capital "A" that would civilize the teeming masses, across the coming decades a divergent array of cultural products, many of them immensely popular and hardly haute, can be traced to Yaddo's support. Yaddo's story, only now emerging from its records made public at The New York Public Library, provides a window on these developments. Yaddo's archive reveals not only the labors of those cultural figures whose names might appear in a survey course of twentieth-century American literature or art but also a sense of the vast expanse of usually underrecognized creative activity and unrecognized administrative labor that contributes to the bedrock of cultural life.

The story of Yaddo's impact on American culture begins with the Trask family in the late nineteenth century. Spencer Trask was a passionate member of an emerging class of financiers who bet on the new technologies and intellectual properties of the Gilded Age and won big. He built his fortune from the expansion of the railways, the distribution of electricity, and by rallying support for the *New York Times* when the paper seemed doomed to bankruptcy.[4] Katrina Trask, in keeping with the gendered spheres of the era, ran the family's multiple households, cultivated her own talents as a writer, and developed a series of salons at Yaddo that hosted some of the most distinguished artists and luminaries of the day. The Trasks shared an abiding faith in creativity as a transformative force that would necessarily improve life for humankind. Creative power would not only ameliorate the conflicts and hardships wrought by modernity's ingenuity but also transmute personal loss, of which the Trasks would have more than their share, into public goods.

The mythology that has sprung up around Yaddo's founding inevitably places individual actors as prime movers in a saga of personal triumph over considerable adversity.[5] However, from other perspectives, Yaddo owes its existence to a convergence of forces. A roiling and rapacious American capitalism that was expanding westward with the advance of the railways allowed Yaddo's founders to accumulate a vast fortune, some $15 million at the turn of the century, roughly equivalent to $1.1 billion today.[6] An economic inequality that Katrina Trask herself found deeply troubling was at the heart of Yaddo's emergence. The prevalence of childhood mortality that just a few decades later would be vastly reduced with the medical advances of antibiotics and vaccines deprived the Trasks of their four biological heirs. The nineteenth-century division of daily life into separate arenas for men and women focused Katrina Trask's considerable talents on develop-

The largest hall in the mansion, known as the Great Hall, houses numerous works of art, including turn-of-the-century portraits of Katrina and Spencer Trask by Arthur de Ferraris.

ing Yaddo as a salon for artists and intellectuals of the day. Perhaps most significantly, these social and material circumstances were animated by a Romantic impulse, an antimodernist sensibility replete with a pre-Raphaelite nostalgia for round-table gatherings in medieval courts, courtly damsels in flowing white gowns, and mystical epiphanies in wooded glens. At Yaddo these Arthurian ideals were inscribed in the baronial mansion itself, with its heralds and the Trasks' own emblems—for her, the rose, and for him, the pine tree. Katrina's image, as the woman in white who would preserve purity and morality from the encroachment of instrumental reason and the monotony, regimentation, and conformity of an advancing industrial era, presides over the mansion.

For nineteenth-century Romantics, creativity was the antidote not only for the shortcomings of any given life but for the failures of modernity as well. The poet was the hero of this world, and the bucolic countryside, rather than the barricaded boulevard, was the site of social transformation.[7] Creative evolution offered an appealing alternative to the political revolution that everywhere threatened to erupt and change the social landscape. Culture—a "high culture" that was not readily viable in the realm of commercial exchange—had begun to be seen as sacred, rarefied, and redemptive, as a civilizing force that would enlighten the populace and transform the unruly masses.[8] Private symphonies and operas became not-for-profit enterprises, and the groundwork for the museum as a nondenominational temple of fine art was laid. Artists' retreats, though not exclusively a phenomenon of modernity, were part of this trend toward alternative means of artistic patronage and a desire to sequester art making from the labor of everyday life and the vagaries of the marketplace.[9] America's artists' retreats, among them the MacDowell Colony in New Hampshire, Byrdcliffe in New York's Catskills, the Provincetown Fine Arts Workshop in Massachusetts, and the Cos Cob and Old Lyme colonies in Connecticut, offered rural or seaside refuge from the noise, congestion, and poverty of urban centers.[10] The new spiritual order that Katrina Trask envisioned was an alternative to the breakneck speed of industrialization and the ruthless competition of capitalism. Yaddo would be a place apart, an alternative universe where shadows—not only of childhood mortality but also of desperate poverty and urban squalor—would be vanquished in the glow of a "sacred fire."[11]

George Foster Peabody was Spencer Trask's business partner for a quarter of a century, a close and influential family friend, and a resolute admirer of Katrina, whom he married in the last year of her life. Shortly after Katrina died in 1922, Peabody set about establishing Yaddo in accordance with the trust the Trasks had set up in 1900. The civic-

Elizabeth Ames, George Foster Peabody, and Marjorie Peabody Waite on the porch at Triuna in 1928.

minded progressive and philanthropist had developed a close relationship with a young woman named Marjorie Knappen Waite, whom he adopted in 1926.[12] Waite's sister, Elizabeth Ames, visited the estate in 1923 and took on the task of cataloguing the Trasks' eclectic art collection. Within the year, the thirty-eight-year-old Ames was named the first executive director of Yaddo.

Although little is known about Elizabeth Ames before her arrival at Yaddo, over the next four and a half decades she would have a lasting influence on American arts and letters through her leadership and administration of the Trask-Peabody legacy. Ames took on the project of establishing the administration of Yaddo with the utmost dedication. She reached out to leaders in the literary, musical, and visual arts to establish a network of confidential advisers, including Lewis Mumford, Alfred Kreymborg, and the Van Dorens—Irita, Carl, and Mark—whose recommendations shaped the earliest guest lists and, in time, the membership of Yaddo and its board of directors. Alfred Kreymborg,

who was editing the influential annual *American Caravan* with Lewis Mumford, wrote Ames in 1928 to alert her to the fact that "Mr. Aaron Copland, the distinguished young American composer, is most anxious to spend a couple of months at Yaddo if the idea is agreeable to you and there is room for him."[13] Ames would find a space for Copland, who visited in 1930, composing his *Piano Variations* in the Stone Tower, a studio that had once served as the estate's icehouse. He also conceived and established the Yaddo Festival of Contemporary Music, which continued for two decades and helped to reposition American classical music. Lewis Mumford was a particularly influential adviser. In 1928 he wrote Ames: "Are the gates to Yaddo closed for the summer? If not, I should like to recommend to you Mr. Newton Arvin. He is a very able young critic & scholar, one of the very best in the country."[14] Arvin visited in the summer of 1928, working on his biography of Nathaniel Hawthorne and developing a relationship with Yaddo and Ames that continued for the rest of his life. (Barry

Werth's essay in this volume considers Arvin's long and complicated relationship with Yaddo.) Mark Van Doren, then an editor at the *Nation*, recommended Lionel Trilling, who in turn nominated Alfred Kazin, who in turn proposed a young Smith College student: "The best writer at Smith, and a very remarkable girl in every way, is Sylvia Plath, she is the real thing. She is graduating in June."[15] Also in 1928, Irita Van Doren, book review editor at the *New York Herald Tribune*, recommended a promising young poet and translator: "I haven't any candidates right off the bat, except one young man, Malcolm Cowley, for whom Yaddo would be perfect. . . . He is a poet of infrequent but distinctive verse, an excellent translator from the French . . . poor as a church mouse with no visible means of support."[16] Cowley's prospects would improve. He went on to join the editorial staff of the *New Republic*, wrote his first book of literary criticism, *Exile's Return*, at Yaddo in 1932, and participated in shaping policies and admissions at Yaddo over the next five decades, supporting the applications of Agnes Smedley, Truman Capote, and countless others.[17]

Determining who was to be invited to Yaddo was of central importance; establishing the routine of daily life at Yaddo was only slightly less so. Ames would develop a regimen at Yaddo that was singularly conducive to any creative art that required solitude. Quiet hours—from 9:00 A.M. to 4:00 P.M. each day—prohibited visiting or loud conversation anywhere on the premises. Deviations from this rule ended in enforced departures. A 1931 guest, Diana Trilling, reported that she was summarily dispatched back to New York City on the next train "without lunch" for having visited a photographer during quiet hours to have her photograph shot in available light.[18] In general, families were supposed to be left behind in the city.[19] The exception to this rule was for couples where both were artists and had been invited on their individual merits or, in the earliest days of Yaddo (between 1926 and 1940), when the corporation also hosted guests at a second estate on Triuna Island in Lake George and allowed some guests with families to stay on at a renovated farmhouse on the north end of the property called North Farm.

The idea that one needed to be sequestered for creativity to thrive, although widely accepted, was one that some writers have found perplexing. The theologian and writer Reinhold Niebuhr, perhaps best known for crafting the Serenity Prayer invoked by millions of recovering addicts, was invited by Ames in 1937 at the suggestion of Lewis Mumford. Niebuhr expressed bewilderment at the idea of leaving his family to isolate himself and do creative work: "I am afraid that even such an inviting project as a month at your place would do me no good if the hospitality is meant just for an individual, as I have a wife and small son."[20] Others invited to Yaddo—for example Robinson Jeffers, recommended by Mark Van Doren in 1926, and Arthur Miller, invited in 1955—declined invitations as they felt well situated to write exactly where they were.[21] The poet Delmore Schwartz, who was recently married when he arrived at Yaddo in 1939 for a visit, defied the ban, smuggling meals to his new bride, Gertrude Buckman, whom he had hidden in his studio.[22] Eventually, Ames relented and allowed the newlyweds to join the group for dinner in the mansion. Novelist Mario Puzo, who had twice visited Yaddo to work on his earliest novels, left early on a third visit, writing Ames: "Sorry I didn't get to see you before I left and I was sorry I couldn't stay. I was having a good time but for some reason I wasn't working too well. Proba-

bly because the older I get the more Italian-peasant I get and so I can't be happy unless I'm bossing a bunch of kids around and hearing a lot of noise."[23]

An escape from family responsibilities and earning a living was not the only sort of refuge that Yaddo provided. Shortly after it began receiving guests, the stock market crash ushered in an era of widespread economic desperation. Ames saw to it that all possible buildings on the property were made ready to house artists and writers whose prospects were crushed by the economic crisis of the Great Depression. As the financial crisis deepened, life at the colony was adjusted so that shrinking budgets could meet the needs of more artists and writers than ever before. A formal breakfast and lunch gave way to a buffet in the morning and lunchboxes at noon, saving on staff time, and guests were asked to take care of their own housekeeping.[24]

Artists and writers counted on their time at Yaddo as a lifeline for themselves and their work, and extending stays became a matter of concern.[25] Until the mid-1940s, confidential advisers made recommendations for Yaddo's guest list, but Ames had extraordinary discretion in deciding whom to invite and to whom extended invitations of more than a month would be made. Beneficiaries of Ames's favor included a young John Cheever, who spent several Depression summers at Yaddo, including at least one working as the boatman ferrying guests back and forth across Lake George to the Triuna property; novelist James T. Farrell, whose wife, Dorothy, worked as Ames's assistant, drawing a paycheck that supported the couple while they lived at the North Farm property; and husband and wife visual artists Philip Reisman and Penina Kishore, each of whom created illustrations for Yaddo.

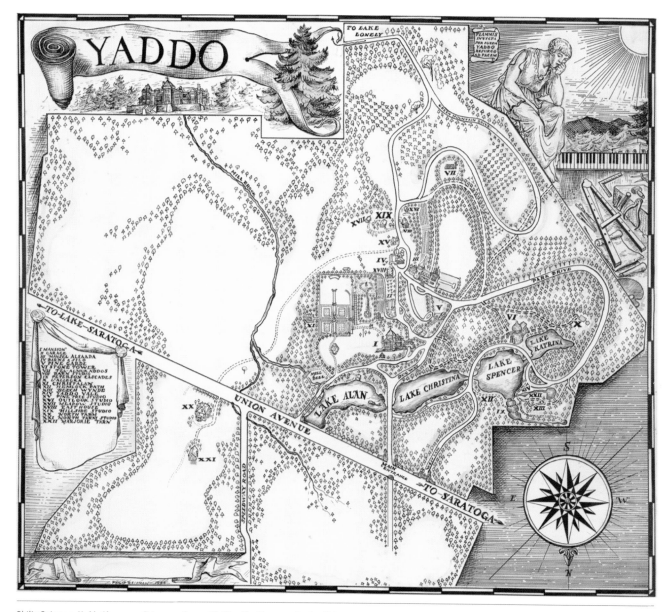

Philip Reisman. *Yaddo Map*, 1934. Reisman, along with his wife, illustrator Penina Kishore, was a guest in 1933 and 1934.

As the economic crisis of the Depression precipitated the rise of European fascism and World War II, Yaddo increasingly came to host individuals escaping the expansion of the German Third Reich. When the mansion reopened for the summer of 1939, Yaddo's guest list included six refugees from Germany and Austria, including Hermann Broch, author of *The Sleepwalkers*; Rudolf Charles von Ripper, a painter and printmaker; and Richard Berman, a newspaper correspondent, who would

die of a heart attack in his room at Yaddo when he learned of the German invasion of Poland.[26] By the summer of 1943, Yaddo's guests also included the Danish novelist Karin Michaëlis, whose support for Jewish refugees ultimately forced her to flee the advancing German army.

Although artists at Yaddo were insulated from the demands of daily life—from familial obligations and the labors associated with making a living—isolation was (and remains) an occupational hazard of many creative pursuits. While

solitude may be productive, isolation can be stultifying. At Yaddo, the hours spent writing, composing, and painting, largely alone, are alleviated both by the social life that unfolds in the late afternoon and evening and by the sense that one is surrounded by the history of artists and writers who have labored at Yaddo. In later essays in this volume, literary critic Helen Vendler describes her experience of solitude and community at Yaddo, Allan Gurganus hails the legacy that launches and supports ongoing

YADDO
Yesterday and Today

MARJORIE PEABODY WAITE

With Illustrations By
PENINA KISHORE

SARATOGA SPRINGS, NEW YORK, 1933

THE STONE TOWER STUDIO

by a pleasant walk through the Queen's Woods at sunset to a cheering cup of tea or other refreshment at the Mansion.

In the first season of Yaddo's functioning in the new life, the summer of 1926, this sequestered Stone Tower became the much-prized Composer's Studio. The deep silence of the surrounding woods contributes to the pliancy of the artist occupying this studio to the Muses' inspiration, as each successive occupant has declared, and the creative work has been far more fruitful than anticipated. The walk to and fro in the heavily shaded woods on the pine-tassel carpet along the edge of the ravine in whose depth lies the gemlike lake, forms a preparing way out of and into the world of people.

OTHER STUDIOS

The Outlook Studio was the first of the outside studios to be built in the summer of 1926 at the edge of the

65

---

verse for tomorrow as a prophecy for the new Yaddo.'

" I found it at last and opened to the morrow when we should arrive at Yaddo. This is what I read — 'The glory of this latter House shall be greater than of the former, and in this place will I give Peace.'

" We cut the last part of that verse upon the cornerstone of the new house — at the base of the tower structure.

" For the hall, Spencer had Tiffany make for the great fireplace a beautiful Mosaic — a Phoenix rising from the ashes — and underneath are the Latin words:—

Flammis Invicta per Ignem
Yaddo Resurgo ad Pacem

THE MANSION

32

Penina Kishore prepared the illustrations for Marjorie Peabody Waite's 1933 book, *Yaddo: Yesterday and Today.*

---

205 West 57 Street New York City.

1st of May 1943

Dear Mrs Elizabeth Ames:

I would be more than happy to come to Yaddo this summer, as I have heard what a wonderful resting-and-working place it has proved to be. Every time would suit me, but still I would greatly prefere, if possible to come in June, also because Mr Kantorowicz then will be there and we are so good old friends. But of more importance is, that I, if so in the beginning of the summer stay there, it will be more easy for me to find out about when the book- my autobiography- can be finished, which the publishers are interested to know.

Through the little booklet I see that some introduction letters are craved, and it will be easy for me to procure such- if necessary. In such a case I think it suitable to ask Mrs James Laidlow, our Danish Minister to Washington Mr. Kaufmann and madame Litvinoff or Dorothy Thompson. But as I have written about fifty books, translated in more than twenty five languages, I have a feeling, you do not insist upon such. I will ask Kantorowicz.

Since I came over here, and stayed, it was in 1939, I have had a rather difficult time, because I came only for visiting my sister and remain half a year, Then the wife of our minister for foreign affaires in Denmark, Mrs Elna Munck came over, and we travelled together all over the S States. She left in Summer and wrote me in September a letter, which showed me, that it would be dangerous for me as a close ennemy of Hitler

---

to return. I now was here without money, without manuscripts or anything which would be of help. Of course only what happened to thousands of people. Anyhow, while in Europe I had a pretty position, I seem to be rather unknown here. And so a little depression a new thing for me, made me feel afraid trying to find my way. My sister, the baroness Dahlerup and her husband took me into their home, but as they by no means are well to do, also this worked as a heavy load on my shoulders. Therefore, if I now could finish my memoirs, which will be interesting because of my life and the people I met and who became my friends, everything will turn out well.

Again, I would be so very happy to come to Yaddo this summer.

With the best greetings

yours

Karin Michaëlis

The immensely successful Danish novelist Karin Michaëlis was forced to flee the Nazi occupation of her country. With this letter, she accepted an invitation to Yaddo in 1943.

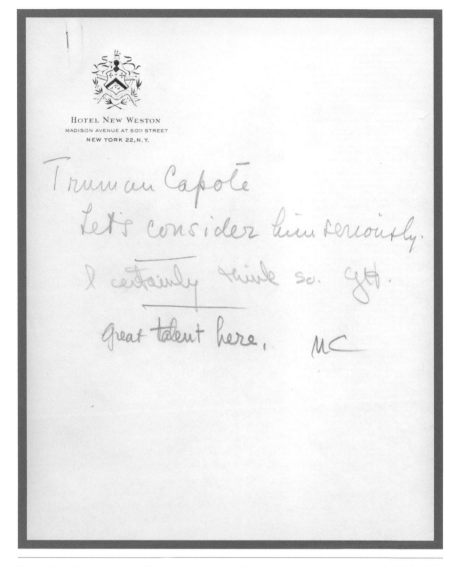

HOTEL NEW WESTON
MADISON AVENUE AT 50ᵀᴴ STREET
NEW YORK 22, N.Y.

Truman Capote

Let's consider him seriously.

I certainly think so. GH.

Great talent here. MC

Truman Capote's application to Yaddo in 1946 was considered by an admissions committee that included Granville Hicks and Malcolm Cowley.

accomplishment, and Marcelle Clements captures the inspiration that comes from working in a room where literary legends have also toiled.

Social life at Yaddo, especially dalliances and liaisons of any variety, has become the material of literary lore. Newton Arvin, the refined and closeted literature professor from Smith College, met and mentored the young, unabashed Truman Capote at Yaddo in the summer of 1947. The three-year relationship that followed was life-changing for each of them, but espe- cially for Capote, who benefited from Arvin's passionate support.[27] Henry Roth, whose 1934 novel *Call It Sleep* used the groundbreaking modernist stream of consciousness of James Joyce's *Ulysses* to portray New York's Lower East Side, came to Yaddo in 1938 at the recommendation of his Greenwich Village lover, Yaddo adviser Eda Lou Walton. That summer he met and married the singer and composer Muriel Parker, who put aside her career in music to support their life together. The novelist Josephine Herbst visited Yaddo in 1939 and fell in love with painter Marion Greenwood, forming a deep relationship that ultimately led to the end of her long marriage to fellow writer John Herrman.[28] On a later Yaddo visit, Herbst met the poet Jean Garrigue, and the two formed a passionate and lifelong attachment.[29] An infatuated Carson McCullers, visiting Yaddo for the first time in 1941, is said to have prostrated herself outside the door of Katherine Anne Porter's room until a disgusted Porter, anxious to avoid being late to dinner, stepped over the younger writer without saying a word.[30] The enmity that followed peppers the letters of McCullers, Porter, and their mutual friend, composer David Diamond, who attempted, often to no avail, to maintain good relations with each of them. Porter wrote of McCullers and a fellow guest, Rebecca Pitts: "My personal feeling about them is very simple: so long as they do not get near enough to me to behave as they so barbarously do to me . . . I cannot care what they do or where they are. I think— and this opinion was formed on a first reading of Carson's first book long before I ever saw her or any one who knew her—that it was a peculiarly corrupt, perverted mind and a small stunted talent incapable of growth: and her further work has borne this out in my mind."[31]

The constant flow of guests, some distinguished and some emerging talents, created a heady mix that allowed for what social networks theorists call "the strength of weak links."[32] A community gains strength in the numbers of connections and relationships rather than simply by the intensity of the relationships or the frequency of contact. Close friends or mentors may offer the occasional assistance. For example, Katherine Anne Porter sponsored the young and unknown Eudora Welty for a visit to Yaddo in 1941 and wrote a critically important introduction to the

Monday

Precious Spooky:

A pretty full day, again--for of course I had the exam at eight o'clock, and now have twenty-five blue-books to read for my sins, and this afternoon I have to spend at Charley Hills helping to read honors exams--an engaging prospect. Fortunately some of my own blue-books are pretty good--as well as pretty rotten, too--and this does something to relieve the grind.

Did you ever hear of a young writer named McGehee? He is applying to be admitted to Yaddo, and a few pages of the ms. of a novel he submitted strike me as rather remarkable. He is recommended by R P Warren and, oddly enough, by my college friend, Harold Ehrensperger, with whom I have been out of touch for 20 years, but who is now, I learn, editing a magazine in Nashville entitled _motive_. Do you know it? I don't--but H E sent me, without further communication, the carbon of a letter he had written to E A about McGehee and his work: I'm afraid that (I mean, the silence) suggest some bitterness, and probably a justifiable one. But McGehee (who also included a summary of his novel) strikes me as a possibility.

Reading the last chapter or two of Karen Michaelis's auto-biography made me repent a little my having been so contempt-uous in speaking of her book--not that these chapters are any better writ-ten or any more "important," than the rest but that they are humanly rather touching and really poignant. Apparently--and she was once enor-mously popular in Europe and quite prosperous--after the Nazis invaded Denmark (she was living in New York) K. M. lost about every-thing she had, and was living during the War on a few cents a day.

She was an old lady by that time, late sixties or early seventies, and one could forgive her for indulging even in a little public self-pity, or striking a note or two of Hard Luck. But not one. No, on the contrary, she alleges that she always found N. Y. a delightful place to live in, and describes at some length the various forms of entertainment one can have there at no expense at all. There is something really touching in the image of the old girl, once an "eminent" and certainly a rich Danish novelist, the Gertrude Atherton of Copenhagen, traipsing about on subways and buses to free museums, to the Cloisters, to the Natural His-tory Museum, etc., and apparently enjoying herself genuinely as she did so. That much passion for experience is surely a kind of genius in itself, and it makes me imagine that, bad as her novels probably are in the strict sense, they must have a cer-tain quality, of energy, of warmth, of expansive feeling, which might keep them from being beneath contempt. I don't know--and you must have heard quite enough about Karen Michaelis by this time. (Though the note on Yaddo is mildly amusing. She speaks there being of forty or fifty outdoor studios on the place--with a fine dis-regard for statistical literalness that may also be genius.)

Now to run down to Rahar's for a bite of lunch, and then to the Hills'. I love you, my darling, and send you a thousand kisses to prove it.

In 1946 and 1947 Newton Arvin maintained an intimate correspondence with Truman Capote in which many Yaddo guests and applicants were discussed.

younger author's first book of short sto-ries, _A Curtain of Green_.[33] But a larger network of support, inspired by the amicable surroundings that Yaddo fos-tered, provides more extensive and long-lasting assistance. So, for example, sev-eral Yaddo guests rallied to support the work of ailing composer Dante Fiorillo, assisting him in securing the first of two Guggenheim foundation grants.[34] Yaddo friends John Cheever, Saul Bellow, Al-fred Kazin, Leslie Katz, and Hilton Kramer ensured that realist novelist and political activist Josephine Herbst would not live out her senior years in penury by facilitating support from the Rocke-feller Foundation, the National Institute of Arts and Letters, and, in Kramer's case, by handling the Beinecke Library's purchase of her papers.[35] Robert Lowell and Flannery O'Connor would leave Yaddo in the winter of 1949 in part so that Lowell could introduce the younger writer to his editor, Robert Giroux, whom he thought would be more sym-pathetic to her singular vision.[36] As Ames observed, "Yaddo brings together naturally and in amity a wide range of backgrounds and personalities, minds and interests. Probably nowhere else is this diversity of minds and experience to be found coming together, not for a purpose common to all, but each for its especial achievements, the contribution to the whole being a by-product. The important contributions which our guests make to each other are spontane-ous and occur because of Yaddo's un-programmed leisure."[37] The secret of Yaddo's success in supporting artists was in kindling the affectionate affilia-tion among members that would build a network of support for them far beyond the gated enclave in Saratoga Springs. As painter Clyfford Still wrote to Ames after a 1934 visit: "Yaddo has given me friends to paint for: you, and Dante, Jimmy, Harris, the Norrises--ever so many."[38] These creative communities, as Karl Willers points out in his consider-ation of the visual artists who have worked at Yaddo, are in great measure the source of an artist's creative power. Although an artist's work may seem to be authored alone, an artwork is a social activity, situated in a dialogue with the conventions that preceded it and, if widely enough disseminated, the art-works that follow.[39]

Although never at the center of Yad-do's mission, collaborations were also an inevitable outcome of Yaddo's pattern of mutual aid and community building. The early avant-garde photographer and filmmaker Ralph Steiner, who was a guest in 1929, collaborated with Yaddo advisers Lewis Mumford and Aaron Copland (as well as with Willard Van Dyke) on the 1939 film *The City*, a visual essay articulating Mumford's vision for environmental planning. Critic and memoirist Alfred Kazin, a guest numerous times between 1942 and 1971, and photographer Henri Cartier-Bresson, a guest in 1946 and 1947, published a text-and-image homage to the Brooklyn Bridge in the September 1946 issue of *Harper's Bazaar*. The two had been guests at Yaddo in 1946 when Cartier-Bresson, who had been in hiding throughout World War II, arrived in the United States to put finishing touches on his Museum of Modern Art retrospective, an exhibition that the museum had originally imagined would be a posthumous memorial. In 1959 poet Mona van Duyn and printmaker Frederick Becker collaborated on a limited edition book, *Valentines to the Wild World*. Mischievous and informal partnerships flourished as well—painter Philip Guston adorned the body of novelist William Gass; poets Jane Mayhall and May Swenson wrote and performed the "Yaddo Blues," an insider's lament of being cast back out into the real world at the end of a stay.

Perhaps the greatest number of collaborations took place in the more formal settings of the Yaddo music festivals. Despite the financial hardships of the Depression era, Ames and Yaddo's directors took the remarkable step of sponsoring the Festival of Contemporary American Music in 1932. Instituted

at the urging of Aaron Copland, the festival was intended to establish a place for America's classical composers to share their work and to develop a more congenial dialogue with music critics who had been openly hostile to newer musical explorations. Tim Page's essay details the history of this seminal project and the sense of community and collaboration that the festivals engendered. In 1937 Ames and Yaddo's board again defied the economic constraints of the period by investing in a recording system that preserved many of the performances of the 1937–1940 seasons.[40] Over the following two decades, there would be nine festivals (later renamed Music Periods) that fostered collaborations between musicians and writers that often continued long after the festivals at Yaddo had concluded. Marc Blitzstein composed an opera based on Bernard Malamud's short story "Idiots First" (1957); Ned Rorem wrote "Conversation" (1957), a song for piano and voice based on a poem by Elizabeth Bishop; and David Diamond composed "Twisted Trinity" (1943), a cycle of songs based on texts by Carson McCullers and others.

"Community" and "collaboration"—these words invoke a sense of an unambiguous goodness, a vision of cheerful cooperation of the parts resulting in a seamless whole. But any community or collaboration that exists without contention is fictive, utopian precisely because they exist nowhere.[41] Yaddo is no different in this respect. Often controversies concern the boundaries of the community itself: who shall be included and who shall be excluded, or in some cases banished. In the earliest years of the community, sponsors made these decisions, identifying and recommending possible guests. Later, admissions committees evaluated work samples in a more formal process that determined

who would be invited. The fabric of a community is woven by these many modest moments of admitting one and rejecting another, in the reinvitation or refusal of the next. An institution, although conceived in its papers of incorporation, is made and remade in the minutiae of such actions. Over time and in the aggregate, these decisions accumulate into a sense of who made an appropriate Yaddo guest—and who wasn't quite suitable.

Thus the efforts of editor Dorothy Norman to secure Henry Miller an invitation to Yaddo were fruitless.[42] Though the archival documents are silent on the particulars, Miller was never a Yaddo guest, and one imagines that his roguish reputation preceded him. Members of the Beats were not sought out as guests; admissions committee member Morton Dauwen Zabel, a long-standing editor of *Poetry* magazine, listed Allen Ginsberg and Lawrence Ferlinghetti under the heading "Doubtful cases" in his 1960 admission commitee notes. Zabel commented: "I recommend that they be passed over; it is fairly certain that difficulties would result from their visits. Moreover, I myself do not believe they merit consideration as writers, whatever their present reputation may be."[43] Sculptor Eva Hesse, applying in 1967 with enthusiastic letters of support from critics Brian O'Doherty and Lucy Lippard, did not gain admission. One admissions committee member described her early postminimal string sculpture as "sprayed glue, strings attached, all sprayed gray," concluding with the judgment: "Bad taste and weak form." Another commented, "I would like to see more craftsmanship in her work."[44]

These judgments and occasional misjudgments were typically anonymous and confidential, and therefore appear seamless. However, on occasion the warp and woof of the social fabric is stretched or torn as it comes into contact with larger social forces. At Yaddo some of the most notable moments of disjunction coincided with the significant issues of social justice at stake during the twentieth century: the segregation and discrimination that marked the Jim Crow era, the paranoia and betrayals that characterized the red scare of the McCarthy period, and the secrecy and the sensationalism that accompanied the outing of homosexuals prior to the gay rights movement (and that regrettably continues today). Yaddo, though imagined as a place of respite from the affairs of the world, was anything but sequestered from these conflicts.

To Yaddo's credit, and in keeping with the values of its founders—who had sponsored Adolph Ochs to take control of the *New York Times* when anti-Semites would have opposed the move, hosted Booker T. Washington in their home, and, in the case of George Foster Peabody, devoted the second half of his life to cultivating educational institutions for African Americans—the artists' retreat was significantly ahead of the rest of the country in voting to end racial segregation among its guests. In 1941, some six years before Jackie Robinson would cut through baseball's color line and play with the Brooklyn Dodgers, Yaddo's directors made the controversial decision to integrate admissions. Urged on by literary critic and longtime adviser Newton Arvin, who had been deeply troubled by the racial exclusions of the admissions advisers with whom he served, the Yaddo leadership voted to open Yaddo's doors to "Negroes properly qualified."[45] (For a more detailed discussion of this, see Barry Werth's essay.)

In 1942, Yaddo's doors opened to African American writers, composers, and visual artists including first Langston Hughes and composer R. Nathaniel Dett (in 1942) and later poet Margaret Walker

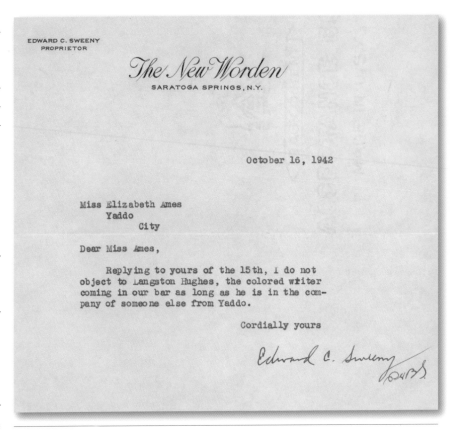

EDWARD C. SWEENY
PROPRIETOR

The New Worden

SARATOGA SPRINGS, N.Y.

October 16, 1942

Miss Elizabeth Ames
Yaddo
City

Dear Miss Ames,

Replying to yours of the 15th, I do not object to Langston Hughes, the colored writer coming in our bar as long as he is in the company of someone else from Yaddo.

Cordially yours

Edward C. Sweeny

Yaddo executive director Elizabeth Ames reached out into the Saratoga Springs community to insist that Langston Hughes be admitted to segregated establishments. In this letter the owner of The New Worden, a hotel and bar, allowed that Hughes could be admitted with conditions.

(1943), sculptor Selma Burke (1946), sociologist and memoirist Horace P. Cayton (1946, 1947), editor and folklorist Arna Bontemps (1947, 1948), painter Beauford Delaney (1950, 1951), composer Ulysses Kay (six times between 1946 and 1971), and novelists Chester Himes (1948) and James Baldwin (1955), among others. Elizabeth Ames would take a personal interest in the integration of Yaddo and the surrounding Saratoga Springs establishments, writing to the owner of The New Worden, a local hotel and restaurant, to ensure that Langston Hughes would not be excluded. Despite these extraordinary efforts, a question raised by correspondence in the Yaddo records but not yet fully answered by research, is to what extent the formal integration of Yaddo was subtly undermined by "well-inten-

tioned" inquiries about the behavior of African American guests. An initial review of the files of several African American men at Yaddo—Baldwin, Cayton, and a young Caribbean American novelist of the 1950s, Alston Anderson—suggests that African American men were held to a different and higher standard of conduct than their Caucasian counterparts. Overweening concerns about drinking, sexuality, and the payment of debts, specifically the payment of toll charges on the house phone, characterize the correspondence in these files. Concerns about offending the sensibilities of the surrounding community of Saratoga Springs and causing embarrassment to Yaddo were articulated in internal correspondence.[46] One lesson from Yaddo's integration may be that even when the leaders of institutions courageously seek to rectify racial injustice of the time, the unconscious attitudes of the individuals charged with carrying out their policies, coupled with pressure from the surrounding environment, may play a significant role in preserving inequality.

Perhaps one explanation for a decreased tolerance of guests who might cause embarrassment to Yaddo in the surrounding and then-segregated Saratoga Springs community of the 1950s can be found in the events of the late 1940s, when Yaddo was again on the forefront of American cultural politics. While "McCarthyism" would not be coined until 1951, Yaddo experienced its own red scare in late 1948 and early 1949.[47] That winter the poet Robert Lowell, along with fellow guests Flannery O'Connor, Edward Maisel, and Lowell's soon-to-be-wife Elizabeth Hardwick, sought to have Elizabeth Ames removed as Yaddo's executive director for supposedly harboring Communists and fellow travelers. The events that followed—now known as "the Lowell Affair"—were precipitated by the long residence at Yaddo of Agnes Smedley, a novelist, journalist, and China activist who was a guest almost continuously between 1943 and 1948. Smedley's biographer, Ruth Price, tells this story in detail in her essay in this volume, but in short, Smedley's renown as a journalist who had covered the rise of Mao Zedong's Revolutionary Army, along with her information-gathering activities for the Soviet Union during a period when the Soviets and the Americans were allies, made her an early target of Cold War army and FBI investigations. Her stay at Yaddo, in turn, brought Yaddo under FBI scrutiny.

On Valentine's Day 1949, two FBI agents visited Yaddo and interviewed two guests, Edward Maisel and Elizabeth Hardwick. Disturbed by the intru-

NOTE FOR FILES: BALDWIN PHONED FROM NYC TODAY WANTING TO COME TO YADDO AS SOON AS POSSIBLE OR ANYTIME. ENDING HIS REQUEST HE SAID HE OWED $35 PHONE BILL AND FOR US TO SEND HIM ANOTHER BILL.

P.H.

10 April 1959

Dear James:

Elizabeth will pass your request on to the members of the Admissions Committee and will write you as soon as possible.

You had itemized statements for your phone bill. The total was $35.49. Please make your check out to The Corporation of Yaddo. And mail it to Elizabeth as soon as you can.

All best to you, James,

Very sincerely,

secretary

Mr. James Baldwin
81 Horatio Street
New York City, New York

pd 35.49
4/24/59

Poet Pauline Hanson served as Elizabeth Ames's secretary in the 1950s and managed correspondence with guests, following up with James Baldwin and others regarding their phone bills.

sion on the retreat and beginning to feel the first paranoia of his not-yet-diagnosed manic-depressive illness, Lowell was seized with the idea that Yaddo must be purified by the removal of Elizabeth Ames, whom he accused of being "somehow deeply and mysteriously involved in Mrs. Smedley's political activities."[48] The events that unfolded, including an emergency board meeting for which Lowell insisted that a typed transcript be kept as if a court proceeding were under way, represent a remarkable moment in the long annals of America's culture wars. The crisis became a cause célèbre in New York City's literary and cultural circles, with petitions circulated supporting the continued tenure of Ames and letters calling for her ouster. Ultimately, those in favor of Ames prevailed, but the costs to her were high. Personally devastated by the betrayals, she retreated to a hospital to recover from the strain, and her long-standing latitude in extending invitations as she thought appropriate came to an end as more active board oversight of the admissions and day-to-day affairs of the colony were instituted.[49]

In each of these defining moments for Yaddo, literary critic Newton Arvin played a pivotal role. In the case of integrating Yaddo, he had instigated the move to racial equality in admissions. In the Lowell Affair, his anxieties about having his own personal life and past political activities scrutinized may have led him to lend a sympathetic ear to Lowell's pronouncements and accusations. By the late 1950s, it would be Arvin's own personal story as a closeted gay academic that collided with the cultural politics of the period, ending his official relationship with Yaddo, even as his Yaddo friends rallied to his support. Arvin, as Barry Werth chronicles in his essay, was caught in a Massachusetts morals crusade that led to his indictment for supposedly trafficking in gay pornography. Once convicted, Arvin was asked to step down from Yaddo's board. Although he was personally welcomed back as a distinguished guest by Ames and his deeply concerned Yaddo friends, he never returned to the estate that had supported him and his work for more than three decades.

Yaddo's more discordant moments suggest that the creativity fostered at the artists' retreat and the constraints of social conventions are, at best, uneasy bedfellows. There may be more than cliché in the notion that creative individuals are necessarily socially unconventional.[50] Indeed, some social theorists have argued that creativity is even more alive at the margins of a society, as individuals at the periphery have a distinctly different perspective from those at the center and are compelled to seek novel solutions to the problems that their outsider status creates.[51] Although there are competing and contradictory views on this topic—some might cite Flaubert's maxim that one should "be regular and orderly in your life, so that you may be violent and original in your work"—the lives of many of Yaddo's most celebrated guests were far from conventional. The sense of support and camaraderie that Yaddo afforded allowed for an alternative community,

Life at Yaddo was governed by a set of guidelines developed by Elizabeth Ames in the earliest years of operation. This list dates from the early 1930s.

particularly in the years before the Lowell and Arvin affairs shattered the retreat's sense of itself as a world apart.

One of the hazards of working in a world apart, of being what some would call "an artist's artist" or "writer's writer," is that one's work may fail to garner either recognition among a broader public or a spot in the literary and artistic canon. Between 1926 and 1980, the period that the exhibition accompanying this volume considers, nearly seventeen hundred artists, writers, and composers enjoyed Yaddo's hospitality. Of these residents, only a handful of names would be readily recognizable to even an educated public. While some might find this lamentable—a sign of the staggering futility of most creative under-

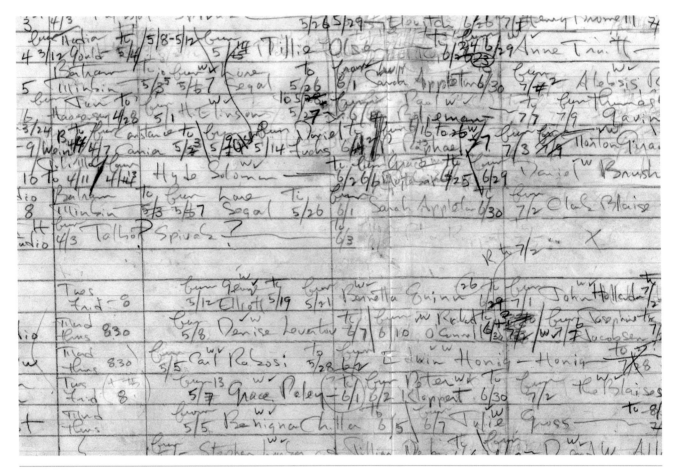

Notes of guests' accommodations have always been kept on handwritten charts, a practice that continues today. This detail of a 1975 chart shows the locations of studios and rooms for guests, including Grace Paley, Denise Levertov, Tillie Olsen, and Lore Segal.

takings—others have argued that any of the works we think of as "masterpieces" or the people we label "genius" would not be possible without the unsung work of fellow artists, not to mention the incalculable labors that support the workings of any art world—the gallerists and collectors, publicists and literary agents, editors and publishers, curators and art handlers, music copyists and piano tuners, bookstore clerks and theater ushers.[52]

Even those artists and writers who do achieve a measure of acclaim are subject to both the fiat of fashion and the power of political change. So a James T. Farrell or a Josephine Herbst, whose working-class realist novels of the 1930s enjoyed both critical and popular success, found their reputations waning in the postwar

McCarthy period. During the Cold War era a more privatized aesthetic arose, an approach that lauded the more intimate stories of John Cheever and the confessional poetry of Robert Lowell and Elizabeth Bishop. The feminism of the 1970s took the poems of a young Sylvia Plath, herself a student of Lowell, and, with the personal reenvisioned as political, installed Plath as a feminist icon. Likewise the figurative prints and drawings of Philip Reisman, Hugh Botts, or Agnes Tait, artists working in the midst of the mobilization of laborers in Depression-era America, would fall out of fashion with the ascendancy of Abstract Expressionism, which better served the international identity of the United States as an ascendant global postwar power.[53] As David Gates points out in his essay,

literary and artistic reputations are fashioned and refashioned in the broader contexts of political and social transformations, making folly of any quest for artistic immortality.

While shifting political landscapes can displace an entire generation's aesthetic foothold, unequal social positions can bury the contributions of others. Poet Marcia Nardi's vehement proto-feminist letters to William Carlos Williams in the early and mid-1940s were incorporated without attribution into the second volume of what most of us think of as *his* modernist masterpiece, *Paterson*, published in 1948. Even as Williams appropriated the letters of many writers—Josephine Herbst and Allen Ginsberg, among others—in the case of Nardi, Williams elected to obliterate her identity and authorship, rechristening her as the fictive character Cress. Amazingly, the title page of the manuscript for the second volume of *Paterson* indicates that Williams originally intended to list Nardi as a coauthor, but changed his mind before the manuscript went to press. Ultimately, feminist scholars have recuperated Nardi's role in the creation of *Paterson*,[54] and Nardi narrowly succeeded in securing two stays at Yaddo despite an October 1951 recommendation letter from Williams to Elizabeth Ames that described her as "a difficult woman, an insignificant little woman of forty perhaps, foolish, frightened but gifted, who has somehow existed among the unfortunate beaten wastrels of Greenwich Village and the Bowery in New York. Yet, believe it or not, she is gentle and though erratic very intelligent. She has had a hell of a life—much of it her own fault. . . . She is not a parasite, but one for whom we must all share the guilt—that such people exist in the world."[55] Similarly, Wallace Stegner, a guest at Yaddo in 1937 and 1938, won the Pulitzer Prize for fiction in 1972 for *Angle of Repose*, a work based on the life and letters of Mary Hallock Foote (later published as the memoir *A Victorian Gentlewoman in the Far West*). While cultural appropriations constitute a particular form of collective authorship, the material in Yaddo's records forces one to consider who retains the privileged status of authorship. Recognition for creative work is subject not only to shifting political climates and the caprices of aesthetic fashions but also to our unexamined ideas of who fits the bill of "great artist," "literary genius," or "exemplary scholar."

———— ✣ ————

The poetry scholar and critic Helen Vendler, whose reminiscence of the community and creative solitude that Yaddo afforded her appears in this volume, writes persuasively elsewhere of the ways in which the poets who speak most profoundly to each successive generation are those who take the given circumstances of their lives and enter into a dialogue with the particulars of their individual lives and their historical moment.[56] What is given matters, of course, but what remains at the end of a life is what one has made of it. Following from Vendler's thesis, but transferring the principle across the art-life divide that Yeats had so carefully delineated,[57] the Trasks' success follows from their embrace of their late nineteenth-century moment, their ability to live at the edge of that century, singing the praises of a bucolic country retreat for artists modeled on a feudal estate with a storied mansion, while embracing—and investing in—the electrification of the city that would accelerate the industrialization and mass production of the emerging century. Creative power could be the epiphany in the wooded glen *or* the lightbulb moment at Thomas Edison's workbench. Such creative catholicism—the Trasks' abiding belief in human creativity and ingenuity in its many forms—has yet to achieve the economic and social equality that Katrina Trask envisioned, but it did go a long way toward eliminating the high culture–low culture divide that characterized the beginning of the twentieth century.

By the time Yaddo opened its gates to guests in 1926, the project of defining a distinctly American culture was much on the mind of the critics of the day. The recognition of American authors as literary auteurs (Melville, Hawthorne, and Whitman among them) was under way and Yaddo, through its support not only of artists but also of critics such as Van Wyck Brooks, Newton Arvin, Lionel Trilling, Malcolm Cowley, Alfred Kazin, and Philip Rahv, played an integral part in the project of establishing an American culture, what Brooks called "creating a usable past"—one from which a future not just viable, but vital, could be built.[58] For Brooks, critics had a central role to play. In his 1918 book *Letters and Leadership*, Brooks called for a criticism that would, in Matthew Arnold's words, "make an intellectual situation of which creative power can profitably avail itself."[59] Observing that a young generation of America was deficient in creative power, but had "more creative desire than it knows what to do with," Brooks called for a criticism that would support the country's youthful inventive energies.[60] Yaddo helped remedy the problem Brooks identified by supporting countless critics and scholars from both the literary and visual arts. Art historian Meyer Schapiro (at Yaddo in 1958) would demonstrate how artistic styles reflect the economic and social conditions of those who have produced those works. Novelist and art critic Robert M. Coates (at Yaddo several times between 1934 and 1970) would apply the term "abstract expressionism" to the movement he saw emerging in the work of a new generation of American painters.[61] And the Yaddo music festivals took on the challenge of fostering links between America's classical composers and its music critics who, at the time, continued to have their eyes trained on European masters.

When Elizabeth Ames retired as Yaddo's executive director in 1969, much of the work of establishing an American culture, both at home and abroad, was well under way.[62] When Brooks had called for an American criticism and culture that would bridge the chasm between "high-brow" and "low-brow," Yaddo answered, as Marcelle Clements explores in her essay. Yaddo had hosted an astonishingly diverse array of artists with widely divergent artistic agendas. From the realism of James T. Farrell's novels and Philip Reisman's drawings and lithographs to the southern gothic of Carson McCullers, Flannery O'Connor, and Truman Capote to the abstract expressionism of Clyfford Still and the politically charged figuration of Philip Guston, Yaddo had remained true to Ames's description, first voiced in her letters to guests in the midst of the political battles of the 1930s, when she wrote: "Yaddo supports exclusively no social or artistic philosophy, and . . . it is most decidedly a meeting place for ideas, a place for free discussion rather than propaganda."[63]

By remaining a home to which creative workers came for "Rest & Refreshment," Yaddo helped populate the American imagination with an astonishing cast of characters. Patricia Highsmith's sensational first novel, *Strangers on a Train*, written at Yaddo in 1948, provided the basis for Alfred Hitchcock's popular masterpiece and paved the way for her memorable Mr. Ripley. America's immigrants and ethnic people—the very unwashed masses for whom a rarefied high culture had been planned as a curative—unleashed their creativity in a flurry of works. There was not only the Jewish stream of consciousness of a Henry Roth in the 1930s but also Philip Roth's equally masterful, if psychoanalytically couched, stream of consciousness in *Portnoy's Complaint* in the 1960s. There was not just the Irish ghetto, with its *Studs Lonigan* that James T. Farrell conjured up from his Chicago's South Side past while housed securely at Yaddo, but also the good man, so hard to find, that Flannery O'Connor would call forth after launching her career from Yaddo. There would be James Baldwin's heartbreaking Giovanni of *Giovanni's Room* and Alice Walker's courageous Sofia in *The Color Purple*. And, of course, the blockbuster Corleone family of *The Godfather* trilogy, born of Yaddo's support of the young Mario Puzo as he shaped his craft.

Critics may find it easy to locate the occasional gaps in Yaddo's reach—most of the Beats took refuge elsewhere, pop and minimalism found other venues, and the mighty forces of jazz and rock 'n' roll had no need of the quietude that Yaddo offers. What is more difficult, perhaps impossible, to imagine is twentieth-century American culture without the work of the artists Yaddo fostered. A world without Katherine Anne Porter's *Ship of Fools* or Saul Bellow's *Augie March* or Carson McCullers's *Lonely Hunter*? Without Holly Golightly's blue-boxed aspirations in Truman Capote's *Breakfast at Tiffany's* or the horror of the horse head in the bed of Mario Puzo's *The Godfather* or the Jets and the Sharks of Leonard Bernstein's *West Side Story*? Without the poetry of Sylvia Plath and the paintings of Milton Avery? It is hard to imagine—even unthinkable—and only so because a bereft millionaire and his wife, poised on the edge of two centuries, embraced the possibilities before them and imagined a parallel world where, until more equitable arrangements might be made for all, at least creativity would reign somewhere. The creative power that they—and a host of others—unleashed at Yaddo continues to illuminate American culture.

2 / REFUGE AND CRUCIBLE

NEWTON ARVIN'S YADDO

Barry Werth

L IKE SO much else, Newton Arvin owed his introduction to Yaddo's world-within-a-world to his mentor Van Wyck Brooks. In the 1920s, if you were a bookish young writer dreaming of a life in letters, Brooks was your man—a socialist critic whose call for a muscular native literature tantalized America's pioneer generation of literary scholars. Arvin had been a frail, skinny, sexually conflicted Harvard senior when, just weeks after his father denounced him as "tinctured with Sovietism" and on the cusp of the Jazz Age, he presented himself to Brooks, who took him in hand. Although Arvin resented suspending a

writing career to feed himself, Brooks steered him toward teaching and, at age twenty-seven, he began working as an English instructor at Smith College and was living miserably in a rooming house in a small Massachusetts town that he despised, churning out reviews for *Commonweal* and the *New York Herald Tribune* while struggling to complete his first book, a biography of Hawthorne.

"My Dear Mrs. Ames," he wrote from Northampton in April 1928:

Thank you very much indeed for your letter and your invitation to Yaddo. I shall be very happy to be there at the time you mention, and

I shall look forward most eagerly to my stay. Naturally, I should not be sorry to be there as long as you were able to let me, and if, as you suggest, my time may later be lengthened, I shall be still more grateful to you.[1]

Director Elizabeth Ames, a gracious and formidable war widow from Minnesota, had begun welcoming guests just two years earlier. Other than that they work hard while enjoying their stay and leave their fellow guests alone to do the same, the standards and conditions for whom to invite and how long to let them visit were entirely up to her. At the recommendation of Brooks and an-

Painter Marion Greenwood was a guest in 1927, 1932, and 1940. While in residence, she created this portrait of fellow guest Newton Arvin in 1932.

despised. Already balding, nattily dressed and groomed, he appeared timid but spoke richly and eloquently at meals, with an air of preternatural authority. The young book and theater reviewer Louis Kronenberger found that Arvin's "immersion in literature argued no disassociation from life. . . . Politics, morals, intellectual movements, social atmospheres, cultural patterns, economic pressures all went into his thinking about literature itself."[2] He especially impressed Ames, who though nearly deaf dined regularly with her guests and invited them back to her house for drinks and conversation.

From Arvin's first weeks in residence, Ames began to seek his advice about new guests, and he took the opportunity to recommend fellow neophytes in Brooks's order, critics who exalted the social responsibility of writers and were scouring the American scene for new voices and what Brooks called "a usable past."[3] Soon after the crash on Wall Street brought the Jazz Age to a shuddering halt, and most Lost Generation intellectuals lurched further left, Arvin's fellow Harvard alums and Smith faculty radicals Granville Hicks and Howard Doughty joined him within the developing inner circle of Yaddo regulars, standard bearers, and literary talent scouts—a group that quickly grew to include Kronenberger and the humanist poet and critic Malcolm Cowley, who like Arvin had been influenced by Brooks's literary socialism as a Harvard undergraduate.

Hawthorne, published in 1929, propelled Arvin to the front rank of those writing about American books and writers. He discovered in his subject, whom Brooks called the "most subterranean" native author, much about himself and America—most urgently, "the dark connection between guilt and secrecy."[4] Arvin's keen interest in the subject arose from concerns far more personal than

other of his protégés, the critic Lewis Mumford, she had offered Arvin a room for a month, possibly two. With four chapters completed and four more in outline, he anticipated a quiet work space, pleasant company, and a monastic atmosphere—a brief, unexpected furlough from what he feared was turning into a life term of toiling over student bluebooks.

At Yaddo, Arvin drove himself "like a dragon," as he now wrote of Hawthorne during a similarly productive siege, ecstatically finishing his manuscript in two months before dismally returning to "That Place"—Northampton, hometown of President Calvin Coolidge, who still shared a duplex with his mother a few blocks from Arvin's apartment and whose catchpenny materialism Arvin academic. As a homosexual, his gravest fear was being discovered. He lived two lives, bulkheaded from one another, and he wrote with pressing immediacy about the pain of living in Hawthorne's America, where sinners are punished more harshly for their secrets than their crimes. "The essential sin, he would seem to say, lies in whatever shuts up the spirit in a dungeon where he is alone," Arvin wrote at Yaddo with scarcely concealed excitement. "All that isolates damns; all that associates, saves."[5]

This first great insight as a critic also served to caution Arvin. Depressed by guilt, seclusion, and drinking, even as his reputation and influence grew, he feared he might collapse. And so he set himself goals of a fuller, richer social and political life. As the Depression took hold, he urged Hicks and Yaddo's other Brooksians to study, discuss, and inevitably write about communism. And he and Doughty had a short-lived love affair, broken off in shame and terror that Smith would find out and fire them both.

The more Arvin put his small-town Indiana past and family behind him and the more cloying life at Smith and in Northampton grew—he now complained to Hicks that he found it "quite unreal" to try to cure the world's ills while teaching English literature and reading student themes at a "ladies seminary"—the more Yaddo came to represent his true home: *beau ideal*, sanctuary, clubhouse, base.[6] In 1932, he hastily courted a student of his, Mary Garrison, giving her Walt Whitman's homoerotic Calamus poems to read as a coded way of informing her of his sexual ambiguity.[7] Although she never read them, he took her apparent forbearance as a sign of "miraculous" acceptance, and after buying an engagement ring and proposing marriage, Arvin sped to Yaddo to tell "everything important" to Ames,

In August 1932 Arvin married a former student, Mary Garrison, at Yaddo. The newlyweds honeymooned at Triuna on Lake George.

who invited the young couple to have their wedding there. Ames, who had no children, made most of the arrangements for what Arvin called the "big day," allowed the newlyweds to spend their honeymoon at Triuna, the Trask estate on Lake George, and even recommended where to buy furniture. "It begins to seem extraordinary," Arvin wrote her soon after, "that we sh'd buy pots and pans without your guidance and advice."[8]

Like many young academic couples during the harshest years of the Depression, Arvin and Mary lived mostly apart: he, traveling to research and write a biography of Whitman, for which he received one of the new Guggenheim fellowships; she, moving among secretarial jobs in New York until she dumped herself, more and more estranged from her marriage and out of sorts, on her parents in West Hartford. In 1932, they both voted for William Z. Foster, the Communist candidate for president. Hicks soon joined the Communist Party as an open, card-carrying member, but Arvin, though he wrote for CP publica-

tions and worked hard for several front organizations, found the party too dogmatic and blunt to submit himself to its discipline. Still, with his dual investment in the crusading populist Whitman and the modern proletarian movement, his democratic impulses soared. Arvin's activism increased at Smith, where he was president of the faculty union, and at Yaddo, where by 1935 he and Ames, albeit decorously, clashed over the colony's racial exclusivity.[9]

"Dear Elizabeth," he wrote in mid-August of that year:

This is an extremely difficult letter for me to write, but perhaps it will not have all the bad results I fear. I realize that I am in no position to express a responsible opinion on the subject of color at Yaddo, and, that being true, I can see that the only honest thing for me to do is resign from the literary committee. I am *extremely* sorry, as perhaps I don't need to say, to take such a drastic and apparently (though only apparently) unfriendly step as this, but you can probably believe that I have not taken it without a great deal of arduous thought on the subject. I find on reflection that I cannot argue myself into an indifferent attitude toward the neo-confederates and their pro-slavery apologetics or towards the treatment of Negroes that seems inevitable when one has (no) social or practical relations with them. You can no doubt see that on the literary committee at Yaddo I am in a false position. [10]

The question of racial integration—"our difficulty," Ames called it[11]—haunted Yaddo as it did the nation. Arvin was zealous, impatient, and vocal, and two years later Ames felt compelled to reprimand him, sharply:

What I chiefly want to say is that I have no desire that you should stop discussing the matter of Yaddo entertaining Negro artists. All I ask is that you take more care, and use greater emphasis in stating what I have said is Yaddo's point of view. Even if you have little confidence in it, you can at least quote me, I should think. I find that, due to the number of persons with whom you have talked, and their propensity—which most of us have—for spreading the news, that Yaddo has a considerable reputation for being anti-Negro. Which is manifestly untrue and unjust. It is also dangerous and unfortunate that this reputation should be contributed to just now when people are so quick to seize upon any racial point of view and opinion.[12]

As the 1930s—his thirties, too—ground to a close, Arvin faced a crucial reckoning. He diligently tried to channel his waywardness into a manly political stance and a loveless marriage. But his true self—unleashed at Yaddo, where he could fully speak his mind and, however guiltily, have sex with Doughty and a few other male artists—groaned more and more under the weight of a double life. In April 1939, Mary, no longer able to bear his conflicts—or her own—suffered a nervous breakdown, spending three months in a psychiatric hospital in White Plains. She was still there, trying to determine whether and how to get a divorce, when in late July Arvin, exhausted and feeling "seedy," left for Yaddo, now—as for many others—his one refuge against life's turbulence.[13]

⁂

A month later, he and most of the other guests huddled in shock and dismay around the one large radio upstairs in the mansion, as the world outside Yaddo's gates—and, as it would turn out, the one within it—suddenly turned more dangerous and confusing when Stalinist Russia agreed to a nonaggression pact with Nazi Germany.[14] Hicks, his faith in communism shattered, drove to Yaddo to consult with Arvin, then renounced his party membership. The literary left reeled, confronted by a sudden and vehement backlash. After Mary sued for divorce, Arvin, again irremediably alone in Northampton, started keeping a journal, though he was reticent, even here, in his most private writing, to confess his secrets or submit to any strenuous self-reflection. Initiating his first affair at Smith since the disaster with Doughty, he wrote guardedly the next morning: "Oskar here for breakfast all morning."[15]

Confronting the full reality of his sexual needs for the first time—he was again living alone, no longer with the cover of a wife, a legal and moral outcast in a small town—Arvin suffered a nervous breakdown. In February 1941, his colleague in the English department Daniel Aaron, another Harvard Americanist who came to Smith "because Newton was there," committed him to Northampton State Hospital, the enormous asylum atop a neighboring hill overlooking the campus.[16] Taking a leave of absence, discovering himself "in great and poignant need of love" even as he also considered himself affectively "impotent," Arvin spent the next several months at the same sanitarium where Mary had gone. Returning to Northampton only long enough to tell Smith's president that he could not possibly teach the coming fall, he left his apartment within days for Yaddo.

Having recently been elected a trustee, Arvin settled in not as a visiting artist but an esteemed "director in residence." The political disagreements of the 1930s, when Stalinists and Trotskyites refused to dine together, now gave way to other schisms. A fellow guest, the poet John Malcolm Brinnin, recalled that Arvin "wore dark suits to breakfast, sat like a furled umbrella, and buttered his toast to the edges," but he gravitated without hesitation to what one heterosexual visitor called "the table of the sensitives."[17] There he befriended twenty-four-year-old Carson McCullers, New York's newest literary darling after the publication a year before of *The Heart Is a Lonely Hunter*, who was unhappily married to her teenage sweetheart but mostly attracted to other women. Arvin invited McCullers on a weeklong car ride with the Hickses to Quebec—"one sustained conversation with moving scenery," he recalled—during which they checked into a hotel together as Mr. and Mrs. Newton Arvin, then came down, shaken, the next morning asking for separate rooms.[18] As fall approached, Arvin decided to return for the "small season" when the mansion would be closed and he could think through his next book, a biography of Melville.

The first reaction after December seventh and its fateful events
was to feel that we must **conserve** and mostly close up.   Then came
the realization that this war is being fought in great part that
the life of the mind and fruits of civilization may endure.   That
seemed to make it obligatory and natural for Yaddo to carry on, if
possible, as usual; and so we shall, simplifying and economizing
as never before.   At this writing it looks as though about forty
guests would come this summer.   The season will be in two parts
of about seven weeks for each.   The vote of the Directors to
admit Negroes, properly qualified, to Yaddo puts Yaddo in the good
society of those who are fighting against racial discrimination.
Our composer directors have believed that it would be neither wise
nor practicable to have a Music Period this year, but they hope
that one may be planned for 1943.   Meanwhile Yaddo will carry on
with its major work of offering hospitality to carefully selected
and invited workers in all the arts.   This will be our seventeenth
summer of such endeavor.

We began in a period of peace and plenty the work designated by
the Founders of Yaddo; we continued it into and through the
depression; now we prepare to carry on under the impact of war.

In her 1942 report to Yaddo's board of directors, Ames discusses the organization's decision to integrate admissions.

That summer, the activist journalist and author Agnes Smedley gave a nationwide lecture tour that drew the attention of Cowley, who recommended her for an invitation to Yaddo, which aided the war effort by shuttering the mansion and shrinking the number of guests. Smedley, who generously helped care for Ames's dying sister, remained in residence through the following summer, when Arvin served as chief "fire warden" for the colony and Yaddo's first two African American guests—Langston Hughes and Nathaniel Dett—arrived following a board meeting at which two trustees letters of resignation were accepted, at least one as a result of the decision to integrate.[19] By now Arvin realized he might never leave Smith despite being wooed by other schools; his past there dragged behind him. With residencies at Yaddo scarce, he exulted near the end of the war at finding a large quiet apartment near campus, a third-floor walkup with good views in every direction. His "cave," he called it. Drinking more, having more and more black days, he hunkered down in solitude.[20] One winter night, after watching the skaters on Smith's millpond, he stumbled home, opened a bottle of liquor, put on a recording of John McCormack singing, and swallowed sixteen Nembutals. Aaron found him and took him to the hospital.[21]

This was the hidden, subterranean Arvin who returned to Yaddo in June 1946, as the country plunged toward "peacetime normalcy," an orgy of self-celebration undergirded by quickening, whipped-up anxieties about the Soviet Union, the Bomb, and communists in society.[22] Smedley, enjoying Ames's gratitude and unwillingness to put out a politically unpopular figure, had stayed on during and just after the war, though no longer in the mansion. Doughty already had arrived and was bedding the tow-headed, twenty-one-year-old Southern short story writer Truman Capote, who had already begun stirring the pent-up colony into what Brinnin called "a dance of bees."[23] Arvin, despite his weariness and gloom, was smitten at once. He and Capote tumbled into the most formative love affair either would ever have. "I can't down the desire to tell you, and only you," he wrote to Doughty a few days after; he had been hit by "this Thing that one can surely expect but once or twice in a lifetime."[24] "Newton," Capote rejoined, "was my Harvard."[25]

If falling in love so unexpectedly with someone so outwardly his opposite wasn't enough to jolt Arvin into fretting anew about the problem of his two lives, he shuddered when word reached him that fall about a *Life* magazine photo spread on Yaddo's own postwar return to "normalcy."[26] The display innocently featured side-by-side pictures of Arvin in a linen suit, making his bed, and Capote sitting at his typewriter in Katrina Trask's white-walled hideaway, the scene of their recent trysts. Still more provocative perhaps, as Arvin understood the country's return to anti-Red evangelism, was a photograph of Hicks, himself, and Ames—a former openly avowed communist, a well-known fellow traveler, and the colony's director—sitting casually beneath the full-length portraits of the Trasks in the Main Hall. Trying to head off what he feared could only cause embarrassment, even scandal, at Smith and among the school's alumni, he urgently wired Ames from Northampton:

ADVISE AGAINST LIFE ARTICLE NO GROUND FOR CERTAINTY THAT SENSATIONALISM WOULD BE AVOIDED NO REAL GAIN TO YADDO AT BEST CHEAPNESS UNAVOIDABLE.[27]

Saturday

Dearest Spooky, my darling:

This morning, as I predicted, I am cutting both classes and determinedly taking it very easy-- just dawdling about the office, nipping now and then at some blue-books, taking a note or two, and generally being a lazy Peter, if not a shiftless one. Susy is cleaning the apartment, so I can't stay there. I needed this let-down, but certainly not because I am suffering from any serious organic ailment: I went to Hayes yesterday, and learned from him not only that my xxxx blood is much redder than it was the last time but that I weigh one hundred and thirty-two (132) pounds, fully dressed, to be sure (I assure you), but still--that's an alarming seven pounds more than I ever weighed in my life before, and I am beginning to worry seriously about my figure: I can't go losing that!

I'm so glad Linscott liked the chapter, honey: I'm sure it does mean something, but in any case you won't be much ruffled by these opinions, one way or the other. I think the chapter is beautiful, and the xx whole book wonderfully delicate and subtle and affecting; so there.

Of course I bought Life eagerly yesterday, hoping that my boy friend was in it--and naturally was let down when he wasn't. Drat those people! Can't they make up their minds when they want to run an article?

No, my dear, I didn't see the news of W Cather's death in the papers. How could I have missed it? And it affects xx me, too, emotionally, a little, somewhat to my surprise. How short a time ago she seemed to xx us a new and even a young writer!-- and how fresh, and how delicate.

That Concord book is a mess, à mon avis, and I've written to Margaret Marshall to say so. It's all written in this style, straight goods, I'm not making it up:

Daniel Bliss looked like a brilliant, though venture-some choice. True, he was very young--perhaps too young --not yet twenty-five. He was also from that new and up-start college, Yale, down at New Haven, where Jonathan Edwards showered fire and brimstone on the people, roar-ing that only the few elect would be saved. Etc., x etc.

When professors go Time-ish, they go it with a will and a ven-geance. Imagine reading 416 pages of prose like that carefully! One would be dead of thirst long before the half way point.

No, darling, as you see, I am not working on Portraits this morning, but I purpose to, tomorrow, and though I probably can't quite finish it, I can undoubtedly get very close to the end. I'm afraid your boy friend demands a lot of patience in these affairs.

The jacket hasn't yet come, but I would hardly expect it yet, and it may well come today, in which case you will hear from me.

Such wonderful sweet letters from you, Spooky precious; they warm me inwardly and outwardly like a pure flame of tenderness and goodness. They are all that make it endurable to be separ-ated from you--whom I love unbearably, and to whom I send more kisses than can be counted.

Arvin provided ongoing support and encouragement to Truman Capote as the young author worked to complete his first novel, *Other Voices, Other Rooms*, published in 1948.

Ames had really only ever had one charge, which was to bring creative and talented artists to Yaddo and let them work in peace. Politics, sex, squabbles, publicity—all mattered only insofar as they affected the general health and welfare of the community. Arvin's fears aside, she was pleased to see Yaddo celebrated as it got back to business, as was the board of directors, which consisted largely of Saratoga business and civic leaders and prominent Wall Street investors. With the Trask fortune proving insufficient for Katrina Trask's dream of generations "creating, creating, and creating,"[28] increased public awareness—though it collided with the cloistered nature of the place—had become a belated necessity.

In February 1949, as Arvin began to grapple with the densest, most contentious section of his book on Melville—the chapter on *Moby-Dick*, which he called "The Whale"—Yaddo faced its first, all-too-public crisis. It was a destructive, suspicious time, the aftermath of the Alger Hiss trial. Rocked by a page one story in the *New York Times* identifying Smedley as a wartime spy for the Soviets, Yaddo became a "stricken battlefield," as Cowley wrote.[29] Within days, two FBI agents arrived to interview all the guests, but in particular, Ames. Her secretary, it turned out, had been an FBI informer since 1942, passing along the comments of Ames and visitors alike. Although the War Department soon conceded that it had no evidence to support the charges against Smedley, who denounced the allegation as "a despicable lie" and who, paradoxically, had left Yaddo the previous year after Ames had quarreled with her about her political activities, the agents told the thirty-five-year-old poet Robert Lowell that the colony was "permeated with communists."[30] Drinking violently, heavily influenced by the anticommunist and anti-Brooksian New Critics, and verging on a nervous breakdown, Lowell enlisted the other three guests to demand an emergency board meeting to remove Ames at once.

Arvin reeled. "Down into the pit," he wrote in his journal, after receiving an anguished phone call from Ames.[31] Realizing that any investigation into communist activity might quickly engulf Hicks, Cowley, himself, and the other leftist critics on the board, he frantically phoned Hicks and then raced by train to Hicks's farm, where they formulated their response. He and Hicks were now Truman Democrats, but that scarcely mattered. Arvin understood that the focus of such hunts were the shadows in

IN A MULLIONED BAY of what was once the boudoir of Lady Katrina, and is now a study for Yaddo authors, Newton Arvin props himself up on long window seat with a portable typewriter on his knees. Arvin is a director of Yaddo, a professor of English literature at Smith and a biographer of Hawthorne.

BED-MAKING, here demonstrated by Author Arvin, is sometimes done by Yaddo guests because servant problem has cut original staff of 20 down to 5.

IN THE TOWER ROOM, once the secret hideaway of founder, Lady Katrina, who wrote poetry, young Author Truman Capote writes his first novel.

STROLLING GUESTS like authors Jerre Mangione and Granville Hicks are discouraged from dropping in on other guests in studios before 4:30 p.m.

YADDO'S FOUNDERS are buried on estate's highest hill. Katrina's carved ledger stone is in center, flanked by two smaller stones for her husbands.

A *Life* magazine spread in July 15, 1948, featured images of Newton Arvin making a bed, at left, and Truman Capote at work in Katrina Trask's study, known as the Tower Room.

IN YADDO'S GREAT HALL, Marguerite Young, author of *Angel in the Forest* (LIFE, Sept. 17, 1945), likes to sit in a bishop's chair stuffed with pillows. Her companion is 21-year-old Truman Capote, short-story writer. Guests all gather in the hall after dinner to discuss life and literature, are discouraged from reading manuscripts to each other.

In 1946 Yaddo sought news coverage to alert its public that the artists' retreat was once again operating at capacity after reducing operations during World War II. The July 15, 1948, *Life* article also featured this photo of Marguerite Young with Truman Capote.

he named more than two dozen poets and critics, including T. S. Eliot, Lionel Trilling, and Robert Frost, if their demands, including Ames's dismissal, weren't met.[33] "I can assure the members of this Board," Lowell threatened, "that this is the most important meeting in its history, one that involves its welfare and perhaps its existence."[34]

Although Cowley and Slade staunchly stood behind Ames, Arvin and Hicks feared that while the communist issue might be negligible, she had been lax in allowing Smedley to stay on. They were concerned that the admission process was now hopelessly corrupted and that Yaddo could be destroyed if it wasn't overhauled. "I am frankly completely hopeless of combating this situation as long as Mrs. Ames is Director," Hicks declared at the end of the meeting. "I am sorry to say this, but I think situations of this kind grow. Therefore, I am handing in my resignation and Newton's, as Directors of Yaddo. I am sure that would be Newton's view."[35]

"Got my will, the bonds, etc. out of the safety deposit," Arvin wrote ominously two days later.[36] If a sympathetic liberal like Ames, a Quaker, could be attacked this way, what hope was there for him? As always, Arvin's sole antidote to quicksand fears and black depressions lay in his ability to move ahead with his work, and he dug deeper into *Moby-Dick*. Soon after, the affair died out. At a second five-hour meeting on March 26, the board supported Ames, who went to recover in a nursing home; censured Lowell, who within weeks suffered a psychotic break so forceful that it took four Chicago policemen to subdue him; and adopted reforms making Yaddo more efficient, and in the process, less vulnerable to charges that it was dominated by radicals. Decisions regarding visits were shifted to the admissions committee. Hicks and Arvin withdrew

one's past, and that because of his political and sexual histories, he was doubly vulnerable. He was frantic that he might be "turned"—bullied by investigators who knew about his homosexuality and would threaten to reveal it if he didn't cooperate.[32]

For two weeks, Arvin wallowed in despair, taking mostly to his bed. He was too shattered to attend the board meeting at Yaddo on February 26, when Lowell told the trustees it was the guests' "impression that Mrs. Ames is somehow deeply involved in Miss Smedley's political activities," described Ames as "a diseased organ chronically poisoning the whole system," and vowed to "confer with certain people in New York"—here

Arvin's arrest on pornography charges stemmed from his possession of periodicals such as *Grecian Guild Pictorial* and *Trim*.

their resignations. "An ordeal for everyone," Arvin wrote numbly in his journal.[37]

⚬⚬⚬

As the 1950s began, Arvin's literary reputation flourished. So did his suicidal misery and surreptitious sexual life. "The will to live burning low," he wrote in his journal on February 4, 1950.[38] Two and a half weeks later Hicks, a member of the literary jury, called to tell him his *Herman Melville* had won the new National Book Award for nonfiction. He had an affair with a young Smith professor, Wendell Johnson, marking their sexual encounters with a penciled X in his journal, and with violently conflicted emotions he inched toward the "set of gay ones" at the college—young homosexual men who began to drop their masks and mingled openly together. Six months after being inducted into the American Academy of Arts and Letters, the country's most distinguished cultural society, he prepared to leave Northampton to teach for a year at Harvard, where

Aaron, who would finish his own career there, believed he might have received a permanent offer if he "had shown any interest or if he could make people confident that he wouldn't break down."[39] On the eve of his departure, he notified Harvard he wouldn't be coming, and traveled instead to Cincinnati, where his sister lived, to receive electroshock treatments for his depression.

Although Arvin made it to Cambridge the following semester, he now believed that remaining in Northampton for the rest of his days "was his destiny," Aaron recalled. "He couldn't leave. He was affixed, doomed to be in this circle, and though he loathed it, it was the only place he could come back to and feel at home in."[40] Through his contact with Wendell Johnson, he began traveling to New York on weekends, occasionally bringing back copies of beefcake magazines now available on newsstands and other "goodies."

He had removed himself to the far margin of the teeming, contentious postwar period, yet, as at Yaddo, the Red-hunts reached closer and closer to

his inner world. In February 1953, the House Committee on Un-American Activities, after finishing with Hollywood, took on communist subversion on college campuses. To Arvin's generation the ultimate capitulation was to turn state's witness, yet Hicks cooperated fully with the committee, naming names. So did Smith English professor Robert Gorham Davis, another close friend of Arvin's. Then William F. Buckley Jr.'s sister Allie, a Smith alum, charged Arvin and four other senior professors with communist activities, inviting the attention of the state's antisubversion unit, which sent examiners to Northampton. "A nightmare, all of it," Arvin recorded in his journal.[41] He managed to testify without incriminating himself or anyone else, but his terror further weakened and isolated him.

Arvin all but stopped visiting Yaddo as a guest, preferring solitary drinking and reading on his secluded screen porch in summer to the hothouse life of the colony, though he remained involved with reviewing admissions lists. In 1958 he was reelected as a director— "despite my lapses," he wrote to Ames.[42] Meanwhile, telling Aaron that his sexual urges had become more powerful than ever, Arvin decided no longer to deny them. Approaching 60, he began to live the life of the aging, proper small-town sexual adventurer: cadging rides to nearby Springfield, a transportation hub, to cruise the bus station and the bars; taking trips to Manhattan and the Everard Baths, the "sodomist's paradise," he called it; buying an 8-mm projector and inviting discreet groups of friends up to view grainy, black-and-white films of youths in posing straps tumbling over one another; once having another teacher and two university students stay overnight for sex and an "all-male breakfast party."[43] As he wrote to Doughty, "If it is a risk, so be it."

It was. The collapse—the collision of Arvin's two lives—came catastrophically, all at once; "the Avalanche," he called it.[44] On September 2, 1960, several nights after he had hosted a small going-away gathering for a young instructor at which several Smith teachers showed one another pictures of naked men and he "ran off one of the pretty silly reels I have," three state troopers, a federal postal inspector, and a local policeman climbed the narrow, twisting stairs to Arvin's apartment.[45] Panicked, Arvin let them in. Claiming that a package containing homosexual erotica had "broken open" in the Springfield post office, they searched his rooms, confiscating what one of them called the usual "fag shit."[46] They also took Arvin's journals, shattering the last of his privacy. As they were arresting him, he blurted the names of several others who he said had similar materials, including two popular young faculty bachelors.

Cowley was one of the first to respond to the news. "Dear Newton," he wrote. "Just a hasty note to say that your friends are standing by you. Let me know if there is anything I can do. Prescription: At the first unencumbered moment plunge into some *work*. . . . our only justification and refuge."[47] Yet privately, Cowley and many others were less certain how to react, confessing to Hicks in a pained letter the following day:

I am shocked and disturbed about Newton. He's been so discreet in manner and at times overcautious about many things. Why was he so indiscreet and incautious in that one direction. Why did he give names? Has he a good lawyer? . . . Of course, one's worry is that he'll go to pieces under the shock.[48]

The police, as Aaron put it, "smashed Newton's nest."[49] They claimed that he

31 October 1960

Miss Alita Hodgkins
Parole Officer
District Court
Northampton, Massachusetts.

Dear Miss Hodgkins,

We are told that Mr. Newton Arvin would like very much to spend a month or two here at Yaddo, and that his attending doctor thinks he would be helped by doing so. Yaddo is a Foundation for offering hospitality to writers and workers in the other arts. Mr. Arvin has been associated with it through many years.

Before our Executive Committee will make a decision, it would like to hear from you the terms of the parole arrangement for him: what he is obliged to do, what if any, are the duties of others in this matter. The Committee would also like to see a copy of the paper or document by which this matter is arranged for him.

I shall be very grateful if you will write me as soon as possible. If this matter is to be arranged, it must be taken care of immediately.

Yours sincerely,

(Mrs.) Elizabeth Ames
Executive Director of Yaddo.

Elizabeth Ames wrote Newton Arvin's parole officer on October 31, 1960, to inquire whether Arvin might come to Yaddo as a guest.

was the central figure in a multistate pornography ring, which meant—with troopers poring over his diaries and culling names and information—that his friends all faced new dangers, too. With no place left to turn, yet too anxious and depressed to remain in his apartment and too ashamed to show his face in Northampton, Arvin retreated to the last safe place he knew—the state mental hospital—to await trial. His literary friends—Brooks, Hicks, Cowley, Kronenberger, Capote, McCullers, Lionel Trilling, and especially Edmund Wilson, whom he had known since recruiting Wilson to teach at Smith for a semester in 1942—all rallied to his side, writing testimonials, voicing encouragement, and sending money for his legal defense. In late September he was convicted on a lesser charge, and Smith retired him on half salary.

As Cowley suggested, once Arvin decided *whether* to be—with nothing left to lose or fear, he made no further attempts on his own life—the critical question was *where* to be. Without his knowledge, for fear he would be crushed if the effort failed, Hicks and Cowley began urging Ames to offer Arvin a refuge at Yaddo. "I think," Cowley urged her, "an invitation to him would outweigh, in common humanity, any objection that might be raised against it."[50] Ames, at Slade's request, surveyed the directors, who split sharply over the question. On October 23, somewhat misinformed about the fate of the others involved in the scandal but staunch in her convictions and friendship toward Arvin, she reported back to Cowley:

The matter most on my mind is the tragedy and ruin of Newton Arvin. This matter has been reported all over the country, and also the European capitals. . . . There is said to be great bitterness against him among Smith faculty people for the ruin he brought on two men so much younger than he. Those two are now in jail.

We have had an Ex. Comm. Meeting about his being invited to Yaddo. John (Slade) is violently opposed because he thinks it would be a mistake in respect to public relations. Granville is all for it; the others wavering. I have written the sanitarium doctor in whose care he has been asking him to answer, if he will, certain specific questions. . . .

It is a terrible situation for a man like Newton. When I can't keep my mind away from his plight, I wonder how long he can go on living. It is dreadful to be rejected, and tragic at his age after having lived a life of distinguished service and with the regard of others.[51]

To which Cowley a week later replied:

All this presents Yaddo with a double problem. If we invite Newton for the winter, we do run the risk of unfavorable publicity, (though not a great risk, I think.) If we don't invite him, then members of the literary and artistic public will accuse us of cowardice and disloyalty. Balancing the two dangers, I think the second is worse, especially as inviting Newton would be the courageous and honorable thing to do.

Pointed memories remained fresh of the Lowell-Smedley affair, when Slade and Cowley defended Ames, and Hicks and Arvin, offering to resign over the "hopeless" state of her administration, did not. Yet despite these conflicts, present and past, Ames believed Arvin's coming to Yaddo to be "almost a life and death situation," she told Cowley. "I don't see how he will put his life together again unless he can take up his writing, and this he would be more likely to do in the ordered atmosphere of Yaddo."[52] Rejection, she feared, might set off a sharp collapse from which he would

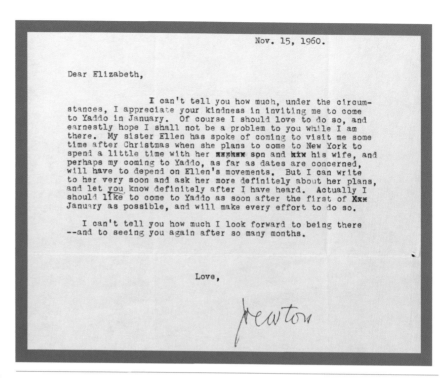

Although Arvin was invited to Yaddo for the winter of 1960–1961, he never returned as a guest.

never recover. On November 11, after the executive committee voted 3 to 2 in favor of an invitation, Ames notified Arvin, who, after a short, uneasy visit to Hicks's farm, had landed back in the state hospital.

Dear Newton,

You are invited to join the pleasant and interesting people who will be coming to Yaddo after the holidays. We shall be ready for you Jan. 2 or 3; I hope you will come then and stay through March . . . .

I'm glad you are with Granville, and I hope you will be seeing other friends later. I think of you often and send you my love,

Yours,

Arvin replied at once:

Dear Elizabeth,

I can't tell you how much, under the circumstances, I appreciate your

kindness in inviting me to come to Yaddo. . . . Of course I should love to do so, and earnestly hope I shall not be a problem to you while I am there.

I can't tell you how much I look forward to being there—and to seeing you again after so many months.

Love,

Perhaps the ultimate measure of the impact of Yaddo on Arvin is that by the time he might have needed its promise of work and sanctuary most, he was able to find it elsewhere. Throughout November, Arvin began considering a book on Longfellow. He discovered he could make it through nights in his apartment and face people in the library, however awful. Smith let him keep his office. In late December, apologizing, he wrote to Hicks, abruptly canceling his visit to Saratoga.

I dislike to seem ungrateful to you and the others who spent time and energy to get me invited: in fact I was deeply touched by all that, and will not forget it. But it seems to me unwise for me to be at Yaddo, set up as it is, so long as I am in any danger at all of having a setback. . . . I cling to the idea of going ahead with the book about HWL and, the fact is, it would not be at all easy to do so at Yaddo. The problem of books, reference works, etc., is a serious one there, and I know it would mean one frustration after another. Here I can use my office as I have always done, take books out of the library, borrow books *through* the library, etc. This is what I strongly feel like doing. I can easily see how people feel that I ought to get away from Northampton, and indeed I feel something of that myself. But here is where I have got to be, sooner or later, and if I can stand the gaff, perhaps it is just as well for me to be facing up to it now. In some respects it has already proved less grim than I feared it would be.

It was around the time that Arvin realized he could survive without Yaddo, even under the direst circumstances, that Ames began to wrestle with his future there. Treasurer C. Everett Bacon and Assistant Treasurer Inslee Clark vehemently opposed Arvin's coming at any time. Just days after Arvin's arrest, Bacon had come over to Pine Garde, Ames's house, to ask that the matter of his resignation be taken up at once by the board. "I am absolutely sure he is not going to leave this matter alone," she wrote Cowley. "He is always, you know, thinking of the welfare of Spencer Trask & Co. and its position in Wall Street. Once he was frightened about Communist charges, and while I think he doesn't consider this quite so evil—yet it is 'no go,' with him."

In May, as the board prepared to meet for the first time since September,

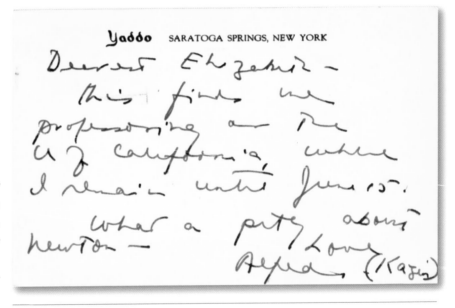

Yaddo board member Alfred Kazin wrote to Ames the day after Arvin's death in 1963 from pancreatic cancer.

Arvin, having returned twice more to the hospital, got permission from his probation officer to visit Hicks's farm. "Newton is far from well," Hicks wrote Cowley.

At first we were struck by the great improvement since last November, and indeed, at his best, to which he rose several times during the week, he seemed quite himself. But he could fall woefully low. He spent one whole day in bed, only getting up now and then to get a drink. (By fits and starts he drinks quite heavily all day long.) He is doing only little pieces of work. I am afraid the future is dark.

Ames, not incidentally, wrote Cowley the same day:

John Slade received a letter from Newton immediately after he had received the announcement of the Meeting. I

The mansion's Tower Room.

have been hoping that both Newton and The Corporation would be saved some difficulties by his resigning now. Instead, he says he cannot continue as a director but would like to remain as a member. John has written him that this will be taken up by the Corporation. I suppose you think, as you did earlier, and as I found out many others do, that he ought not to continue in the Corporation.

By the May meeting, thirty-three years after he first arrived in Saratoga, Newton Arvin no longer was a member of Yaddo. His feelings went unrecorded,

but others felt the expulsion sharply. John Cheever, who hid his bisexuality, panicked, his daughter Susan recalling later that Arvin's fall was "huge" in her household: "Maybe I heard Malcolm [Cowley] talking about it—this innocent man hauled off to jail by brutes because he was homosexual. I may have asked Daddy, in all innocence, how it happened. Now I know he was scared out of his mind."[53] Remarkably, Cheever was elected to fill Arvin's position.

And yet if others were terrified and perplexed, Arvin surprised them—and himself. Discovering he could go on, unencumbered by teaching, severed from

the intimate friends and sexual partners whose names he had given to the police, he finished his *Longfellow* in less time than he allowed and plunged into several major new projects: "at the flood-tide of his energy and power," Kronenberg wrote, "never more enthusiastic about what he planned to do, or more eager to set about doing it."[54] Living less than three more years, Arvin discovered more and more in his final solitude the deep serenity and optimism he had first glimpsed possible at Yaddo. "Never mind," he comforted Capote from his deathbed, "At least I've grown up at last."[55]

3 / THE TRAILBLAZER

AARON COPLAND AND THE FESTIVALS OF AMERICAN MUSIC

Tim Page

THE WORD *unique* has been so debased by overuse that some publications have all but forbidden it from their pages. Still, eight decades on, the *New York Times*'s 1926 description of Yaddo as "a unique experiment which has no exact parallel in the world" continues to fit, and the more one investigates, the more fascinating the history becomes.[1] And yet, because Yaddo has always protected the privacy of its artist-guests so assiduously, while generally shying away from institutional publicity, the remarkable—indeed, *unique*—contributions it made to twentieth-century music in America have too often been overlooked.

From the start, Yaddo fulfilled the Trask family's vision of "liberal devotion to artists and the arts" and provided a haven of solitude, where creativity could flourish far from the intrusions and distractions of urban life. Yet composers have very different needs from those of authors and visual artists, who have the opportunity to rush home from Yaddo to share their Saratoga-engendered accomplishments with a loved one, mentor, publisher, or gallery. When a composer completes the creative process, the work is nowhere near finished. There are any number of hurdles yet in store—hiring interpreters, copying parts, locating rehearsal space, and, of course, securing the funding to make sure this can all be achieved—before a piece of music will ever reach an audience. To this day, there are many thousands of chamber works, symphonies, and operas in America that have never been heard, except in the minds of their creators.

And so one contemplates the accomplishments of the Yaddo Festival of Contemporary American Music (later the Yaddo Music Festival) with a sense of appropriate awe. During Yaddo's nine Music Periods (1932–1952), a total of 137 American composers participated directly in the series. No fewer than eighteen festival participants went on to win Pulitzers, including nine of the first eleven composers ever awarded the music prize. All but two people on the *Harvard Dictionary of Music*'s 1972 list of thirty leading twentieth-century American composers born before 1919 had their music presented by Yaddo, and even the occasional ones that Yaddo missed, such as Gian Carlo Menotti, attended the festival as visitors.

Predictably, the indefatigable organizer Aaron Copland served an essential role in the establishment of the Yaddo festivals. In 1930 the composer was in residence, putting finishing touches on his magnificent *Piano Variations*. To the Trask estate came a wealthy and talented Bostonian, Theodore Chanler (1902–1961), and the two men became fast friends. Both delighted in an escape from their respective cities. As Copland later recalled, it was a "grim and difficult period." The Great Depression was deepening, and, in Copland's words, "the artist is always the first to suffer, particularly in America, where he does not have the respect enjoyed by creative artists abroad."[2]

Within the refuge of Yaddo, Chanler and Copland had long discussions about the deplorable state of American music, observing how repertory from the Old World—mainly German, Italian, and

Group at Triuna in 1931. Elizabeth Ames and Aaron Copland are seated second and third from the right; the others are not yet identified.

French—filled concert halls in the New. Tellingly, the hotbed of contemporary American composition was not Manhattan, Boston, or Chicago, but France, where the legendary Nadia Boulanger held court (she would eventually teach as many as 100 U.S.-born composers). As Copland and Chanler spoke, a shared, utopian fantasy of an American music conference slowly took shape.

Still, a conference in itself, if it was limited to an exchange of ideas, lectures, and dialogue among colleagues, would hardly differ from programs that were already offered by several extant organizations. What composers really needed was the ability to hear their music and to share it with others—and so Copland believed it imperative that composers write music specifically for Yaddo, to be played at Yaddo.

Chanler urged Copland, whose command of musical politics ranked second to none, to suggest such a conference to Elizabeth Ames, Yaddo's executive director. Ames herself expressed little en-

thusiasm for the idea, but she took the proposal to the board of directors, which swiftly approved it.[3] Ames gave Copland free rein but reiterated the eco-

The Stone Tower, once the icehouse for a self-sufficient estate, serves as a secluded studio for composers. Copland completed his *Piano Variations* there in 1930.

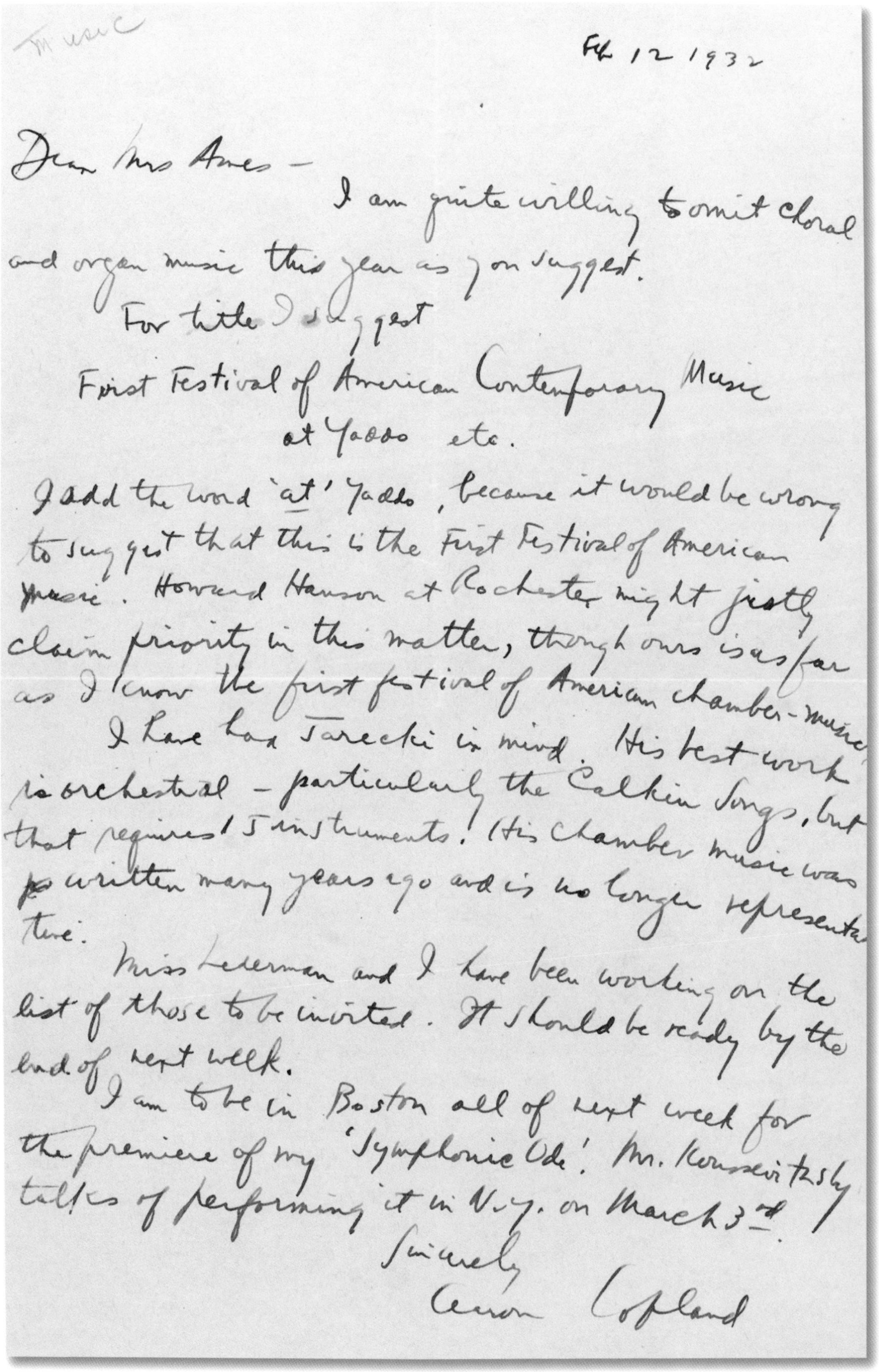

Music

Feb 12 1932

Dear Mrs Ames —

I am quite willing to omit choral and organ music this year as you suggest.

For title I suggest

First Festival of American Contemporary Music
at Yaddo etc.

I add the word "at" Yaddo, because it would be wrong to suggest that this is the First Festival of American music. Howard Hanson at Rochester might justly claim priority in this matter, though ours is as far as I know the first festival of American chamber-music.

I have had Jarecki in mind. His best work is orchestral — particularly the Calkin Songs, but that requires 5 instruments! His chamber music was written many years ago and is no longer representative.

Miss Leberman and I have been working on the list of those to be invited. It should be ready by the end of next week.

I am to be in Boston all of next week for the premiere of my "Symphonic Ode". Mr. Koussevitzky talks of performing it in N.Y. on March 3rd.

Sincerely
Aaron Copland

Composer Aaron Copland first proposed that Yaddo establish a festival of contemporary American music in 1930. By 1932 the idea was a reality, and Copland corresponded with Ames regarding a name for the event.

nomic restrictions: no matter how opulent the Trask estate appeared to be, the Depression had affected everyone, and Copland promised to remain within a strict budget.

Not surprisingly, the first composer he contacted was Roger Sessions (1896–1985), who had been living abroad for years, first in Italy and then in Germany, but continued to visit the United States annually for performances of his music. From 1928 through 1931, the two had cosponsored the Copland-Sessions Concerts, which presented nine events every year, eight of them in New York and one in Paris. As Copland later put it, "What had started with the Copland-Sessions Concerts in an attempt to promote the younger generation of composers, I hoped might continue at Yaddo."[4]

Copland next consulted with Virgil Thomson, with whom he evaluated a wide variety of Boulanger's disciples for consideration. Back home, he reached out to the very youngest generation, to composers still in their teens (Henry Brant and Vivian Fine) and early twenties (Paul Bowles and Israel Citkowitz). Another resource for Copland's search was the League of Composers, which had been founded in 1923.

And so Yaddo's week-long First Festival of Contemporary American Music solidified, slated to begin on April 30, 1932. Three concerts were planned for the weekend, featuring eighteen composers (Robert Russell Bennett, Marc Blitzstein, Louis Gruenberg, Roy Harris, and Walter Piston, among others) and a public discussion, with the four subsequent days taken over by conferences for musicians only.

For the public events, Ames adhered to meticulous, if unconventional, Yaddo standards. The festival would be neither a high-society occasion nor aimed at the local community, she declared. In-

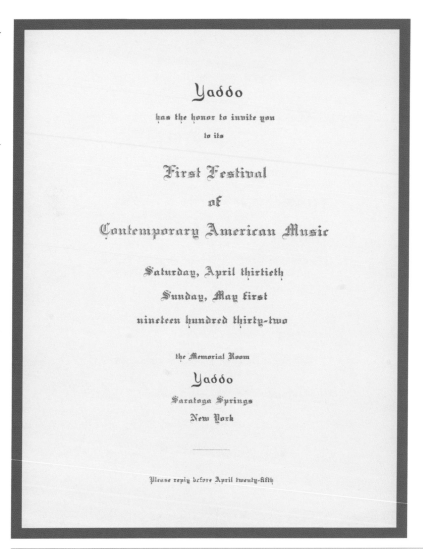

Yaddo's First Festival of Contemporary American Music took place in the spring of 1932.

stead, Ames and Copland devised a hierarchical mailing list that was topped by fellow composers, critics, and conductors, after which came "friends" of Yaddo, and finally directors of northeastern orchestras and concert venues. (Although the events had the obvious potential to secure future engagements for composers, no concert promoters or publicists were invited.)

The targeted one hundred people received what resembled a wedding announcement, with raised gothic script spelling out the "Nineteen hundred thirty-two" schedule. An embossed reception card permitted the bearer entrance to concerts on Saturday morning, Saturday evening, and Sunday afternoon, as well as to Sunday morning's "Conference for Critics and Composers."

The initial conference created considerable controversy. In the 1930s and 1940s, critics tended to focus on execution or performers of known repertory, so contemporary American composers found themselves competing with Beethoven and Tchaikovsky for coverage. With so few opportunities to have their music heard, composers viewed critics from a vantage point different from that of other working artists: in their minds, newspaper attention mat-

Composers and players from the First Festival of Contemporary American Music. *Top row*: Lehman Engel, Israel Citkowitz, Charles Moross, Marc Blitzstein, Bernard Herrmann. *Second row*: Henry Brant, Harrison Kerr, Herbert Elwell, Walter Piston, Aaron Copland. *Seated*: Wallingford Riegger, Randall Thompson, Robert Russell Bennett, Wesley La Violette, Vivian Fine, Richard Donovan.

tered—and mattered greatly—to their personal success. As such, a "gathering of critics and composers to further mutual understanding" promised to enormously benefit hungry American composers.

Yet only four music critics, two of whom wrote just for monthly journals, attended the First Festival. Copland took the floor, feeling, as he later recalled, that "it was up to me to express the anger and frustration felt by the composers" about the paucity of attention Americans received. He accused critics of "neglect and lack of curiosity"

about new music: "Under such circumstances I consider daily newspaper criticism a menace, and we would be better off without it."[5] The words sounded harsh, but not so much in the context; besides, composers made up the majority of the empathetic audience. At the discussion's end, preparations were under way for the afternoon concert, and no one noticed the young Associated Press reporter who slipped out to write a story.

The next morning's *New York Times* and *New York Herald Tribune*—the most intellectually distinguished papers

in what was then the undisputed musical capital of the United States—were two of the countless dailies that published the wire service account, which emphasized not the concerts but the attack on the perceived extramusical "menace" of the press.[6]

The article embarrassed Yaddo and infuriated George Foster Peabody, financier and Katrina Trask's widower, who let his displeasure be known. He dashed off long letters denouncing the story, including one to the Associated Press management, emphasizing that he was mailing carbon copies to his "good friends," the chairmen and editors-in-chief at the *New York Times* and *New York Herald Tribune*.

Peabody may not have known that Copland sent his own letter to the *New York Times*, which the paper's music critic, Olin Downes, reprinted and responded to at unusual length.[7] Downes suggested that composers should be grateful for any crumbs of attention they received, and insisted that any perceived public apathy toward American music was owing to the dearth of any works worth hearing. Neglect in the press came "not from indifference to the composer's interests, but after much practical experience of American music—even recent music—to which it has listened."

In essence, Downes turned the festival premise topsy-turvy and came out swinging. He argued that deserving American composers had more than enough critical attention, awards, and outlets to be heard. "If he has any talent, it is likely to be sought out and published far and wide," Downes insisted. "The time is past when native composers should complain of neglect when failure is likely to be due to lack of creative and technical power." Lest anyone thought that Copland exaggerated the possible "menace" of some critics in the struggle for acceptance of American music, Downes handily proved the point.

Reactions were hardly unanimous, nor was all the attention negative. Charles Ives, the oldest person in the inaugural concert, received more acclaim at Yaddo than he had to date. Nevertheless, in each of the six Yaddo Music Periods that featured Ives's songs, he received the consistently best reviews—to the surprise of many. One critic phrased the reversal as "the first time [Ives] heard applause, not cat-calls."

One composer, a protégé of George Gershwin who briefly studied with Arnold Schoenberg, went on to achieve international acclaim—although not for his composition. Oscar Levant, a phenomenal piano prodigy, became an award-winning Broadway and Hollywood composer, actor, author, and television star. In 1932, somewhat impulsively, he announced his ambition to compose seriously. Copland met him through Gershwin, whose jazz-inspired traces of ragtime and blues echo throughout Levant's *Sonatina*, which received its premiere at the First Festival.

For the Second Festival Copland once again oversaw a large part of the composer selection process, working with the Central Music Committee—made up of Richard Donovan, Walter Piston, Wallingford Riegger, and Randall Thompson. The 1933 committee took greater artistic risks and peppered the mix with more radical modernists, such as George Antheil and Henry Cowell. (Charles Martin Loeffler, the conservative elder statesman, was invited to balance the two.) The combination of such disparate creators offered audiences a broader cross-section of music of the era, and proved the impossibility of pigeon-holing any one "American school."

The Second Festival's public forum intended to explore "the relationship between Composers and Interpretative Artists." One hundred and fifty composers attended, but interpreters were in shorter supply. A majority of pieces were scored for one or two people, and skilled composer-performers played their own and others' music. The dialogue covered a lot of ground, with some blame put on formal education; it was felt that prominent music schools taught little, if anything, except acknowledged classics. Elie Siegmeister, a young composer who was on the panel but not represented in the concerts, blamed society and modern music's fail-

ure to connect with the masses. Sessions, who chaired the forum, injected money into the debate, decrying the way interpreters were trained to pursue "breadwinning" pieces. Inspiration and ideas proliferated, and the milieu was nothing if not stimulating.

Copland immediately set to work on the Third Festival, but musicians and critics had begun to state outright what had been hinted at since 1932—that his reliance on a cohort of Boulanger's students and members of his social circles had resulted in what the otherwise sympathetic critic Paul Rosenfeld called "too many Coplandites." Copland himself was working at Yaddo on his *Short Symphony* (Symphony no. 2) when Ames informed him that the board had unanimously decided that the festivals needed a new direction. Without bitterness, he agreed to step down, but he would not return to Yaddo until the final season.

With 137 composers' works accepted for concert performance at Yaddo over the years, listeners should have heard 137 different styles. But in fact, more than 137 composers were heard, informally, owing to sweeping changes enacted for the 1936 festival. After a three-year hiatus, a new Central Music Committee, consisting of Luening, Porter, Richard Donovan, and the harpsichordist Ralph Kirkpatrick, brought a fresh approach to the entire festival. The overhauled Yaddo Music Festival omitted the words "contemporary" and "American" from its title, but it did not diminish the quantity of new music. From then on, each festival was called a "Music Period," and all composers and interpretative artists belonged to the "Yaddo Music Group."

A lot more than mere terminology changed during the hiatus. The Yaddo Music Group's interpretative contingent now included a twenty-two-piece cham-

From their inception, Yaddo's music festivals received wide press attention. This 1938 photograph appeared with Olin Downes's report for the *New York Times* on the event. *Left to right*: Elizabeth Ames, Ralph Kirkpatrick, Otto Luening, Richard Donovan, Quincy Porter.

ber orchestra, pianists, vocalists, and a separate string quartet. Repertory was far less limited. And there was a new emphasis on personal communality. Three weeks before the public festival, all interpreters and composers lived and worked together, with, as Luening later stated, two noble ideals: "to establish an intimate and informal relationship between composers and performers as they prepare for concerts," and to eliminate those "aspects of competition and professionalism and to make music for its own sake." The new philosophy worked brilliantly and efficiently, as interpreters read through composers' works and both learned much in the process. In 1936, for example, the players sight-read sixty new pieces, of which twenty-seven were chosen for public presentation.

Of the five concerts in 1936, three were devoted to contemporary American composition, with two additional programs devoted to music of the past. The board decided that the festival

would include some traditional music—not hackneyed standards, but neglected gems from the baroque and classical eras. And so the pianist John Kirkpatrick—who performed throughout two decades of Yaddo concerts, notably in music by Ives, Copland, Ruggles, and the unjustly forgotten Robert Palmer—would share programs with Ralph Kirkpatrick (no relation), who specialized in the eighteenth century.

It is impossible to imagine a single greater contribution to contemporary American music than the study records the Yaddo Music Group produced during those weeks. Quincy Porter conceived of the venture when state-of-the-art recording equipment had been installed in the Trask mansion. Of varying technical quality, the extant 162 recordings were not intended for retail sale. Rather, they were traded at cost to universities, libraries, associations, and other institutions. Such invaluable tools permitted students and composers to

listen to the realized scores that, up to that point, could have been studied only visually.

Union members of the Yaddo Music Group donated their services, and a staggering forty-nine records were issued in the 1936 Music Period, with another fifty-four records in 1938. Much of the music had never before been heard outside of a single performance at Yaddo. The manner and extent to which the mere existence of these recordings assisted and educated a new generation of American musicians cannot be overstated. A complete collection of the Yaddo discs, remastered and reissued with proper annotation, would be a significant contribution to our understanding of our musical culture.

In the late 1930s, composers' advocacy for their field and their struggle for public recognition took a new tack. The 1932 Yaddo press battle with critics was indirectly remedied as American composers themselves became critics, of whom Virgil Thomson was by far the most prolific. Thomson, who literally wrote volumes of daily criticism, paved the way for a younger cohort of composers to write reviews on a freelance basis for the *New York Herald Tribune* at the time of Yaddo's festivals. Members of the Young Composers Group, including Bowles, Henry Cowell, Elliott Carter, and Arthur Berger, supplemented their income as critics for the paper during the Yaddo era.

Cowell promoted American music overseas, as well. Before his attachment to Yaddo, he had been the first American composer invited to the Soviet Union. Now he founded the Pan-American Association of Composers, *New Music Quarterly*, and a record company offshoot, the last two of which involved other participants from the festival family. And in the face of a dire personal crisis—Cowell was arrested, convicted,

A rehearsal for the eighth music festival in 1949, Dean Dixon conducting.

and then imprisoned on what officials euphemistically dubbed a "morals charge"—Luening, Riegger, and the Central Music Committee secretly came to his rescue, voluntarily running his magazine and record company in the interim.

The 1937 performances continued to combine the old and new. During the Fourth Music Period, the resident ensembles read through 125 contemporary compositions and performed 37 of them. Ralph Kirkpatrick's masterful selection of baroque- and classical-era pieces may have won over the public, but it was hardly planned as a sop to members of the press threatened by new music. The chance to experience uncommon works of the past brought satisfaction to the musicians themselves.

Increasingly, the media recognized the value of Yaddo's music ventures. At the 1938 series, the *New York Times*'s music critic, Howard Taubman, interviewed composers and sat in on rehearsals as well as performances. The *Times* allotted a large space for his positive review. Taubman even injected a plea to ornery concertgoers: "Like it or not, [contemporary music] represents our time, and its direction should be of as much concern as trends in other pursuits."[8]

In 1938 New York's WNYC radio instituted live concert broadcasts of the Yaddo festivals, bringing thirty-nine new compositions to a huge audience in the largest metropolitan area in the country. By 1940, concerts from the Trask mansion were aired nation-wide on the NBC radio network: listeners tuned into American contemporary music on the same stations more famously associated with Arturo Toscanini.

The good times were not to last. World War II and the war effort intervened between Music Periods, and the next festival did not take place until 1946. Significant pieces were written by Carter, Louise Talma, and Lou Harrison. The year 1946 also marked the Yaddo debut of a new generation, most famously Jack Beeson; Peter Mennin, who would later direct the Peabody Conservatory, and then hold the presidency of the Juilliard School for twenty years; and Vincent Persichetti, who would be a crucial force in the composition department at Juilliard for four decades.

After the Yaddo Composers' Conferences, Festival of Contemporary American Music, and Yaddo Music Festival had supported American music for eighteen years, the board contemplated its end. The Corporation of Yaddo, its mission, structure, and design, was never meant to be a public institution. Elizabeth Ames, who remained faithful to the Trasks' vision until her death at the age of ninety-two, believed that Yaddo satisfied artists' needs best when it satisfied them simply, and she felt that the festivals had grown too complex. Finances became overwhelming with the expenses and number of guests and visitors. The press coverage and public audiences' intrusion distracted from the Yaddo spirit and purpose—a sacred provision that any tangent from the artists' retreat must not violate.

Nevertheless, the festivals had promoted contemporary American composition and a profound understanding of it in a way few institutions approached before or after. And the nation had transformed dramatically in the early 1950s. In the peacetime prosperity, "Music Appreciation" was taught in grade schools, and the G.I. Bill afforded a higher level of education throughout America. It was hoped that a better educated public would result in greater respect for the arts. The new decade brought with it tremendous advances in technology that assisted composers in realizing their creations, and it opened up a new frontier in musical language. (Luening, for example, helped found the Columbia-Princeton Electronic Music Center.)

The board of directors chose to draw Yaddo's musical era to a close in 1952. The 1949 Central Music Committee agreed with Ames, who thought the festival should go out with a bang—a joyous celebration after twenty years of music. Yet no one left so soon. Yaddo had hosted its first composer-guests in

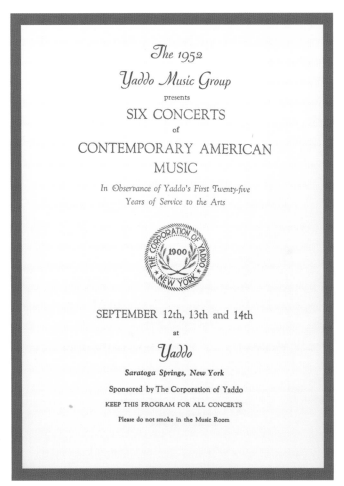

Program for the 1952 Yaddo Music Group.

Rehearsing for the 1952 music festival. *Left to right*: John Kirkpatrick, Frederick Fennell, and Dorothy Fennell. The 1952 festival was the last of the nine seasons of performances.

1927, the year after it opened, and by 1950, much of the Yaddo Music Group had privately worked in residence at some point. And so Elizabeth Ames included the five years leading up to the First Festival to title the Ninth Music Period, "Twenty-five Years of Music at Yaddo."

This grand finale was a retrospective of a quarter-century of American composition. Copland came back to Yaddo, as did other members of the "Boulangerie": Chanler, Diamond, Finney, Harris, Sessions, and Thomson. Nearly one hundred musicians performed works by the thirty American composers selected by the Central Music Committee. By 1952, many of the brash young adults who had taken bows at the first and second festivals had achieved considerable fame. The Pulitzer Prize for composition had been awarded only since 1943, but eight winners were scheduled for the last Music Period. In keeping with the festival's original purpose, a dozen composers came from the youngest generation, and there were Yaddo debuts by Irving Fine, Nikolai Lopatnikoff, Robert Evett, and Ben Weber, who had grown up in a society much more accepting of American music, thanks to the elders with whom they shared the stage.

The Yaddo Music Festivals set out to present a snapshot of American music in the 1930s and 1940s and managed instead to present a panoramic vista. The Music Periods gave composers the opportunity to hear their own music and a massive amount of their peers' music, to learn and teach, share and debate, form associations and arrange for one another to have music published, recorded, and performed.

These two decades were a time of fertile creativity, a turning point when American composition finally felt liberated from Europe's sway. Over the years, its programs offered the music of stark modernists, such as Wallingford Riegger and the young Elliott Carter, as well as late Romantics, such as Mary Howe. Eastern and Western idioms combined in the work of Peggy Glanville-Hicks and came together in an utterly different mode in works by the prolific Alan Hovhaness. Israel Citkowitz almost exclusively composed art songs for soprano, while Roger Sessions specialized in symphonic works. Henry Leland Clarke wrote tonal music based on scales of his own invention. Alvin Etler, from Cleveland, was part of five Music Periods. Rooted in twelve-tone practice, his music nevertheless exuded jazz influences. Themes from all manner of

popular songs pervaded the choral works by Randall Thompson, a Central Committee member. Protestant hymn tunes appear in different guises in Virgil Thomson's works, as they did in music by Richard Donovan, a professor at Yale whose dedication to the Yaddo Music Festivals was unparalleled.

Looking back on the Copland-Downes controversy of the first season, Irving Kolodin wrote: "One may be sure that there will be adequate press coverage of this year's festival, that there will be no occasion for complaints about 'neglect.' Many of the same men and women are gathered here again, but if the air is less charged with excitement, the reason is simple. Yaddo has accomplished its pioneering mission and now can reap in confidence the fruits it sowed in rebellion."[9]

When the curtain came down on the final Yaddo Music Festival, the artists' retreat recaptured its peace and quiet, which has been mostly unbroken in the years since. Even so, dozens of American composers have continued to take advantage of the generous support at the Trask estate where Copland once wrestled with his *Piano Variations*. If the music *at* Yaddo has quieted down, the music *from* Yaddo will, one hopes, be with us forever.

[OPPOSITE] Louis Lozowick. *Roofs and Sky*, ca. 1939. Lozowick, a Precisionist printmaker, was a guest in 1929 and 1930. As with many of Yaddo's artists, he was also supported by the Federal Art Program of the Depression-era Works Progress Administration.

4 / IN GOOD COMPANY

VISUAL ARTISTS AT YADDO

Karl Emil Willers

[I] have thought so long and often of the wonderful spirit and continuity of Yaddo, and always feel more prepared to go on with the direction of the intangible when one knows that somewhere others have faith and courage.

—BEAUFORD DELANEY, 1950

THE ROSTER of artists who have worked at Yaddo over the years provides a unique and alternative perspective on the visual culture of the last century, one that both inflects and augments the canonical story of American artistic endeavor. There are certainly many Yaddo residents in every discipline whose contributions have yet to be fully recognized, and even the briefest overview will include individuals whose work is yet to be wholly integrated into the traditional narratives and lessons of art and culture. However, the history of art is undoubtedly largely synonymous with the history of taste, and much that remains underappreciated today may yet prove of interest to future audiences. Ultimately, the idea of Yaddo is not based on the cultivation of new art-stars to serve the excesses of a current market. Rather, it embraces the concept that all cultural life is fundamentally a social activity. At Yaddo, good company nurtures great endeavor.

That said, clearly the story of the visual arts at Yaddo during the twentieth century is largely coextensive with the history of art in America of the same period. During the early decades of the twentieth century, the influence of European modernism on American artists intermingled with a variety of figurative modes that often addressed the economic deprivations of the 1930s. Precisionist paintings by Louis Lozowick (resident in 1929) depicted the New York skyline and streetscape, combining an urbanism and modernity that characterized American visual culture of the 1920s. Drawing on machine forms and industrial architecture, the photographs and films of Ralph Steiner (resident in 1929) as well as the paintings and drawings of Elsie Driggs (resident in 1935), expanded on this modernist vocabulary. The prints and drawings of such graphic artists as Hugh Botts (resident in 1928), Nikolai Cikovsky (resident in 1931), Philip Reisman (resident in 1933–1934),

LOUIS LOZOWICK

20 West 56th St,
New York, N.Y.

Nov. 2, 1930

Dear Mrs. Ames:

Probably as a reaction against extreme zeal at Yaddo I have done nothing this past week but walk the streets and visit exhibitions. Beginning tomorrow, however, I am starting on my first job of the season. I have to serve on Jury duty; probably help straighten out some kinks in the eternal triangle or put the fear of God into a pickpocket and help him on to bigger game.

I have been looking over my drawings and paintings of the summer which taken together make quite an impressive showing — at least in bulk. My stay at Yaddo was really the full equivalent of a Guggenheim Fellowship, plus

LOUIS LOZOWICK

the personal care and interest, naturally lacking in that Fellowship. My sincerest gratitude.

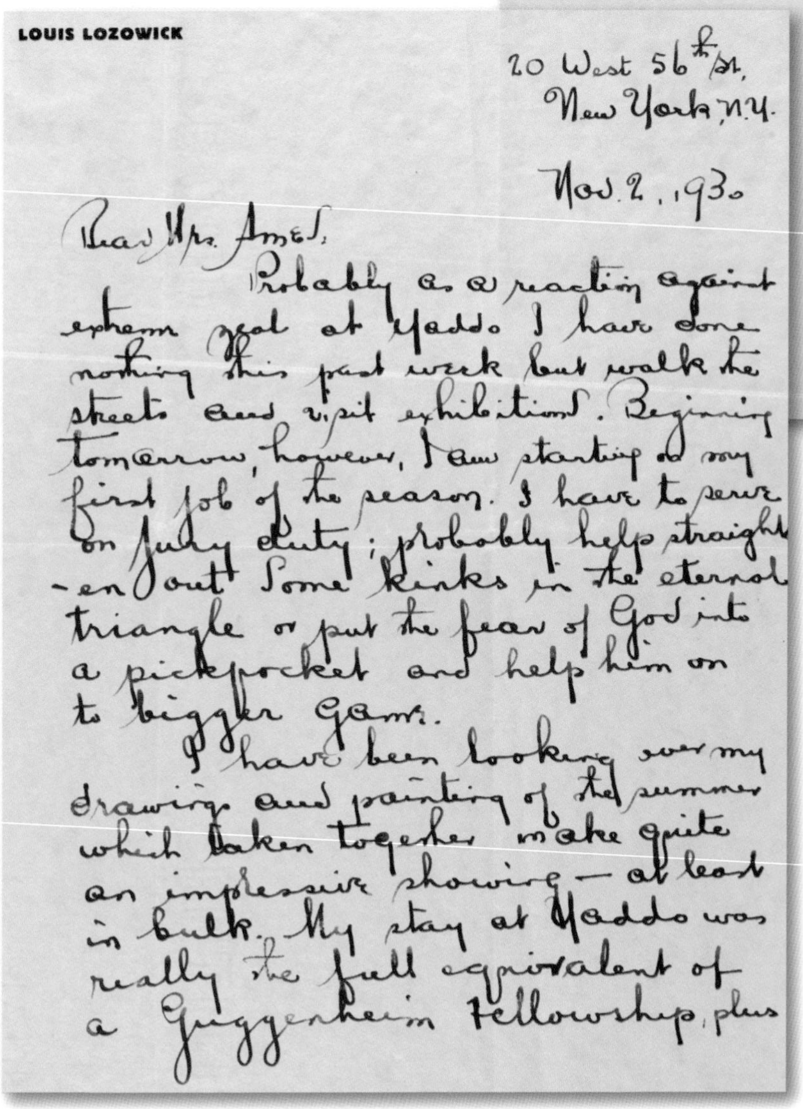

I would be happy if you found leisure to see me sometime in the winter. My warmest wishes for your trip to Europe.

Friendly greetings to Miss Gard, Mr. Wright (and thanks for the lift to Albany), Mrs. Waite and everyone else I knew as well as to the lakes and woods of Yaddo.

As ever,
Louis Lozowick

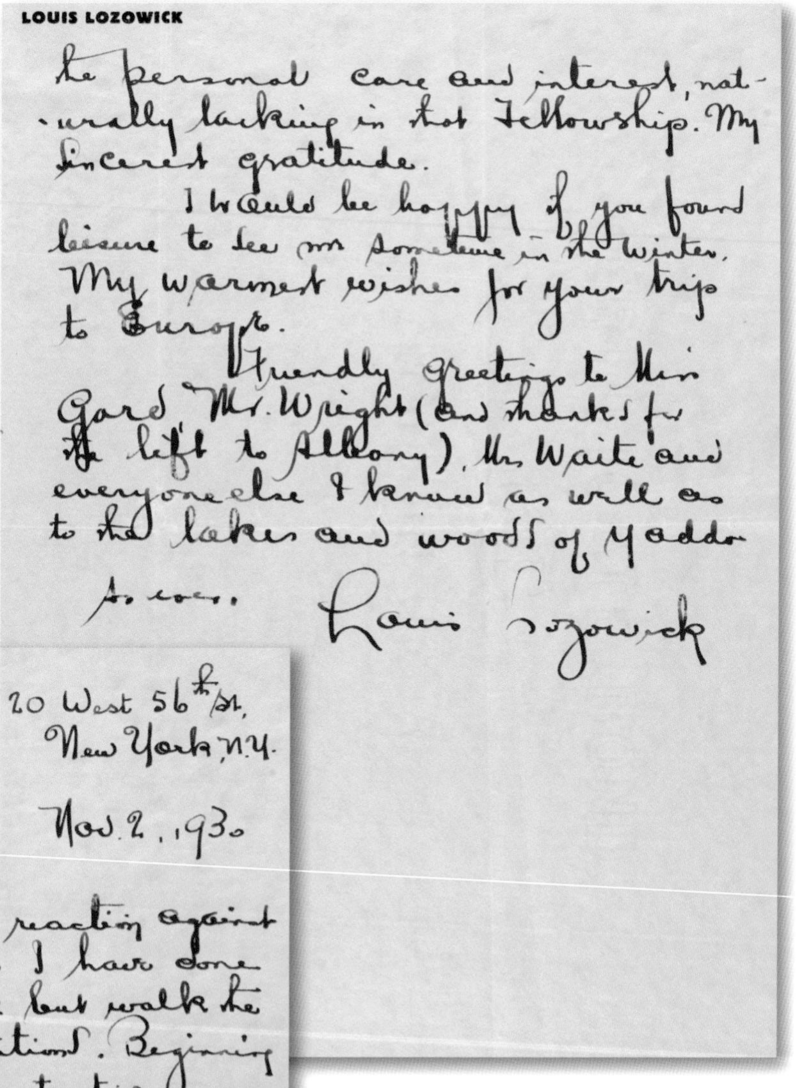

Louis Lozowick expressed his appreciation regarding his stay in a letter to Elizabeth Ames, November 2, 1930.

Hugh Pearce Botts. *Columbus Circle*, n.d. Botts was a guest in 1928.

Nicolai Cikovsky. *Union Square*, 1934. Cikovsky was a guest in 1931.

and Agnes Tait (resident in 1933 and 1940), among others, exemplified the political activism and social realism that emerged with the economic struggles of the 1930s. Although not a resident at Yaddo until the mid-1950s, Adolf Dehn created art that was a gritty and powerful critique of American society and the politics of the Depression era.

The mid-1930s through the mid-1950s brought to Yaddo artists working in a variety of styles, ranging from a hard-edged formalism in painting that evoked utopian ideals to more literal explorations of the social and personal implications of war and its aftermath investigated through diverse new media. The couple Ilya Bolotowsky and Esphyr Slo-

Philip Reisman. *The South*, 1934. Reisman's graphic rendering of a lynching was a controversial image during the Jim Crow era. Reisman, a guest in 1933 and 1934, inscribed this print to Elizabeth Ames.

bodkina (residents in 1934), as well as others associated with the American Abstract Artists group, championed Neo-Plasticism in America, a pure geometric abstraction that sought universal ideals across the divides of nation-states and native languages. With the advent of World War II, Surrealism and Dada found expression in the psychosexual landscapes and biomorphic figuration in the art of Frederico Castellon (resident in 1939), Ruth Gikow (resident in 1942), Nan Lurie (resident in 1942), Minna Citron (resident in 1946), and Sari Dienes (resident in 1953). In photography, both reportage and montage were advanced through the chance revelations captured by Henri Cartier-Bresson (resident in 1946) and in the anomalous juxtapositions explored by Vladimir Telberg (resident in 1953). Directly addressing racial and social injustice, Jacob Lawrence (resident in 1954) produced a series of screen prints that explored the African American experience in a society marred by segregation and inequality.

In the postwar era, the increasing dominance of gestural abstraction in New York was also apparent in a generation of artists who worked at Yaddo. However, the latent content embodied in the very refusal of representational modes would arise in a multiplicity of styles during the 1960s and 1970s that paralleled the rise of political and social protest. The paintings of Milton Avery (resident in 1955) proved to be idiosyncratic precursors to the rise of Abstract Expressionism in postwar America. Though a resident at Yaddo as early as 1933, Clyfford Still would become a pioneer of the gestural abstraction characteristic of the New York School, a tradition furthered and extended by painters such as Lawrence Calcagno (resident in 1963) and Jules Olitski (resident in 1971). Philip Guston, another first-generation

Ilya Bolotowsky. *Untitled*, 1937. Bolotowsky and his wife, artist Esphyr Slobodkina, visited Yaddo in 1934.

Agnes Tait. *Front Street, New York*, 1936. Printmaker Agnes Tait came to Yaddo in 1933 at the recommendation of Lewis Mumford.

Ruth Gikow. *Flood*, 1936. Gikow was another of the printmakers supported both by the WPA and Yaddo. Gikow visited Yaddo in 1942.

Minna Citron. *Men Seldom Make Passes*, 1946. Citron was a guest in 1946. Dorothy Parker, from whom she borrowed the title for this image, was a guest in 1958.

Nan Lurie. *Technological Improvements*, 1937. Lurie visited Yaddo in 1942.

Jacob Lawrence. *Confrontation at the Bridge*, 1975. Lawrence was a guest in 1954 and 1955.

Abstract Expressionist, did not visit Yaddo until 1969, when his painting had come to embrace a politically infused figuration that continues to influence contemporary art half a century later. Anne Truitt (resident several times between 1974 and 2001) was one of the few women to make early contributions to a Minimalist aesthetic that questioned traditional relations between the art object and the viewer. With the rise of consumer culture and the pluralism of identity politics, the artistic contributions by guests of Yaddo expanded almost exponentially. All in all, it is no exaggeration to say that the numerous

artists who have worked at Yaddo at some point during their careers not only replicates, but also generously expands, the standard history of American visual culture of the past century.

In taking advantage of the refuge offered at Yaddo, visual artists face obstacles that writers and composers do not. To work effectively and productively, visual artists often require a unique accumulation of raw materials and studio infrastructure. The sculptor Martin Puryear (resident in 1979) addresses this:

The main memory I have of the place is just how privileged one feels to have your work and your life as an artist supported like that—and protected in such a special way. Artists, unlike writers, do need a special kind of place to work. (These days, I think of writers as people who can pretty much put down their word processor anywhere—even in a Starbucks.) Artists tend to need a base to operate from. I spent two months at Yaddo after my studio in Brooklyn was destroyed by fire. And even though my familiar base of operations was gone, I was surprised to learn how

Philip Guston. *Sea*, 1969. Late in his career, Guston developed an animated figuration.

focused my work habits could be at Yaddo, and how much work I was able to accomplish without the everyday distractions I was accustomed to.[1]

Even assuming that it takes all artists in any medium a period to adjust to new surroundings, painters obviously require pigments and brushes and canvas and stretchers and easels—as well as adequate space in which to work. Sculptors (or those who build, construct, mold, carve, chisel, assemble, accumulate, or arrange three-dimensional objects—as well as those who make entire installations and overall environments) face even more cumbersome challenges in terms of acquiring the physical mate-

rials and studio space to practice their art. Even in our age of digitization, such arguments can be extended to recognize the encumbrances that accompany other reproductive and new media, including photography, film, video, and computer-based arts.

Nevertheless, visual artists did produce at Yaddo, and often made significant work. While recognizing the impediments of being away from one's usual workplace, the sculptor and painter Mary Frank (resident in 1970) summarily dismisses the limitations:

I want to go back to Yaddo. I really do. It was superb. Not infrequently when I go into my studio, I've thought, "Oh,

I wish I was at Yaddo." It can be difficult working away from one's studio, but it depends on how you work, of course. If you work on a painting for years—not good. I wasn't going to take up big canvases there. I wouldn't have been able to work on sculpture, but I wasn't really working on sculptures then. I did a lot of work on paper—drawing, acrylic, and oil. A number of them were included among a wall of portraits that were recently exhibited at DC Moore Gallery—others were incorporated into collages. Yaddo gets you out of your daily routine, and when I later looked at the work I did there, it looked different.[2]

Mary Frank. *Man in the Water*, 1987. Frank first worked at Yaddo in 1970.

It can be argued that new surroundings, new methods, new materials, and new experiences often spur on the creative process. That is indeed one premise on which the artistic retreat is founded. And if this is true, then logically the greater the challenges posed by an artist leaving habitual places of work or study, the greater the possibility of creative breakthrough or redirection or accomplishment. Rejuvenation and achievement may very well be the outcome and result of any escape from the habits of everyday life and regularity of studio work.

This brings us to a fundamental point about Yaddo and what it contributes to visual arts, or for that matter what it accomplishes for culture itself. It is an obvious point, but all the more reason to state it plainly—it is the mix of practitioners working in a variety of disciplines that makes Yaddo exceptional and distinctive. Mary Frank comments at length on this aspect of her stay at Yaddo:

Yaddo was full because it was summer—not only visual artists, of course, but also writers and musicians. I made one very good friend there. The reporter Jacki Lyden was reading parts of a piece she was working on about Iraq. She's a very courageous woman. She has been in Iraq and Afghanistan at least twenty, maybe thirty times. She has written an unforgettable book called *Daughter of the Queen of Sheba*, her memoir about life with her mother who was bipolar. It is so moving and wildly funny in an unlikely way—beautiful. I don't always want to be only with visual artists—I have such a desire to do more collaboration with writers, poets, and playwrights. The composer and pianist David Del Tredici was also there, and sometimes he played. Oh, that was wonderful. There were so many people working intensely. I only wish I had had more time to see

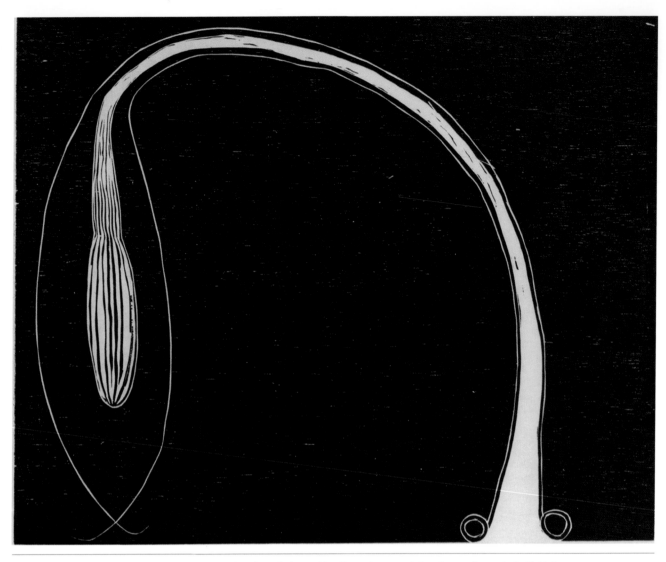

Martin Puryear. *Karintha*, 2000. Woodcut for the 2000 Arion Press limited edition of Jean Toomer's 1921 novel, *Cane*. Puryear first worked at Yaddo in 1979.

their work and listen to them. Partly because I wanted to work in the studio a lot, I did not get to talk with everyone. Yaddo was so good—not only about meeting people I didn't know, but about having people from other fields right there.

For visual artists, Yaddo is frequently a place to meet and develop a rapport not only with colleagues working in similar media but also with individuals practicing in creative fields very different from their own. It is a place where visual artists are thrown together with individuals pursuing writing, performance, sound, and movement in all their disparate practices and genres. Martin Puryear also notably cherished his exposure at Yaddo to diverse fields of inquiry:

For me, the interesting thing about it was the chance to be around people from different disciplines—writers and composers—people who I'd never really had much contact with. It was just extraordinary. I remember one of the writers—Paul Auster, who I had not met up until then—did a reading of one of his early works. He invited us on a Saturday, and a group of us sat through the entire reading. We showed up and sat in the main room in West House and listened to readings all day. We had a break for lunch, came back and read in the afternoon. Then we had a break for dinner, came back and read up until bedtime. I saw Paul Auster again last year and we had a very fond mutual recollection of our time there at Yaddo. It was just extraordinary.

It is something of a cliché to say that the ability of people to associate and commune with individuals working in other arts—of artists having contact with disciplines different from their own—has the potential of enriching all. The culture at Yaddo certainly cannot be described as officially promoting interdisciplinary practices or formally advocating cross-fertilization of the various arts. On the contrary, the pattern of life at Yaddo frequently encourages concentrated and isolated work—residents are forbidden to interrupt one another's periods of concentrated activity. In this sense, the rituals of Yaddo can even be described as formulating an almost monastic sense of self-absorption and solitude. The extensive property and spacious grounds at Yaddo, to which all guests have easy and unlimited access, often enhance this experience, particularly in a time of social crisis, when the world can seem to be closing in on the imaginative space of the artist. Marion Greenwood (resident in 1927, 1932, and 1940) wrote to Yaddo's executive director, Elizabeth Ames, of this effect in 1940:

> Your letter [inviting me to return to Yaddo] was like a burst of sunshine for me in this grey city, of rushing and worrying and war news—and once again I knew I would be free to paint and gather my thoughts and my scattered self, and be in the country. After years of constant disciplined production I feel like a machine that's running down. The plan is a spiritual hauling over, and the motto will be "less quantity, and physical labor, more quality and searching thought" and the hope that peace and quiet in Yaddo will help me get a start towards it.[3]

Martin Puryear corroborates the restorative powers and beneficent force of Yaddo's natural setting:

> My stay at Yaddo was close to two months. I saw fall turn into winter, which was just so beautiful. I remember watching the Gingko trees from my studio window shed their leaves all at once. I had a studio that was down behind one of the main buildings—maybe the building where we all had meals—and it looked out over this quiet area without much traffic around. Looking out from my studio window, it seemed that I had the whole place to myself. What I loved was the way you could take a break anytime during the day and just wander through the grounds—or run through the grounds for exercise. I did both. I explored every nook and cranny of Yaddo's property in my ramblings between work sessions. It was just heavenly.

Mary Frank also found the grounds at Yaddo an integral and formative part of her experiences there. The outdoors provided a site for communing—not only between the self and nature but also among the staff and residents:

> I loved the gardens. I went around deadheading flowers, because I missed my garden at home. Yaddo has this strange landscape of evergreen trees that were planted long ago when nobody realized quite how big they would get. They form sort of imposing dark allées that actually look more European than American. I talked to the cook about solar cooking, which is being taught in many parts of the world to prevent deforestation. He was very interested. I went mushroom hunting and did find Chanterelles. I cooked them outside with a solar cooker. People came by and wondered what was cooking without a fire of any kind. They smelled the food and got to taste it. They were amazed. The time at Yaddo was rich—rich and also peaceful, which is maybe an unusual combination.

In the same way that the opportunity for sustained work is enforced, open and free exchange among guests also is subtly encouraged, even insisted on by the requirement that all residents take their evening meal together. Whether this scheduled meeting results in interactions and exchanges, the potential for association among practitioners of different arts and letters can be said to do much for building communities of interest and support. Painter and author Alfred Leslie (resident in 1986) believes this spirit of community is more important than ever in the current climate. "I think it has something to do with real estate," he has said. "At the end of World War II, there was plenty of space for everybody. Today you don't have that easy access to space or an understanding of how to make community happen."[4]

Yaddo has an exceedingly admirable record of extending invitations to artists when they are most appreciated—and this is a point to emphasize, for it is one of the principal revelations of its archives. Puryear commented on how Yaddo's hospitality seemed timed to help him move forward at a moment when he was at a particularly difficult impasse in his career:

> I was astounded at how much work I got done when I was there. I went to Yaddo some time after there had been a fire in my studio, so I really didn't have a good workplace. I had lost my studio in Williamsburg, Brooklyn, and was working in different places on some large-scale projects. This may sound a little disjunctive, but I'm just trying to put it in order and set the scene for how useful Yaddo was for me. I'd had the fire in the late 1970s. That was during the winter, and that following summer I was at Art Park up in Lewiston, New York. I also had a show of work that I had

George Rickey. *Two Slender Lines Excentric*, 1977. Rickey first worked at Yaddo in 1969 and later became a deeply committed supporter and board member.

managed to collect together at the Corcoran Gallery of Art in Washington, but by autumn I still didn't have a good working situation. Yaddo was the place where I was really able to consolidate my thinking and my mind after that fire. I was able to produce a body of work at Yaddo, and it was amazing just how much I did produce.

The organizational process of how people come to be invited to Yaddo for periods of stay assures that the largess is bestowed for optimal benefit. Yaddo is largely a self-generating phenomenon. Residents enter into something of a family—past guests sometimes serve on admissions panels, recommend other artists, or even return as residents. This inherent, consistent building of continuity can suggest exclusivity, yet in actuality the qualified individuals who collectively provide input and feedback within this process have become extensive and varied. Ultimately, there can be no better source for information about talents that need nurturing, as well as what personal or professional setbacks can be mitigated or remedied by a Yaddo stay.

For some residents, Yaddo provided an opportunity for exploration and experimentation relatively early in their careers. Over the years, however, Yaddo also gained a unique and prestigious reputation as a place for concentrated work by experienced and mature practitioners. The tendency to name and celebrate some of the most renowned visual artists who have resided at Yaddo misses and overlooks much, especially the subtleties of Yaddo's impact on American culture. Yaddo provides that opportunity to leave the studio, to temporarily escape the contingencies and distractions of personal and professional life. Yaddo's role in the larger culture is tied up with how widely the net has been cast to make that opportunity count.

[OPPOSITE] In the late 1930s, writer John Cheever served as Yaddo's boatman, ferrying guests to the Triuna camp on Lake George. *Left to right*: unidentified man; Elizabeth Ames; Ames's dog, Brownie; Cheever; and an unidentified man and woman.

5 / THE GHOSTS OF YADDO

WHAT THEY TAUGHT

Allan Gurganus

If I am not for myself, who will be for me?
And if I am only for myself, what am I?
—HILLEL

There are those who have seen ghosts. And those who have not seen ghosts yet.

YADDO, THE artist colony now a century old, chose to situate itself in one immense shadowy nineteenth-century mansion surrounded by four hundred evergreen acres. One look tells you: the dark house is highly likely to be crawling with spirit boarders. To have really seen one there seems a bit too obvious.

And yet, during my very first visit at age twenty-four, even as I worked to finish one short story and learn my craft,

a stalwart from some other zone made herself manifest not ten feet from my desk. Ever since, I associate my own good work habits, sunset itself, and the simple luxury of Yaddo's cloistered silence with this strange translucent sentinel. She taught me something.

Do you mind if I tell you? I survived that face-off with the first ghost of my career. (Just as some persons forever attract mosquitoes, others tend to magnetize buzzing leftover energies.) Since that first spirit, yes, there have been others. I am, after all, sixty now. And Yaddo is a round one hundred. Since my first ghost, how many have I *had*? (Or, no,

how many have had me?) A gentleman never deals in numbers. Therefore, I can tell you: six.

But, as with sex, it is your first that matters most.

———✀———

If you still feel cynical about someone's seeing the departed-still-on-hold, just wait. One has not yet found you? Maybe you're still shy. Maybe they are. But not to worry—when you least expect it, something in the room will prove as unexplainable as undeniable. Only then should you come back and read this. Only then will you be ready.

For what Yaddo showed me: about writing toward an awkward truth, about the even-harder chore of existing alongside those not-quite-fully-alive but as yet unable to lie down. Writing fiction is mere preparation for facing those who, against their will, somehow overstay.

———— ✺ ————

You turn left off Route 87 North not too far short of Montreal. Just past the interstate, you'll enter a wooded redoubt. The car crosses a narrow spit between lakes always a wee bit stagnant. These lakes are named, you somehow sense, for two children who died a hundred yards uphill and dead ahead.

At the crest of the hill, rising zig-zagged gothic against an Adirondack sunset, one stone mansion offers to become your crash course in art, your dorm and doom, your home sweet home.

The great house, favorite nighttime playground of light-starved bats, imitates an Austrian *Schloss*. Robber baronial, it claims a gardened terrace that itself supervises one great lawn sloping toward a fountain. There, white marble water-nymphs remain, as in one's sex dreams, perpetually yawning, perpetually wet.

Hidden in the woods are countless outbuildings, barns transformed to painters' haunts, groundskeeper domiciles where writers now secrete their narrative landscapes. But Yaddo's major structure is correctly called "The Mansion." Its fifty-five rooms have known more than a million artistic births and at least four human deaths. Most old houses endure and enclose such a tally. Few retain the essences of those stuck in transit, not-quite-departed but always packed, intending to.

The Spencer Trasks, a spirited couple, stood ready to offer their children this

In 1888 Eastman Johnson painted posthumous portraits of the Trask children Christina and Spencer Jr.

Guests in the first season, 1926. *Top row*: William Waltemath, Tadeusz Jarecki, A. E. Johnson, Joseph Warren Beach, Thomas H. Dickinson, Marian Calkins. *Bottom row*: Dagmar Beach, Louise Jarecki, Elizabeth Ames, Lillian Louise, Joseph K. Hart.

Guests in 1934. *Top row*: John Duke, Arthur Berger, unidentified man, Martin Craig, unidentified man, James T. Farrell, Joseph De Martini, Alexander Godin. *Near flowerpot*: Irving Fineman, Muriel Rukeyser. *On bench*: Dorothy Farrell, Roy Harris, Walter Quirt, Jean Liberté, Elizabeth Ames, Eugene Joffe, Ann Rivington, John Cheever. *On pillows*: Louis Hechenbleikner, Christl Hechenbleikner, unidentified man.

estate and more. That included all their New York Central Railway and *New York Times* stock. Spencer had helped found both concerns. Of course, the children were pretty and bright. Their mother fell ill. The doctor wrongly adjudged her recovered. The children, too long quarantined and missing her so, were allowed upstairs for many postponed hugs and kisses. The kids were dead within two weeks. Their portraits by Eastman Johnson were painted posthumously larger than life in some belated act of grieving compensation. These images still cast a chilled whimsy on the Music Room.

The house looks far too haunted to be credibly haunted. It would be far more original to see ghosts in La Guardia Airport or on its parking decks. Therefore, as an aesthetician, I have kept silent all these years—not exactly ashamed but wary of seeming too garrulous a witness. And yet, the hundredth anniversary and my own galloping mortality make me think, If not now, when? Seems time to speak of what I saw that evening. Make of it what you will.

Seeing ghosts along these dark-paneled corridors is about as likely as spying aluminum putters on most miniature golf courses. Mansion residents have long used ghosts as "cover." One such story is told about the young John Cheever at age twenty-five and at his most satyr-like. The tale might be apocryphal but has proved immortal anyway. The brilliant, handsome young story-writer, sneaking naked from the room of tonight's conquest and back to his own quarters upstairs, got caught en route. Trapped in the hallway by other artists returning from drinks in Saratoga, Cheever, pale in the gloom, took a frozen pose as if a suit of armor. The scene makes me know how James Thurber would have drawn it. Once campers paused around the naked youth, he said in monotone, eyes glazed, "I am a ghost."

—And now, of course, he is, God bless him.

————— ∞ —————

And yet actual phantoms, needing no hall-pass explanation, stalk these corridors, too. I do not speak of anything merely ectoplasmic. Nor do I propose to offer here the "Key to All Knowledge of the Underworld's Above-Ground Afterlife." Instead, I shall try to describe what physically happened and in language as plain as I can bear.

The rest will be up to you. Yaddo is generous. Along with providing me the quiet shelter that let me write ten complete stories and the better chapters of at least two novels, maybe Yaddo's greatest gift to me has been precisely this: a first glimpse, beyond even art's own lens, into a parallel and second sort of world. As I write this, early August at my home in North Carolina, I seem to smell the third floor of Yaddo's mansion. The spruce scent of deep woods combines with a mineral cleanliness rising from the sun-cooked roof slates. A healthful Alpine scent rides breezes from Vermont. Even the little generic bars of bath soap, left after the maid's weekly cleaning of your bedroom, contribute to your sense of the place's stark monastic mission. To be left alone, to simply think one's thoughts, to shape each subsequent sentence so it encloses that last thought like its own balanced chalice—what a luxury and privilege. There is something fine and clear and singularly antimodern in Yaddo's scheme. It acknowledges—unlike Hollywood or Washington, D.C.—that art is not committee work. Find one room, put one artist in it, and leave those two alone together for some months. See what such cohabitation might produce.

I tell you the one I saw was as real as these keys I now press in trying to evoke it.

I had arrived at Yaddo in 1971 or so, a kid fresh out of Sarah Lawrence and bound directly for the Iowa Writers' Workshop. I had a twenty-six-inch waist, a head of thick reddish blond hair. My only wrinkles then gathered at my knees and elbows. Though not a virgin, I had never seen a ghost (except in the fiction of Henry James, H. P. Lovecraft, Edith Wharton, and Poe). Yaddo legend claims that Poe, visiting the present lakes where a fishing camp stood, was

inspired to write his "Raven" here. He scared a local boy by repeated baritone cries from the deepest woods, "Nevermore!" If not here, where?

My first full day at Yaddo, I took a walk along its allée of immense spruces. Planted yards apart ninety years before, treetops now met and mingled, hands in prayer, far overhead. A breeze made branches shush, then rustle.

This setting almost does the contemplating for you. Unlike your usual stride, you fall into a walking imitation of one brilliant Jesuit seminarian, head nodding from that wise head's weight, hands clasped behind your back. And as I moved in this mindful attitude, something brittle if lightweight struck my skull quite hard. I stopped, retrieved the thing. It proved to be a rabbit- or chicken-leg bone, picked clean of flesh but still, to my touch, revoltingly damp. I scanned overhead in a "Why me, Lord?" attitude worthy of Job.

And there, perched nineteen feet above me on a dead branch, one big

white barn owl stared unblinking down at me and through me. It must have just been beaking into the bone's last calcium when, irked at being interrupted, it dropped the femur square onto my head.

Okay, I felt plainly on notice. I knew I had just left the realm of the literal. Anything merely actual, consolingly suburban, was now lost to me. A set of rules reigned gothic here. A bone had struck my cranium roughly sixty feet from the very grave of the lady whose own contagion had, alas, claimed her beloved children. There were rules in force here. But such inverse laws could not be taught.

Only learned.

Even in my first few weeks I noticed that certain people coming down to breakfast could look miffed, jumpy. They had not bothered to brush their hair and, scratching at it, seemed almost glad to display this wildness. A few men admit-

Guests in 1928. *Standing*: Stanley Kunitz, Elizabeth Sparhawk-Jones, Carolyn Cox, Hatcher Hughes, Granville English, Elizabeth Ames, Carl Schmitt, Paul Reno, Jeanette Garrett, Edgar White Burrill. *Seated*: Helen Pierce, Dorothy Kreymborg, Alfred Kreymborg.

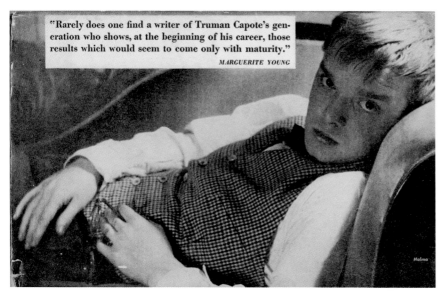

> "Rarely does one find a writer of Truman Capote's generation who shows, at the beginning of his career, those results which would seem to come only with maturity."
>
> MARGUERITE YOUNG

The photograph on the back of the book jacket of Truman Capote's first novel, *Other Voices, Other Rooms*, is said to have inspired Andy Warhol's self-transformation and a series of prints that Warhol dedicated to the author.

ted they had "heard something much of last night." One burly male painter from the Midwest complained, "I was up till dawn, throwing shoes into the corner at it."

"'It'?" one newly arrived Manhattan academic smirked. Already bone-struck, I didn't crack a smile. I dared not risk it. Already I believed. I do I do I do believe.

"Go ahead and laugh," the hearty painter snapped. "'It' prefers one corner only. That's all I know. Its being in that corner's fine by me, as long as it stays put. My room is pretty dark at 2:00 A.M. I didn't dare turn a bedside lamp on it. But I could tell this much: It had a head. Thing stood about five feet tall. And its only sound all night was a kind of steady hiss or clicking. Like the noise some kids make with their mouths. Meant mostly to irritate you. You laugh, go right ahead, Mr. Slick New Yorker. You want to trade rooms tonight? Then we'll talk tomorrow at breakfast, compare notes." The painter sounded angry. The academic, intent on oatmeal, suddenly lacked intellectual curiosity; he declined.

I believed. But nothing had yet happened to me. I now think maybe I wanted it too much.

⁂

I soon heard other tales: the poet Stanley Kunitz arrived one night decades earlier and felt quite happy till the bed on which he slept lowered as if one human leg bearing an adult's weight stepped through the wall, then bounded off the bed again, lifting it nine inches. Stanley Kunitz was gone by breakfast.

But surely they are good ghosts, I decided, in a house that has produced so much. Like all young cultists caught up with Yaddo's legend, I could tell you (and now will) what books got written in which rooms.

Truman Capote's *Other Voices, Other Rooms* was composed in Mrs. Trask's white meditation chapel, up its own narrow staircase. In one of the novel's most memorable scenes, a bird flies into just such a high-ceilinged chamber. The room where Capote wrote his book has no window screen, just a single six-foot picture window whose glass pivots open completely to the sky.

Studs Lonigan had been written just downstairs by James T. Farrell, an angry

Writer Allan Gurganus, *right*, first visited Yaddo in 1975. Four guests from a later visit—*left to right*: Paul Klein, Altoon Sultan, David Vereano, and Ellen Lanyon—appear in this photo, for which Lanyon created the pen-and-ink mat.

young man of the people. His stay was replete with breakfast in bed, then one of Yaddo's sumptuous early privileges. Did this luxury confirm his sense of how corrupt the rich were, or soften his hardboiled anger?

But I, convinced that ghosts were other people's joy or woe, worked happily. Yes, I felt alert to the bats that often made Yaddo's steep hallways a funhouse fear show. True, I noticed many owls. Sure, I felt startled by the sound of white-tailed deer leaping through white-sided birch groves. I saw a great deal of my Hermes portable typewriter and the many pages it somehow manually produced. But, all summer long, nothing more wondrous than luna moths starred my window screens. I got accustomed to gorgeous rosy sunsets. I savored the region's dramatic summer lightning storms all but patented by upstate's first great published writer, Washington Irving.

⸺⸺ ✾ ⸺⸺

It was in August, just as I finished what would become my third or fourth published story. I had typed it so many times over that I'd accidentally memorized the first page and a half. My room was on the mansion's third floor, set inside a conical battlement turret. Twelve windows sweep around it, a river-boat-prow half circle. Views stretch clear to Vermont. And now, sun setting, just at 6:00 P.M., I knew I had, after months of bone-scraping revision, finally completed my tale of an American tour bus caught up in an African revolution.

Eventide brought cocktail drinkers gathering three stories down. They shifted metal garden chairs across flagstone terrace. Working till the dinner gong, I felt soothed by the sweet greeting of ice cubes clinking glasses, mur-

mured confessions about workday efforts, news of one senior poet's big winnings at the racetrack just next door. A slight breeze brought sounds and a moment's coolness through the dozen open windows of my tower room.

The desk sat in the center of the room, flanked by all those windows. My big brass bed occupied its own rear niche. I now bent across its coverlet, collating numbered pages of this story done at last. Tonight, I felt invigorated and enlarged. My new story had been planed and sanded till not one syllable burred a loving touch; I could forever read it without cringing. Yaddo's supple peace had been this work's coauthor.

I'd surely earned a drink. I stacked the last numbered pages as something happened out beyond me in the dusk-pink room. I sensed a change of atmosphere. It felt as if two windows or one door had just blown open. The shift in air pressure registered along my hands, against my face.

I glanced up from the bed alcove, scanning windows as the sun commenced its setting.

Between my own dark corner and the late light a figure stood. Five feet tall, it looked smoothed and faceless. Somehow "human," it resembled a dressmaker's dummy. No inverted *V* of light showed between its legs, so it seemed to wear a floor-length skirt. I knew I was on its front side, its observing side. No specific facial features, but I sensed this was a conscious entity, a female one of those, somehow in charge of this space I'd been content to use these past two months.

I could see right into it but only as far as into some frosted-pane translucence. Through glass, if darkly. I somehow knew, as I held the three last pages of my story, this guardian spirit had some long proprietary claim on this, her room. She

had come back from an unfamiliar storage time, returned to see if her space was being well used. I had somehow met her test. Tonight, especially, she found me elated, busy, overconfident in that rapt breathlessness peculiar to idealistic young men.

I knew its gender to be female. I saw its form was stylized but sensed the thing was fully sentient. It appeared a human-sized, lathe-turned, chess piece granted some half-life and now boldly facing me.

Odd, I studied it with such detachment. My inward thought simply ran "Oh." As if I had turned at a sound, spied no more than a moth in the room, turned back. I did that now, literally went on arranging pages. And only then did I do this huge eye-popping Three Stooges double-take, "What the...?!"

Of course it was gone.

I remember walking over, checking the floorboards. For what? Rocket condensation? Footprints?

How I knew her gender, how I understood her long claim on this space, I have not yet discovered. I'd simply owned these sovereign facts about my guest.

—No, I was *her* guest. I was, now and forever, her guest.

Downstairs, the dinner chime sounded. I placed my story's final pages on the bed. Only after I turned on all the room's lamps, only also after activating the overhead light, did I dare tiptoe down for food.

I told no one. I could not imagine being smugly queried about my "it," much less my "her." Later, I genuinely feared returning to my room. I dawdled. I played two extra games of Ping-Pong. When I finally found the nerve, I paused at my own open door. I craned in for one quick room check before stepping over the threshold.

She did not appear again. I waited. First I feared her. Then I wanted more. Why had I not spoken to her? Or charged in her direction? I ask you to believe this manifestation had not been, as Dickens had Scrooge say of his own first ghost, a bit of undigested beef, a spirit "less of grave than gravy."

That day I had eaten nothing past my box lunch's nonhallucinogenic carrot sticks. I'd drunk not a drop of booze, though I now sure needed some.

All I knew: my work and I had just passed muster. I could not then (cannot now) explain the reversal of Newtonian physics that allowed into my room and hers, the shape I'd just so clearly seen.

Was she a figure who could not help appearing? Did she, having died in this chamber, remain forever Denver-booted to its space and uses? Was she one of those persons who survive uneasily past death, peeved in her electro-static limbo, forever fixed on her one holographic errand? How had she been doomed to endlessly repeat one chore—her sunset walk, her night's last door-lock check? She must have been forever surprised by successive living blunderers trampling on her privacy. Though she shocked me by appearing, I sensed she had not been the intruder. *I* was. I had polluted a claimed space, one for her as sacrosanct as the stilly grave itself.

⸺⸻⸺

Years later, over drinks in Manhattan, I would meet others who had "seen things" at Yaddo. Likewise, they had let these go unmentioned. One man, a sort of shaman who had spent years with the tribesmen of New Guinea, confessed to seeing one lady wearing a trailing white nightdress and carrying a lit lantern down her home's grand stair-

case. I believed him; I did not believe him. Mostly I believed. My own manifestation had lacked props and even features. But she remains mine. I knew what I had seen.

⸺⸻⸺

And yet nothing ever ends at Yaddo. If every artist arriving here is looking for some new way to start a story or a film or a painting, Yaddo continues to resist easy conclusions, even incidental mortality. Here our sense of openings and endings get reversed.

As ever in Yaddo's abounding echo chamber where silence is still sovereign, my one sighting would not be the end of it.

I researched the first person to occupy "Third South," my favorite third-floor perch. That room rested one floor above the Trasks' own lavish bedchambers but one below the parlor maids' crowded warrens. Someone on payroll, if prestigious in her role, must have lived there. I mean a lady not quite help or quite yet company.

I figured that my ghost had likely been a Miss Pardee, the children's nanny. She was a revered member of the original staff. I'd found her portrait hanging in the Great Hall when I first arrived here in the 1970s. And even after the children's awful deaths, this handsome single woman remained on payroll. She finally merited burial beside their sad mother herself. "Ever in the Circle" the gravesite bronze stated.

⸺⸻⸺

It is the dream I'll end with. In it, I was offered some sort of secret that I cannot bear to keep even one night longer. Were I writing this as fiction, I might now place the ghost sighting last. But

that ghost herself, I believe, made this dream possible.

I would return to Yaddo many times. Some summers, I served as a glorified bellhop, showing people to their rooms, telling the place's countless tragic-comic peony-layered tales. I knew and know the history of each painting and statue in the Great Hall and most geegaws elsewhere. One face I knew very well indeed was that of our benefactor, Katrina Nichols Trask. It is easy to make fun of her till you come first to pity then love her. Love arrives, of course, only once you begin to understand her luck, then her loss, and finally her bravery. For years, she staged masques and balls here of which she, incidentally (somehow forever surprised), was always enlisted to reign as queen. "Who, *moi*? Queen of the what? . . . Harvest? Silver Harvest Moon, you say? Well, but . . . only this once and solely if I am the servants' choice as well."

Heavy lies the rhinestone crown, but someone has to wear it. You'll still find several glass tiaras in the home's lead-fronted display cases. Katrina Trask's own poetry and plays were of the inspirational variety, as willed and well meaning as they are forgotten. Contemporary poets she most admired and most often entertained ran to high-minded rhyming devotionalists like Henry van Dyke. The greatest poets of her age seemed lost on her, too "difficult and negative." And yet, when her children perished from her own disease, when it fell to her to somehow survive them, she became inspired—which literally means, of course, "breathed into."

She conceived the notion of inviting artists, writers, and composers to assume her children's logical inheritance. We became her heirs. And before she died, in order to ensure Yaddo's continuation, she moved out of the mansion.

Marble statues representing the four seasons border the Rose Garden.

She lived as simply as she could to save for our future.

The summer after I saw the ghost upstairs, I had one of those dreams that shake you. They are rare and, while occurring, seem far more tinted and hyperreal than life. In the dream, I was just another guest at Yaddo, simply here doing my daily work. One afternoon, I was taken aside by an older woman painter about to end her stay. She invited me for a walk around the wooded

lakes. We had not been close, but I'd always liked her work and face. Now she pressed me for what she said was an important talk. We settled on a rock near the water as she explained.

Through reasons no one ever quite bothered to explain to anybody, Mrs. Trask herself was somehow still alive and hidden in the Mansion. Well over 130 now, she still existed in a secret niche set high in one attic storeroom. Since our hostess had first greeted artists into her home, a curious relay commenced. One artist-guest at a time fed her. And, upon their leaving, they, in

deepest secrecy, chose another then another to sustain her lo these hundred years.

"Will you be next? Then before you go, you should pick from among the newcomers the one likeliest to keep the secret of her being left alive. You choose the one likeliest to feed her, someone guaranteed to pass along the news. Otherwise, she'd just be up there, be left up there. . . . No one has failed Katrina yet, and not one has told the secret she's alive. —Today will be my last time to visit her. You'll need to know where she is. Can you come with me now?" I nodded.

The rest of the dream remains silent. I follow the painter into the mansion, and we greet the few campers reading the *New York Times* in the Linoleum Room. Hushed, we ascend a narrow staircase past the third floor, then find a smaller curving passage up into the attic.

Down one long, dark hallway till we step into a storage room. My leader locks the door behind us. The place is stacked with old furniture scarcely worth saving; boxes of tax records rise in columns to the ceiling. Windows shut, the air is peppery with dust, a room never visited.

My guide now steps before a blind wall ribbed with wainscoting. She shows me how, by simply lifting it away, one low indentation is revealed. I step aside, and daylight lets me see within the niche. Here rests a plain tan camp cot, covered with tattered brocaded blankets. At one end is a child's satin pillow, and on it is the living head of an ancient so thin that she hardly makes a bump under her coverlets.

Here rests a crone so old that she has gone all but transparent, features seeming formed of isinglass or dragonfly wing. Her blue eyes are child-sized, bright with some strange faith, if sunk within a face webbed with infinitesimal wrinkles whose sum effect is one of infant smoothness. She is conscious, and I stand within her gaze, smiling down at her, fearful only of alarming her. She doesn't seem upset at the sight of me, just the latest stranger in an endless series of such. Instead, her awareness offers its own benign solemnity, some dimpled pleasure seen in all portraits of Mrs. Trask.

My guide now opens her own lunchbox, then stoops. She crumbles up a raisin cookie and, with the delicacy of a large man feeding a fledgling bird, she presses some few crumbs at a time into this ancient chewing mouth.

With eyes the startling blue of a young child's, our benefactor receives her daily feeding from the latest of the artists whom she publicly supports and who, in private forever, sustain her. Wordless, I'm invited to feed her by hand a few last crumbs. I squat, and she accepts them. Her eyes fixed on me are calm. She lives past speech, yet she appears to search my face, the cut of my summer clothes, for news of the world, some sight of oil paint on my hands, some hint at the motion below the stairs where, thanks to her, forms and ideas and marble and wood are being bartered and reshaped, reinvented, given content then totally revised.

I leave the room in silence, knowing I am now briefly and tenderly in charge of her. A departed figure yet lives. Not quite a ghost yet no longer a full life. Instead, some promising medium, a continuous hunger strung between life and death, existing on our syllables, our brushstrokes, our crumbs.

I was just a kid then. And yet I had found the greatest lesson-consolations in that dark cubby-holed Mansion. It is a typifying trait of young people to believe they are the first. (And, in fact, any young painter applying oil pigment to a stretched virginal canvas *is* the first to ever approach this particular surface in this particular mood with this set of abilities.)

Somehow, at Yaddo, I reversed the usual boastful youthful wish to be my own Columbus, discovering a world I could then call "New" and claim as mostly mine. Just as I would meet so many of my future friends and several favorite lovers in the corridors of Yaddo, I encountered something even richer, ever newer.

I learned that every one of my stories, however much I felt I'd just invented it, was already haunted by other earlier souls. My attempts at linguistic action met with haunted springy reaction. Ancestry created me and, through that, everyone's sole shared narration.

Therefore, every real story is a ghost story.

There are the people who know
    they are latent ghosts.
And there are those who will
    discover that ahead.
And the first bunch, finally, is
    happier.

I am sometimes asked to name my greatest teachers. The answer usually includes the great writers who have instructed me.

But here, now, I feel finally able to state a fuller truth at last.

I count among my greatest teachers . . . the ghosts of Yaddo.

They showed me how dead children can give way to living artists. How grief must finally move on by allowing the radical act of creation to happen, curative, again and again.

While still young at Yaddo, I saw I did not have to be the *first*. I need not be the most brilliant, the most beautiful and sage. I came to understand how to nod, courteously, toward actual patrolling ghosts. Lives. Coming or going, but lives. Owls anointed me with bones. My cup runneth over once I learned how to feed, with exquisite and secret patience, the not-quite-dead-yet.

Q: So, what is the lesson that the ghosts of Yaddo taught?

A: I might become unique . . . only once I saw I'd been, in art and life, preceded.

6 / LIVING WITH ARTISTS

Helen Vendler

I HAVE BEEN a guest at Yaddo three times: for two months in 1997 and for a single month each in 2000 and 2005. I was generously invited there, the first time, thanks to my Harvard colleague Henri Cole, then a member of Yaddo's board. I accepted with gratitude, but also with some unease, not knowing the circumstances for work at the retreat. At my only previous residency, at Bellagio, I had certainly discovered that I could get more done in a month away than in six months at home, but a residency still seemed to me an odd phenomenon. I had spent so long as a single mother that even though my son was now grown it still seemed unnatural to be away from home for as long as a month. Yet I had, as always, several things in me asking to be written, and so off I went to Yaddo for what became a heavenly two-month stay in June and July 1997. Yaddo was at its most inviting and most populous—and as different from formal Bellagio, with its liveried and gloved dining staff, as one could ever imagine. In the 1980s, when I was there, Bellagio's guests were mostly academics, with an occasional writer at times, while Yaddo was teeming with composers, artists, and writers of all sorts, a vivid company that made me far happier than I had expected to be. Yes, we all worked hard during the day and had our solitary box lunches— but there were wonderful conversations (at chance encounters over the morning newspapers, in the library, or on the grounds, as well as at the nightly dinner). Living with artists is more fun than living with scholars.

During my three visits, there were always writers in residence whom I knew: Chana Bloch, Henri Cole, Peter Davison, Melanie Thernstrom, Susan Yankowitz, Herb Leibowitz, Michael Harper, and others. They made it easy for me to come as a new guest. I also had the delight of meeting composers and painters and sculptors and filmmakers (people I do not spend time with in my usual

Sept. 17 '34

My dear Mrs Ames:

We have arrived safely — Pullman
however much the worse for sleep.
For we drove day & night. The first
1500 miles we covered in 48 hours.
Even so I arrived late for the first
faculty meeting, and was very happy
to miss it! Would I could have found
a way to miss all of them.

Before leaving New York I visited
Mr Craven at Great Neck. We talked
for three hours and had lunch together.
I found him generous and capable in
his criticism and most kindly as
a man. Incidentally we found our
viewpoints almost too coincident.

Mr Dickinson was kind enough
to help me get my pictures properly

Painter Clyfford Still wrote to Elizabeth Ames after his visit in 1934, saying that "Yaddo has given me friends to paint for."

assigned to their respective exhibitions at Bedworth's and gave me the highest hopes for the results. In fact, Mr. Stickman's encouragement and Yaddo's gracious sanctuary have almost unfitted me for anything but the most fanatical application of paint to canvas. I only hope the work this winter will justify my return to this smug town. It will have to be good to be worth it.

Yaddo has given me friends to paint for: You, and Slater, Jimmy, Harris, the Morrises — ever so many. You and all Yaddo have my deepest regard and constant memory.

Remember me as I will you.

With love & best wishes

Clyfford E. Still

Department of Fine Arts
Washington State College
Pullman
Wn.

Clyfford Still. *Untitled*, 1945. Still worked at Yaddo in 1934.

ognize but could never comprehend. Music's invisibility—vis-à-vis words and paint—makes it for me more astonishing than the other arts. It is physically incredible, as instant and weightless as thought itself. "But ah! thought kills me that I am not thought," says Shakespeare; in every other art the weight of the body makes itself felt. Only music is of the ether. I was so joyful to be among composers that I felt translated into another language.

The visual artists "gave me afterward every day" (as Whitman says of his parents) in that I saw for the first time artists working day after day, tirelessly, pursuing one or the other creative experiment—rearranging a subject on canvas, using different glazes, maximizing or minimizing scale, using one or another medium, and at times memorializing Yaddo itself. I brought one painting home with me that first year, and I should explain why. I had bought a cell phone (my first) to use at Yaddo in case the common phone was unavailable, but found I could not get a signal. I called the support line, whereupon a tech said, "Do you have *trees* there?" "Yes," I said, looking around me in awe, "we have trees." "Oh *well*, then," said the tech. I decided it was worth losing a signal to have those sublime trees. The trees became for me the symbol of Yaddo: I had never lived in the middle of huge evergreens before, or seen the dappled glades they produced or the immensely long shadows they cast in the afternoon, or how superb their shadows were against the stars at night. One of the artists at Yaddo with me, Gail Wittwer, painted the trees in a tall-format watercolor that I bought without a minute's hesitation; it hangs where I see it every time I come in my front door and warms my recollections—the nobility of the trees is in it. When I first walked under the trees at night, what

academic life). I loved the variety of their temperaments and their works. Daniel Brewbaker and I struck up a friendship around music and poetry; when I heard of his father's affliction with Parkinson's, I gave him Seamus Heaney's poem on a woman with Parkinson's. Daniel set it to music, and Seamus, seeing the score, wrote the poem out in longhand for Daniel. I talked to Tom Cipullo, another composer, about Emily Dickinson, whose poems he was setting at the time. David del Tredici could be heard at the piano in casual moments of evening gatherings. Paul

Moravec was composing choral works. I felt like Vaughan: "I see them walking in an air of glory, / Whose light doth trample on my days," since music is to me the most unbelievable of human creations: not there—and then unexpectedly and audibly there. "And suddenly, there was with the angels a multitude of the heavenly host, . . . singing": that is how music streams out of the air into its listeners. I know the verbal arts, my subject, as expressive form; I can understand some art at least as a "visible core" (John Ashbery's phrase); but music comes from a form of mind I rec-

Adolf Dehn. *Lunch at Yaddo*, 1955. This pastoral scene by Dehn, a guest in 1955, is a sharp departure from the artist's social commentary of the 1930s.

came to mind was Keats's description in "Hyperion":

> Upon a trancèd summer night,
> Those green-robed senators of
>   mighty woods,
> Tall oaks, branch-charmèd by
>   the earnest stars,
> Dream, and so dream all night
>   without a stir.

Every clear night, I could see Yaddo's senatorial trees "branch-charmèd by the earnest stars." (I always come to know what I am feeling by the quotation that arises unsummoned in my mind; when Keats's lines rose up in me, I knew I was at home at Yaddo.) And Gail Wittwer's trees, here in Cambridge, tell me that I am still, in my heart, one of the residents.

A baronial dining table seats up to thirty guests in Yaddo's windowed dining room.

Tobias Schneebaum, a painter, printmaker, and anthropologist who wrote about his time among the peoples of Papua New Guinea, was a guest first in 1953. Schneebaum would visit several times in the next five decades. In 1954 he created the screenprint illustrations for Vance Nye Bourjaily's limited-edition book *The Girl in the Abstract Bed*. This illustration is captioned "She played in a kidney-shaped playpen built by her power-tooled father, DADA."

Three years later, when I was at Yaddo again, I bought an oil painting by Yee Jan Bao, an intent and tireless artist. He painted relatively small (and often humorous) canvases, standing all day before them and trying out different shimmering glazes, which gave his paintings layers of luminosity. But he also painted larger canvases, often of moments in a sport; I own one of these, an abstract sandy baseball diamond, in which the ball thrown by the pitcher approaches the batter in multiple separate replicated selves, curving over the diamond. It never fails to give me pleasure. Lorna Bieber, whom I met only briefly, was doing imaginative black-and-white photography (more of which I saw when we later had heady days together at Bogliasco). And Gail Gregg, during my last visit, was doing beautiful reticent color

photographs (some of which turned up on small postcards as individual gifts). The artists showed me how freely the world transforms itself under their querying gaze; they made the world I live in seem rigid and immobile by contrast. They helped me see more flexibly—or at least to imagine seeing more flexibly.

Of course there were many guests whose work I never got to see or hear, given the overlapping schedules at Yaddo. And there were guests who found Yaddo not to their benefit or liking: Betty Friedan, restless and unhappy in the solitude of Yaddo, left after three days. There were relatively invisible guests who kept mostly to themselves; and there were the convivial guests who made a party at whatever table they occupied. There were guests who were selfish (such as the woman who tied up

the common phone for hours as she communicated with her shrink far away, or the guests who tried to compose an exclusive clique of a single dinner table but were, of course, unsuccessful). But unpleasant guests were few. Mostly, the guests of a given moment created an ongoing familial house party.

I met many writers at Yaddo whom I might not otherwise have run into: the gifted satirist A.M. Homes, the generous and outgoing Fran Kiernan, the interesting poets Marilyn Chin, Judith Vollmer, and April Bernard, the fine storyteller Nora Sayre (now gone from us), the young novelists Bliss Broyard and Nicole Krauss, the tersely clever Mac Wellman, the genial Joe Caldwell, the theatrical Lynn Freed. (Lynn, when I first met her, had just come from teaching a writing class in a neighboring col-

Tobias Schneebaum's illustration for the last page of Vance Nye Bourjaily's *The Girl in the Abstract Bed*.

lege, where the director had told her she could *not* write "Boring" on her students' papers—someone had apparently complained. "But I'd told them, over and over, that the single worst thing a fiction writer could *be* was *boring*!" cried Lynn. "And if they were being *boring*, *some*body had to tell them so!" I couldn't agree more, and I listened ever after for her lively accounts of life.) I read works by many of the writers I met, and as a result felt more in touch with a broad canvas of American literature than I had ever felt before (or have felt since).

There were two foreign poets present while I was at Yaddo. Gabor Shein was at a disadvantage, since he spoke almost no English, and other guests spoke no Hungarian. (Some, but not Germanless me, could talk with him in German.) Even so, he was a gentle and attractive

presence. But the poet whose work I *could* read, and whom I came to admire very much, was the Honduran Roberto Sosa, a poet of strong political sympathies for the Honduran poor, who had a delicacy of expression that made the strong feelings credible, not propagandistic. At Yaddo, he was working with his American translator, Jo Anne Engelbert. He was the real thing, and I was sorry to say good-bye to him. His modesty made me unaware of his fame in Latin America and Spain; I was glad to learn later (Googling him) that everyone recognized his quality.

Then there was our grand eccentric, the artist, writer, and anthropologist Tobias Schneebaum (1922–2005), "the man who lived among the cannibals" (as was said of Melville). Tobias was ingenuous and sophisticated at once; we be-

came friends over his love of art and literature, his candor as a human being, and his struggles as a novice with the computer. (He was trying, in 1997, to translate handwritten documents into computer-generated pages, and was recapitulating many of my own recent efforts to learn how to do just that. We condoled with each other, and denounced technical manuals together; he was a very sympathetic and original presence.) In the last Yaddo visit during which we were together, in the summer of 2000, he showed the film he had made in old age of returning to "his" tribe, the Asmat, in Papua New Guinea. It was moving to see him clambering with effort out of a boat, and walking with even more effort over rough terrain. His irreverent cheerfulness in his eighties (in spite of disability and rela-

Antonio Frasconi, a guest in 1952, created this broadsheet woodcut to announce the birth of his son that year.

tive poverty) is something I hope to keep in mind.

What did I accomplish at Yaddo in the four months I spent there from 1997 to 2000? Mostly, I was finishing a book on Seamus Heaney that came out in 1998, or I was thinking about Yeats (*Our Secret Discipline: Yeats and Lyric Form* was to come out in 2007 from Harvard). Or I was planning and writing two lec-

ture series: the first, *Coming of Age as a Poet: Milton, Keats, Eliot, Plath*, appeared in 2003; the second, *Poets Thinking: Pope, Whitman, Dickinson, Yeats*, appeared in 2004. But what mattered (and matters) less to me than the actual appearance of these books is the time of thinking spent in the peace and beauty of Yaddo, under the lofty pine trees and among the glowing evening fireflies. In

academic life, thinking often has to be done with respect to proximate events— the next class, the next public lecture. But the luxury of peaceful thinking, as at Yaddo, releases the mind to be itself once again. For me (odd as it may sound), that release means once again being fifteen. I remember fifteen as the age when I came into my own, writing my first "adult" poems (unlike those I wrote from six to twelve), and living in "that perpetual reverie" (Coleridge's words) that makes up "the radiant and productive atmosphere" (Stevens) of an artist. I didn't, in the long run, turn out to be a poet; but that year, at fifteen, taught me what it might be to be a writer. And when I am free from schedules and obligations, as I have been at Yaddo, that reverie and that atmosphere are regained, almost unnervingly so, until thought becomes an area, a field of residence, rather than a linear pursuit.

The directors of Yaddo (in my time, Michael Sundell and Elaina Richardson), with their unobtrusive hospitality, were selfless in their unremitting work for the foundation itself and for the artists passing through. The staff did everything to feed us well and make life easy for us, so that we took no thought for the morrow and could get on, unimpeded, with today. I remember an invigorating evening of Irish music that I was taken to by Cathy Clarke, one of the office staff.

And the open houses of the artists made almost every day a surprise.

The tragic story of the Trasks and their children engenders seriousness in everyone who works at Yaddo. Because four children died, Yaddo artists have inherited their house, their trees, their pergola, their very leisure. Every resident wants to make work worthy of the children and of their desolate parents, who converted unending grief into a project of ongoing creation.

[OVERLEAF] Holiday cards from Yaddo's artists, including Rosemarie Beck, Louis Hechenbleikner, Vincent Longo, Hyde Solomon, Patricia Mangione, George Biddle, Langston Hughes, Minna Citron, Antonio Frasconi, Milton Avery, and Nell Blaine.

NOEL

Happy Holidays to you!

Christmas Cards

I forgot
To send a card to Jennie—
But the truth about cousins is,
There's too many.

I also forgot
A card to Joe—
But I believe I'll let
That old rascal go.

I done bought
Four boxes now.
I can't afford
No more nohow.

So Merry Christmas,
Everybody!
Cards or no cards—
Here's Howdy!

Langston Hughes

Langston

Milton Avery

Hyde Solomon

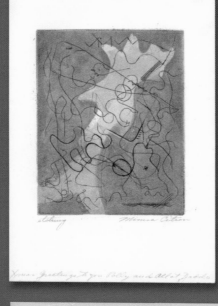

AN OLD
CZECH CAROL
WITH
WOODCUTS BY
ANTONIO FRASCONI

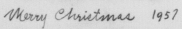

Merry Christmas 1957   from Nellie

[OPPOSITE] Guests in 1943. *Seated*: Isabella Howland, Margaret Walker, Jean Stafford, Harold Shapero, Tamaras Kerr, Agnes Smedley, Karin Michaëlis, Carson McCullers, Alfred Kantorowicz. *Standing*: Kappo Phelan, Elizabeth Ames, Rebecca Pitts, Paul Zucker, Hans Sahl, Langston Hughes. This group of guests was smaller than usual, as Yaddo economized because of the constraints of World War II. Smedley was reunited with her old friend Karin Michaëlis, at whose home in Denmark she had written her first book, the roman à clef *Daughter of Earth*. Smedley was also pleased to be in the company of Langston Hughes, with whom she had corresponded while she was in China. Jean Stafford, the first wife of Robert Lowell, was also in residence that summer.

7 / THE LONGEST STAY

AGNES SMEDLEY, YADDO, AND THE "LOWELL AFFAIR"

Ruth Price

IT WAS not that Agnes Smedley thought loosely about sexual matters, but she had, after all, come of sexual age in Greenwich Village, and the nightly "undisciplined guerrilla warfare" practiced in the bushes of the Chinese Communist base of Yenan in 1937 suggested to her the need for a more advanced sexual outlook. After fitting several hundred female soldiers with pessaries provided by her friend and mentor Margaret Sanger, Smedley hosted private soirées where she taught Chinese Communist leaders to dance. Then she set to work on the troubled marriage of Mao Zedong—a move that earned Smedley a

blow from his unhappy partner, which Agnes met with a punch that laid her opponent on the floor. Five years later, Smedley was ensconced at Yaddo, where she remained for the next five years— the longest tenured guest in its storied history.

No examination of Yaddo would be complete without a mention of Agnes Smedley, one of the most significant American women of the twentieth century, and one of Yaddo's most controversial visitors. A flamboyant, charismatic journalist, feminist, and political activist, she made historic contributions to letters and politics on three continents. Though nowadays she is largely

forgotten, during her fifty-eight years she crammed in enough experience, and enough notoriety, to fill the lifetimes of several lesser women.[1]

If Smedley is remembered today, she is recalled by a circle of conservative scholars and journalists who resurrect accusations that she worked and spied for Moscow during her years in China in the 1930s, both through the Comintern (which provided leadership for the world revolution Smedley and many of her colleagues on the left believed would occur in their lifetime) and in the Soviet military intelligence ring of Richard Sorge. With equal fervor, some leftists argue that Smedley, like other figures accused of Soviet espionage over the past fifty years, was the tragic victim of a McCarthyite smear.[2]

It was not my original intention to expose Smedley's clandestine career. Her writings, which include an autobiographical novel, three books of China reportage, a biography, a memoir, and hundreds of articles for newspapers and periodicals, including the *Nation, New Republic*, the *Manchester Guardian*, the *Frankfurter Zeitung*, the *Modern Review*, and *Komsomol Pravda*, were my intended focus, along with her outsized personality and colorful life. My initial Smedley was an uncompromising rebel who operated independent of Stalin's machinations, outside party strictures.[3] However, the opening of Soviet archives in Moscow, a felicitously timed trip to China, and recently declassified "Project Mask" decryptions from Great Britain ultimately confirmed what I unwittingly began unearthing nearly from the start of my research: that Smedley had indeed collaborated closely (albeit on her own terms) with both Moscow-based entities, her indignant denials notwithstanding.[4]

The controversies surrounding Alger Hiss and the Rosenbergs are well known. But the story of Agnes Smedley—her real story—is worth knowing too, for a more nuanced understanding of what Smedley did and why sheds light on other Cold War battles still being argued by historians, including the 1949 "Lowell Affair" at Yaddo: an epic clash of literary titans that pitted the likes of Robert Lowell, Elizabeth Hardwick, Flannery O'Connor, and Dwight Macdonald against Malcolm Cowley, Katherine Anne Porter, Carson McCullers, John Cheever, and Alfred Kazin—and in which Smedley figured prominently. In the charged climate of the late 1940s, which often reduced the interpretation of political commitments to a simple

Long Meadows Farm, New Paltz, N. Y.
June 26, 1943

Dear Elizabeth Ames:

Malcolm Cowley has suggested that I wrote you and try to secure an invitation to spend the summer in Yaddo.

A few months ago, friends suggested that I try to go to Yaddo. I thought it a charitable place for the indigent, and dropped the idea. Then I learned it was a Foundation of respect and honor. In the meantime, however, I had gone to work as a farm laborer on the farm of friends. I've been here for months, and the work has so completely exhausted me that I cannot write. While in China, I suffered a back injury, and this has also now returned due to physical labor, and I must go to New York this week-end for treatment.

I talked with the Theatre Guild a few months ago about a possible play for this winter's season. Mr. Gassner was delighted with the plot that I outlined. In the meantime, however, I had to finish my new book (Battle Hymn of China), and immediately it was finished, I came to the farm to work. Since then, all writing has been out of the question. I have been asked for articles, but have no energy or time. If I could come to Yaddo, I would be able to rest and start work again.

Can you find a place for me there? If so, I should be grateful indeed.

Sincerely,

Agnes Smedley

Agnes Smedley first inquired about a stay at Yaddo in 1943, at the recommendation of Malcolm Cowley. She had been working on her friend Thorberg Brundin's farm in upstate New York and was in need of a place to stay that would be more conducive to her writing.

"Red or No?," the complexities of Smedley's views and actions split Yaddo into warring camps that left an enduring mark on the colony.

Born in rural northern Missouri in 1892, Smedley was a young girl in southern Colorado when a coal-field strike against John D. Rockefeller's Colorado Fuel and Iron Company turned into all-out class war. That experience, along with her subsequent years on the West Coast, shaped her into an action-oriented radical more along the lines of the anarcho-syndicalist Industrial Workers of the World than of her East Coast peers. Too conflicted about her working-class origins to seek a role in the Socialist Party, too theoretically ignorant to compete in America's fledgling Communist movement, Smedley

initially found a place for herself in the 1910s in California's Hindustan Ghadr Party, an essentially Sikh movement that sought an armed war of independence against British rule in India. The German government financed the movement amply in the years before the United States entered World War I.

In 1918, she was arrested in Greenwich Village and charged with violating the Espionage Act by conspiring with the Germans. Smedley prevailed on influential liberal friends and colleagues, including civil liberties activist Roger Baldwin and Margaret Sanger, to defend her as an innocent victim of wartime hysteria even as she remained on Germany's payroll, dazzling supporters with her magnetic personality and obscuring discrepancies that belied her

Smedley's *Battle Hymn of China*, published in 1943, made her a popular public speaker on the topic of China-U.S. relations.

denials, preferring her own moral compass to a law that persecuted radicals like herself.[5]

Smedley passed most of the 1920s in Weimar Berlin, where she continued her involvement in Indian independence work while honing her skills as a writer, both as a journalist and as author of the powerful novel *Daughter of Earth*. There she met the two people who engineered her 1929 posting to China as a journalist and covert operative and her subsequent involvement with Richard Sorge. One was Willi Muenzenberg, the hugely influential German Communist; the other was Jakob Mirov-Abramov, European chief of the Comintern's Department of International Liaison, the OMS (the important, albeit unpublicized, section of the Comintern's executive committee) and later a ranking official in Soviet military intelligence, the GRU.[6]

Within months, Smedley had fallen in love with China and begun to file groundbreaking articles, becoming the first Western journalist to cover the Chinese Communists since Chiang Kai-shek had turned on them two years previously. But hers was a different trajectory from other Americans who, documentary evidence now suggests, worked for Moscow. For one thing, Smedley was a freelance revolutionist, not a Communist Party member. For another, her gift for turning obscure tales of political upheaval into epic adventures earned her an extraordinary place in the hearts and minds of American readers and the Chinese people.

Smedley was able to operate in China—for a time—with a degree of autonomy otherwise unheard of in international Communist circles. By the summer of 1934, her proximity to the

Chinese Communists and a year in Moscow had opened her eyes to Soviet duplicity in China. No longer willing to "sacrifice partial interests to the whole," as she put it, she opted out of Soviet work to devote herself entirely to China's revolution. The exasperation was mutual. The Comintern's initial attempts to rein her in proved disastrous and, by 1936, Smedley's career as a political operative drew to a close.

For a time, Smedley pursued an outlaw life among the Chinese Communists: the Calamity Jane of their revolution. Her outrageous antics included racing horses, cross-dressing, and providing instruction on birth control, Western dance, and romantic love as described above. But her bohemian lifestyle, individualistic politics, and personal meddling eventually incurred Mao's wrath, and she was expelled. Later, she faced death alongside Chinese soldiers during the Sino-Japanese war.

While Smedley always remained true to her own moral compass, by the time she returned to the United States in 1941, she was a pariah among orthodox Communists everywhere. Her iconoclasm cost her her livelihood. After a Communist-sponsored "smear campaign" dried up her lecture audiences and left her nearly penniless, Yaddo board members Granville Hicks and Malcolm Cowley (who had reviewed several of her books and written an introduction to *Daughter of Earth*) helped arrange an invitation for her to the prestigious writers' colony.

Agnes arrived at Yaddo in July 1943 and embarked on writing a play, tentatively about a Chinese general troubled by his conscience. However, the form did not come easily to her, and by late afternoon she was ready to socialize. Cowley frequently stopped by for a game of checkers and Katherine Anne Porter, a dear friend of Thorberg Brundin, Smedley's former sister-in-law, quickly became a fan. Guests that summer included Margaret Walker, Carson McCullers, Jean Stafford, and Alfred Kantorowicz, along with two old friends, the Danish novelist Karin Michaëlis and Langston Hughes.

Michaëlis, a venerated novelist known for her probing analysis of the inner lives of complex modern women, had known Smedley in Berlin. And though Agnes had initially feared Michaëlis was interested in her for use in her own literary endeavors, Michaëlis had been tremendously encouraging in the writing of Smedley's novel, *Daughter of Earth*. It was at Michaëlis's island home, in fact, that Agnes had composed the first draft of her book. Michaëlis was thrilled to see Smedley again, and the two women often went into town for a drink or ice cream at the end of the day. Even in this distinguished company, Michaëlis reported, Smedley was the center of the crowd. Defiantly *not* urbane, she got drunk and bawdy at cocktail parties and performed or told stories of her life in China, her laughter resounding in the oversized rooms.[7]

Smedley had known Hughes since 1931, when he sent her an inscribed copy of his novel, *Not Without Laughter*, after a reviewer noted parallels to hers. Agnes was already an admirer of Hughes and had committed much of *Weary Blues* to memory. But at that time, she was the better-known literary radical, and she freely critiqued his work in a "comradely" way. By ending his novel happily, its protagonist triumphant, she argued, Hughes had failed to depict the real fate of the Negro masses, which "is not happy—but is beaten and debased by condition of beastly subjection." Perhaps, she speculated, the fault lay in Hughes's petit bourgeois upbringing, which had not taught him sufficient suffering.[8]

To his credit, Hughes had accepted Agnes's criticism without comment. The two had been buddies ever since. Together, they snuck off to the local black church in Saratoga Springs to deliver political sermons and distribute tomatoes from Yaddo's garden. Agnes endeared herself to Hughes with open-hearted gestures like her angry public refusal to join PEN, the international writers' association, because it did not admit African Americans as members—an act that apparently resulted in an invitation to Hughes to join its executive board.[9]

Expectations were high that summer for Smedley's China memoir, *Battle Hymn of China*, as it went into a third printing before publication. But all was not well for long. On July 16, a Mr. Pettigrew from the FBI telephoned and explained that he wanted to speak to Smedley the next time she came down to New York City. In the spring of 1943, her name had appeared in a German newspaper article in connection with the Shanghai phase of the Soviet military intelligence ring of Richard Sorge. On August 13, 1943, U.S. Army Intelligence opened a file on her in relation to the case.

For the time being, life went on as usual. On August 31, Smedley returned to Yaddo, where guests had a book party waiting. Critics declared her depiction of China and the people's efforts to resist Japan—while their old society rotted away and a new one struggled to be built—as moving as anything yet written on that country. Her "great and gallant character," as one reviewer put it, also came in for praise.[10]

The positive reception for *Battle Hymn of China* brought Smedley additional speaking opportunities, and she was a popular radio guest. NBC and the Canadian Broadcasting Network aired radio dramatizations of *Battle Hymn* and her previous book, *China Fights Back* (even though one producer insisted on transforming Smedley into "Mr. Scott" before allowing her character to march with the Chinese guerrillas). All this left little time for Smedley to pursue her literary life. However, Yaddo was rather empty since America had entered the war, and its director, Elizabeth Ames, who was grateful for Smedley's help nursing Ames's dying sister, Marjorie Peabody Waite, invited Smedley to stay on another year.

In the spring of 1944, Agnes brought in the novelist Leonard Ehrlich to collaborate on her play. Ehrlich was the author of *God's Angry Man*, which was based on the life of John Brown and the Harpers Ferry slave insurrection—a book that Simon and Schuster's legendary editor Clifton Fadiman had called "by far the finest first novel that has been submitted to my house during my seven years of editorial experience." Ehrlich was a good choice—and a necessary one.[11] In the years since she had written *Daughter of Earth*, Smedley had expended much of the creative fire that might have made her a great imaginative writer on more active involvements. Now she was in over her head. At summer's end, she turned over everything she had written to Katherine Anne Porter to critique and instructed Ehrlich to complete it himself while she returned to more familiar modes of self-expression.

Smedley's pungent analyses of Chiang Kai-shek's scapegoating of American advisor Joseph Stilwell to divert attention from his own misrule and America's role in bolstering Chiang's regime appeared in the *New Republic*, the *Nation*, and *PM*, a progressive daily. On October 25, 1944, amid a Kuomintang propaganda campaign to induce conservative American Republicans, clergy, and newspapers to brand as "Red inspired" American reports that criticized the Chinese government and silence those who wrote them, J. Edgar Hoover ordered the FBI's Albany field office to open an investigation of Smedley, "In as much as she has been for many years a notorious Communist expert on the Far East."[12]

That same fall, Smedley was active in the National Citizens' Political Action Committee and appeared with Katherine Anne Porter at several Democratic rallies for Roosevelt in upstate New York. "There is something so touchingly warm and good in Agnes, her heart is so tender and her thoughts so wild," Porter later explained, that "it makes very little difference to me what she says or does politically: her feelings are right no matter how misled her acts, some of them."[13] The two friends ushered in 1945 with songs and a drunken ballet performed in Yaddo's ballroom.

At the beginning of 1945, Porter left for Hollywood. Smedley sorely missed her. These days, though, her lectures provided her livelihood, and the first few months of the year were a blur of cities and engagements, during which Smedley spoke frequently on the Chinese Communists' proposal to replace Chiang Kai-shek's one-person, one-party dictatorship with a program of democratic reform and have their joint military forces fight the Japanese. She was particularly popular with college students, including the young women at nearby Skidmore College.

Agnes returned to Yaddo in April 1945, worn down, in ill health, and vowing to put her lecturing days behind her forever. For all her efforts, she had earned only a thousand dollars. "Think of your weekly income!" she wrote Porter. Despite much talk the previous year

about lucrative movie adaptations of her books, which gossip columns reported Bette Davis would produce, Agnes said that in the end the studios had simply stolen whatever they wanted. She urged Porter to hoard her current earnings from MGM and then return to work on her book.

By this time, Elizabeth Ames had invited Smedley to make Yaddo her permanent home. Agnes moved from the mansion where the other guests stayed to a renovated farmhouse on the property and commenced work on her oft-interrupted biography of Chu Teh, commander in chief of the Chinese Communist Army. Unlike most of Yaddo's visitors, Agnes was not bothered by a lack of creature comforts, and the arrangement limited her contact with the sometimes difficult Ames, who, Agnes said, had begun to "press in on her."[14] However, unknown to Agnes, Yaddo was no longer her private retreat.

Beginning in 1946, there was an informer inside the writer's colony: Yaddo secretary Emma Grace "Mary" Townsend. According to Agnes, Townsend believed in two things only—God and Thomas Dewey—and she was soon supplying the FBI with drafts of Agnes's speeches, descriptions of her conversations with other guests, and the contents of her mail. As Townsend later explained, "whenever I heard people talking very brilliantly red, I have written down their name and address and dropped it off at a certain place in Saratoga for forwarding to the FBI, because they do not heckle or hound, and do not make anyone uncomfortable unless they consider it dangerous."[15]

After scrutinizing Smedley for more than a year, though, the agency had turned up little suspect activity in her current life. Reduced to grumbling about her "mannish" appearance and

"boyish" bob, the FBI downgraded its investigation to a "pending inactive" status. The agency did, however, pass on copies of its internal reports to Army Intelligence, which was proceeding with an investigation of its own.

Before he was put to death, Sorge had made a confession that named Smedley as one of his main assistants in the Shanghai phase of his ring. Since V-J Day, American occupation authorities and foreign newsmen stationed in Tokyo had been piecing together Smedley's role in Sorge's operations. Nothing had appeared yet in the American press, but surviving group members in Japan, released from prison at the end of the war, were beginning to tell their stories. After one report that described Smedley as the friend of a deceased ring member appeared in the Japanese press, a friend there informed her.[16] By the spring of 1946, she was worried.

Smedley told friends who remarked on her growing distress that the hardships of her life in China had left her weary and dispirited, and she attempted to burn off her anxiety in rigorous manual labor. But she began to quarrel with the other guests, who over the next two summers would include Truman Capote, Newton Arvin, Robert Lowell, and Marguerite Young, and neither the reissue of *Daughter of Earth* in Germany nor Cowley's interest in writing an article on the book's enduring appeal appeared to lift her spirits.

In November 1946, Americans elected the first Republican Congress since the days of Herbert Hoover, and several announced their intention to insist on a Chinese government without the Chinese Communists. As this new postwar mood began to sweep the country, Smedley would point to men in her lecture audiences she believed were FBI agents and announce that she

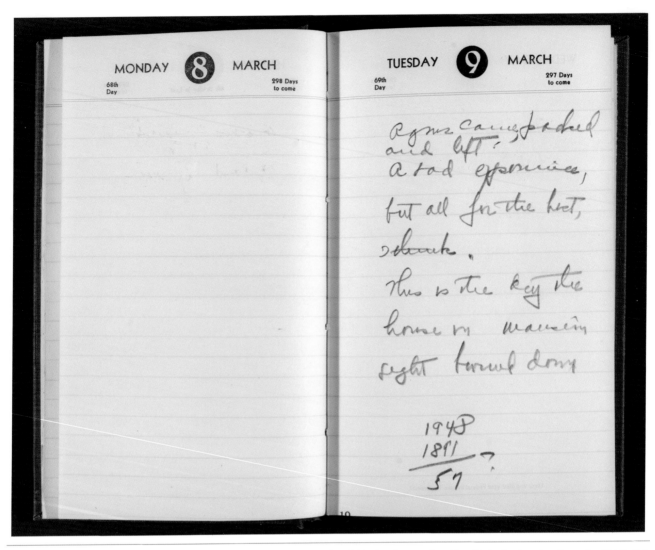

MONDAY **8** MARCH
68th Day · 298 Days to come

TUESDAY **9** MARCH
69th Day · 297 Days to come

[handwritten note]

1948
1891
―――
57 ?

Elizabeth Ames's appointment book for March 9, 1948, the day of Smedley's departure from Yaddo. Ames's note to herself recalls the March 9, 1891, disaster in which Yaddo's first mansion was destroyed by fire.

knew she was being "marked down for a concentration camp . . . but that it was the duty of every American to fight up to the last moment, standing firmly on our Bill of Rights."[17] In the face of danger, she was defiant.

Smedley left Yaddo at the start of 1947 for a series of lectures in New York, Chicago, and Boston. After nearly a decade in existence, the House Committee on Un-American Activities had recently been revitalized, and Smedley said she "rather expected" to be ordered to appear before them. In typically reckless style, she decided to seek advice from the Soviet consul general, Jacob Loma-

kin. While she was in New York City, she wrote, she "rolled into the Consulate around 12 and sent up a scrawled note." Lomakin invited her up. Later, they went out for lunch and "sat talking until 3:00 P.M.," according to Smedley.[18] Grateful for his solicitude, Smedley invited Lomakin to visit her at Yaddo. In the end, Lomakin did not come, but Townsend shared every detail of Smedley's experience with the FBI.

In her agitated state, Smedley was often thin skinned and snappish, and she complained that the current crop of Yaddo guests, who included Edward Maisel, Theodore Roethke, Arna Bon-

temps, Robert Lowell, and Marguerite Young, looked down on her for not spending her days "searching for the perfectly balanced sentence." They cared only about analyzing Kafka, Joyce, and Sartre, she wrote, and tossed "lesser mortals into the burning pit."[19] Ill at ease among them, she preferred the company of tradespeople in nearby Saratoga Springs.

That October, Smedley seriously strained relations between nearby Skidmore College and Yaddo by exhibiting what Edward Maisel described as "brutal discourtesy" toward a Dartmouth professor during a debate at the school.[20]

My dear Elizabeth —

I'm taking the night bus for Albany, then on to New York for a few days. I'd intended to go 2–3 days later & take my mms. along to show my publisher but I've decided to go now instead. I've left my address with Mrs. Townsend.

Smedley left Yaddo on March 9 after a confrontation over her political activism. The "Mrs. Townsend" with whom Smedley left her contact information was Ames's assistant, who was later discovered to have been an FBI informant.

Already disturbed by Smedley's seemingly permanent tenure, Townsend and Maisel complained to Ames that Smedley's political activities reflected poorly on the writer's colony and that her influence over local coeds had outraged townspeople.

Thus far, Ames had defended Smedley's behavior on the grounds of "her being in that terrible spot . . . connected with finishing a book."[21] But then, in an unfortunate, rash piece of timing, Smedley hosted a reception for CPUSA organizer Harold Klein at Yaddo following his local debate with Countess Tolstoy. Afterward, Maisel and Townsend informed Ames (and the FBI) that Smedley had used the occasion to proselytize students. Ames felt forced to take a stand.

Sources she trusted, Ames wrote Smedley, had charged that her radical activities were leading people to believe that Yaddo was itself "a source, or even a promoter, of such interests."[22] The time had come for her to choose. If she promised to work solely on her book, she could remain at Yaddo until autumn. If she persisted in combining her literary and political activities, she needed to leave at once. On March 8, 1948, Smedley returned to Ames a winter coat she had borrowed and a set of cocktail glasses she had used to entertain guests; the next day, she was gone. However, in the escalating tensions of the Cold War, her presence lingered.

That November, following Democrat Harry Truman's stunning upset victory over Republican Thomas Dewey and the reelection of a Democratic majority to Congress, embittered Republicans saw too much political hay to be made with the Tokyo report of Smedley's spycraft to keep it under wraps any longer. On February 10, 1949, Colonel George Eyster, deputy chief of the Army's public information division, released the 32,000-word Sorge spy report, along with a press release even the FBI deemed "flamboyant and bombastic."[23] Not only did the document use Smedley to stoke American fears of the Communist bogey just as they reached critical mass, it also made her the first American to be named for the unexpected turn of events in China. Touching as it did on so many controversial issues currently before the public, the story was front-page news across the country, with Smedley receiving the lion's share of the headlines.

Smedley declared the charges "a despicable lie" and denied that she was now or ever had been a Soviet spy or agent of any foreign government. She blamed MacArthur's attack on the recent defeats of Chiang's government, which, she said, undermined plans of American military authorities. Within a day, various papers, including the *New York Times*, questioned the idea that high American officials had been "hoaxed" by Smedley's writing and challenged the Army report's lack of documentation, paranoid, sensational style, and reliance on opinion in making its charges. In the meantime, Smedley kept up her demand for redress with a widely leaked letter to

of the institution of Yaddo and perhaps its survival. I now
present the petition of the four guests:

We petition that Mrs. Elizabeth Ames the executive
director be fired; that this action be absolute, final and
prompt; that pending a decision she be immediately suspended
from all administrative functions.

Drawing up my notes I made every effort to avoid
invective and emotional rhetoric, but I warn the Board my
statements will be extremely full and frank because of the
gravity of the charges. I shall present nothing that I do
not believe to be true and relevant. I shall now present
the charges.

1. It is our impression that Mrs. Ames is somehow
deeply and mysteriously involved in Miss Smedley's
political activities.   *this is
                                                    libel.*

2. That Mrs. Ames's personality is such that she is
totally unfitted for the position of executive director.

As to the first statement, it would have seemed unbelievable to me had I not been at Yaddo for the past month
or been elaborately informed. The second charge would be
supported by a tremendous majority of the more objective
Yaddo guests.

I shall now ask the patience of the Board while I
present a very relevant figure of speech which I think
will greatly clarify the nature of the charges I am bringing.
I shall compare the institution to a body and the present
executive director to a diseased organ, chronically
poisoning the whole system, sometimes more, sometimes less,
sometimes almost imperceptibly, sometimes, as now, almost
fatally.

I consider the institution in its
a splendid and rare thing, and if prop
that could perform unique services to
I want you to ponder my figure of spee
eliminate certain misleading paradoxes
considerable services the institution
in the past in spite of its administra
the institution and the services it ca
conditions explain why distinguished s
the past. returned, noticed nothing wr
varied impressions, ranging from cordi
tution to obsessive hostility.

Robert Lowell asserted that Elizabeth Ames was
somehow "deeply and mysteriously involved in Miss
Smedley's political activities." Ames emends page 15
of the 75-page transcript, noting that Lowell's charge
is libelous.

Since the last meeting of Yaddo Directors, on February 26,
a group of five persons has caused to be extensively circulated
their two-page mimeographed version of that meeting and of
certain other matters incidental to it. They enclosed a
petition for which, on the basis of that version, they were
widely soliciting signatures.

The five names affixed as signatories to the literature and
to the project of the petition, were as follows: Harvey Breit,
John Cheever, Eleanor Clark, Alfred Kazin, and Kappo Phelan.

On Friday, March 25, a consultation, informal and
off-the-record, took place between a representative of our
group and three of the five signatories. Discussion at this
time centered wholly about an examination of the mimeographed
literature being circulated by the five.

No formal discussion of any kind has as yet taken place
                considering   which the five have
for ~~consideration of~~ the novel situation ~~which the five have
yet~~ precipitated.

The above statement is submitted for entry in the record of
the Yaddo Directors at their meeting on March 26.

                          Robert Lowell
                          Elizabeth Hardwick
                          Edward Maisel
                          ~~Flannery O'Connor~~

The four writers who had challenged Ames's leadership—
Robert Lowell, Elizabeth Hardwick, Edward Maisel, and
Flannery O'Connor—were concerned that New York's
intellectual community had rallied to Ames's defense.
O'Connor had dropped out of the controversy by this time.

President Truman in which she threatened to sue MacArthur for libel. As she had in the past, Smedley confronted her accusers with vehement denials, convincing her liberal allies that her accusers were the real enemy. China correspondents, including Edgar Snow, Annalee Jacoby, Pearl Buck, John Hersey, John Fairbank, Harrison Salisbury (and several others who wished to remain anonymous), raised funds to cover her legal expenses. CBS correspondent Eric Sevareid recorded a sympathetic interview. I. F. Stone and Harold Ickes published numerous columns lambasting the document itself and its effect on the nation's growing hysteria.

On February 18, the Army backed off, pleading that it had made a "faux pas" in releasing what it termed a "philosophical report" on Communist spying in Japan and China.[24] But ripples from the report had already extended into Yaddo. Between February 10 and February 18, when Smedley was "cleared," FBI investigators interrogated Yaddo guests, staff, and officers including Elizabeth Ames, Malcolm Cowley, Newton Arvin, Granville Hicks, Flannery O'Connor, Elizabeth Hardwick, Edward Maisel, Mary Townsend, and Robert Lowell. Apart from Cowley, none evinced any sympathy for Smedley, political or otherwise. Lowell, however, took FBI suggestions of Communist infiltration of the writer's colony to another level. Concluding that the institution had long been permeated "by moods or influences that were politically or morally committed to Communism" and that Ames, its director of twenty-five years, was "somehow deeply and mysteriously involved in Miss Smedley's political activities," he demanded Ames's ouster.[25]

Lowell's acrimonious charges turned Yaddo into a war zone. While Cowley maneuvered to keep the story out of the papers, Lowell supporters O'Connor,

Maisel, Hardwick, and Townsend fed the FBI stories about Smedley's love affair with Sorge and her friendships with other Communists. On February 26, a special meeting of Yaddo's directors was convened to hear the writers out. At Lowell's insistence, the board had the proceedings transcribed.

Acting as spokesman for the other writers, Lowell advised the board that if it failed to respond adequately to their concerns, he intended to confer with prominent literary anticommunists, including Diana Trilling, Philip Rahv, and Sidney Hook, and convene a large meeting of the "more important" former Yaddo guests. He had "influential friends in the world of culture," he warned, "nine tenths of whom in the course of my correspondence and conversation will be informed of this affair within three months." Those he named included George Santayana, Robert Frost, T. S. Eliot, William Carlos Williams, John Crowe Ransom, Marianne Moore, Elizabeth Bishop, Allen Tate, Robert Penn Warren, W. H. Auden, James T. Farrell, Delmore Schwartz, Jean Stafford, and John Berryman.[26]

Mary Townsend described the "aura of subterranean activities" she believed surrounded Smedley, and confessed filing between twenty and thirty reports on Yaddo guests she suspected of Communist sympathies to the FBI. All she required was a "snide type of comment," as in the following: "when we were all in the station wagon . . . an apartment was blown up in New York . . . a man apparently intended to destroy himself and turned on the gas and after the blast it was found that books and pamphlets on Communism were ejected through the force of the blast, and the remark was made, 'In which direction were the books going?'" Townsend reported both listener and speaker, "quite convinced [they] were inclined that way."[27]

Ames, clearly stunned, attributed the crisis to the writers' distress at having been questioned by the FBI. "Here have been these people . . . for several months, living in great apparent harmony and good will toward me . . . every one of them asking for more time . . . no reservations at all. They frequently come to my house for music or cocktails, a harmonious life, with now and then little affectionate notes . . . then all of this change."[28]

"I think Yaddo at the moment is being made the victim of hysteria," she concluded. Cowley concurred. "What do you call it, this action of these four guests, but hysteria?" In response to what Yaddo's president John Slade described as an ultimatum based entirely on "intuitions" and twisted "conclusions drawn from utterly insignificant remarks" that threatened Yaddo with a vicious smear campaign unless it agreed to fire Ames, "reform themselves and overturn everything," the board voted to meet again after the members had time to process everything. The following day, Mary Townsend tendered her resignation. On March 1, the four writers left Yaddo as well.

According to Cowley, there were several groups that had long wanted to rule or ruin Yaddo: "the Communists, the fanatical anti-Communists, the homosexuals, the alcoholics, [and] the Catholic converts." The problem was if any of those groups became dominant, and this winter "the guests were fanatical anti-Communists, with no opposition. Two or three sensible guests with no political religion would have changed the situation," he mused, but it was too late now for regrets.[29]

Katherine Anne Porter "had nothing but contempt," she wrote, "for the ringleaders of this gang, and their followers were beneath contempt."[30] Moreover, after the indecent way her "sweet Agnes"

COMMUNISTS AT YADDO DURING PAST THREE YEARS (majority were
there during past summer)

Vladimir Youshavensky	Cell organizer, Communist composer
Agnes Hart	Communist painter
Joe Presser	Communist painter
Matthew Josephson	Cell organizer *never a guest here.*
Mrs. Matthew Josephson	Translator of Communist poet
Joe Lasker	Communist painter
Stephen Raffe	Communist painter

Ruth Domino — *She had a dollar a day to care for the library, answer telephone & door bell & to assist in the pantry* — German Communist writer, listed by State Department for deportation as dangerous enemy alien, was employed at Yaddo at full time salary for part time work, which included reporting on political opinions of guests. She served Molotov cocktail parties at Yaddo, urged that plot be started to rid Yaddo of non-Communist artists. In the past. she had been successful.

Agnes Smedley — *She was here from July 1943 – March 1948* — At Yaddo eight years, urging overthrow of American civilization and Wall St. capitalism, was writing biography of head of Communist Army in China, spent year as guest of Soviet Union in Russia, boasts openly that she had gold medal from Stalin, may be member of Comintern. FBI has large dossier upon her and Mrs. Domino, who collaborated at Yaddo.

Ralph Bates	one-time Soviet courier in Asia
Leonard Ehrlich	Stalinite – at Yaddo ten years
Henri Cartier Bresson	French Communist
Mrs. Henri Cartier Bresson	In this country to organize Javanese revolution with help of C.P.

A list of "Communists at Yaddo" was part of the documentation prepared against Ames. Ames emended the document by hand.

YADDO - Page Two

Igasaki *??*   Japanese Communist, and various
                               Chinese Communists

Michael Lerner *???*

Alfred Kantorowitz   Right hand man to Eisler, caught
                               up with by State Department day
                               or two after leaving Yaddo, was
                               to have been head of American
                               radio in Berlin, became editor
                               of magazine in Russian zone to
                               which Yaddo writers have been
                               urged to contribute.

Mrs. Alfred Kantorowitz   His wife, an actress   *never at Yaddo*

Not a complete list, but the above may suggest the favor-
itism shown to Communists at Yaddo at a time when non-
Communist artists of greater gifts have been turned away
for lack of space. Those Non-Communists who left at the
end of this summer declared publicly that they could never
return to a place where they are forced to hear their
country cursed at every meal. Mrs. Ames has asked non-
Communists not to engage in political discussions but is
inclined to ignore the discussions of Communists. Was
only frightened by the openness of their attack this summer
as the FBI came.

*not true. I have urged on all
the restraining of over exciting
argument.*

What we are concerned with, and most urgently, is the very grave political accusations that were arrived at overnight, and hurled at Mrs. Ames in an atmosphere strangely comparable to that of a purge trial. We wish to insist on the gravity of the charge. It was of the deliberate complicity of Mrs. Ames in a Communist plot of a kind detrimental to national security, and for which over a long period she was said to have used the facilities of Yaddo. However, during the hours of questioning at the meeting no shred of substantial evidence was produced to support this charge, which had been arrived at, in Miss Hardwick's words, by "intuition." The material mentioned in support of it included the names of Stalinists who at some time had been guests at Yaddo; a story of a group of guests having once served a drink referred to as a Molotov cocktail; names of two or three political suspects with whom no one present was acquainted, but who had been mentioned by the FBI as having been connected with Agnes Smedley years earlier. Mainly the case was made to rest on vague personality factors; Mrs. Ames was said to have been "evasive" at one moment, "nervous" at another, and so on.

No mention was made of the fact that many prominent anti-Stalinists have also been guests at Yaddo, as well as a very large number of artists of no political persuasion. In the minds of the prosecutors it was of no importance that 1) the Army had withdrawn its charges against Miss Smedley; 2) Mrs. Ames was on record as not having sympathized with many of Miss Smedley's agitational activities in Saratoga; 3) Mrs. Ames had finally asked Miss Smedley to leave Yaddo.

On the basis of the record, we consider the whole procedure to have been a perfect example of the use of innuendo and personal disparagement in lieu of evidence. Those responsible for it have made it clear, and have stated privately, that they do not care what happens to Yaddo in the future. Their sole appetite and concern seems to be to create a tabloid case. We regard their action as a thoroughly foolish and nasty performance, dangerous to the extent that it weakens any sober fight against Communism.

The charges are to be repeated at a Director's meeting in New York next Saturday, March 26th. We are therefore asking you to sign the enclosed statement immediately, and return it to us by return-mail at the following address: c/o Kazin, 415 Central Park West, New York 25. If there is not time for us to receive your signature by mail, please telegraph your approval of the statement.

Sincerely yours,

Harvey Breit
John Cheever
Eleanor Clark
Alfred Kazin
Kappo Phelan

March 21, 1949

Dear

On Saturday, March 26th, a meeting of the Board of Directors of Yaddo is to be held in New York City, at which certain vital decisions are to be taken with regard to the future of Yaddo and particularly to the tenure of Mrs. Elizabeth Ames as Executive Director. The enclosed statement, which we feel you will want to sign, will be read at this meeting. The necessity for it arises from a shocking incident which occurred at Yaddo in February and of which we wish to give you as brief a summary as possible. Our account is based primarily on a verbatim transcript of the meeting, lasting many hours, which took place at Yaddo on February 26th.

On February 10th, when General MacArthur's allegations against Agnes Smedley appeared in the press, the FBI, which had been watching Miss Smedley for some time, began questioning the personnel and the few guests then at Yaddo, where Miss Smedley had lived for some four years before her departure in 1947. Of the guests, one left immediately; the remaining four became very busy, and leaped overnight to the conclusion that Yaddo was, or had been, the scene of a dangerous Communist conspiracy in which Elizabeth Ames had played a leading and fully conscious role. Led by Robert Lowell and Elizabeth Hardwick, they took advantage of their unique position as winter guests to press a case that may have been based either on hysteria or on some motive not yet clear. Robert Lowell had recently been proposed as a director of Yaddo. Also involved in their conferences was Mrs. Ames' secretary, Mary Townsend, who, it later turned out, had been acting as informant for the FBI for some two years past, by sending in the names of any guests who made what she considered disloyal remarks.

A meeting of local Directors was convened in the Yaddo garage. The four guests, with Lowell as prosecutor, presented their charges, after first demanding that Elizabeth Ames be unconditionally and immediately fired. The charges were: 1) that Mrs. Ames had been "somehow deeply and mysteriously connected with the political activities of Agnes Smedley"; 2) that she was temperamentally unfit for her job as Executive Director. The guests made it clear that they intended to blacken the name of Yaddo as widely as possible if their demands were not met. Robert Lowell with no apparent irony recited a list of famous acquaintances of his in the world of arts and letters, beginning with Santayana, Frost, Eliot, whose influence he promised to bring to bear toward this end. He also threatened to air the matter among his connections in Washington.

We are not here concerned with the second of the charges, which is clearly not of an order to call for a public inquisition, nor to be dealt with in an air of political hatred, panic and fanaticism.

Alfred Kazin led a group of Yaddo writers and artists who defended Ames's integrity. The group circulated a petition among Yaddo's former guests in support of Ames.

had been treated by MacArthur, Porter thought it despicable that Lowell, whose behavior she found "vile beyond words in any situation at all," would drag Smedley's name through the mud again. During this time, there was much talk of making Lowell a director of Yaddo.

On March 21, a letter signed by Harvey Breit, John Cheever, Eleanor Clark, Alfred Kazin, and Kappo Phelan urged supporters of Ames to sign a petition in her support to be presented at the upcoming meeting.

What we are concerned with, and most urgently, is the very grave political accusations that were arrived at overnight, and hurled at Mrs. Ames in an atmosphere strangely comparable to that of a purge trial. . . . The material mentioned in support of it included the names of Stalinists who at some time had been guests at Yaddo: a story of a group of guests having once served a drink referred to as a Molotov cocktail; names of two or three political suspects with whom no one present was acquainted, but who had been mentioned by the FBI as having been connected with Agnes Smedley years earlier. . . .

On the basis of the record, we consider the whole procedure to have been a perfect example of the use of innuendo and personal disparagement in lieu of evidence. Those responsible for it have made it clear, and have stated privately, that they do not care what happens to Yaddo in the future.[31]

More than fifty former Yaddo guests signed the petition, and prominent writers, including Carson McCullers and Josephine Herbst, as well as dozens of lesser-known writers and musicians wrote letters in support of Ames. Agnes, who found the idea that Ames was in any way connected with her own politi-

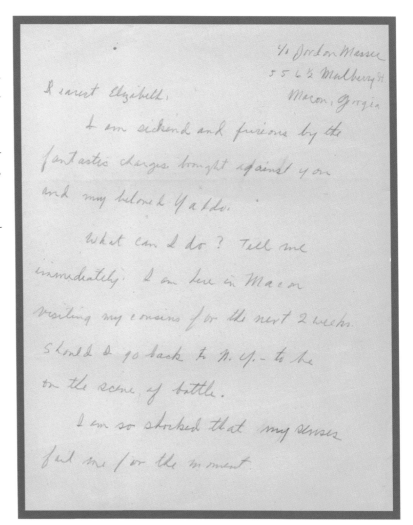

Carson McCullers wrote Ames to express her support.

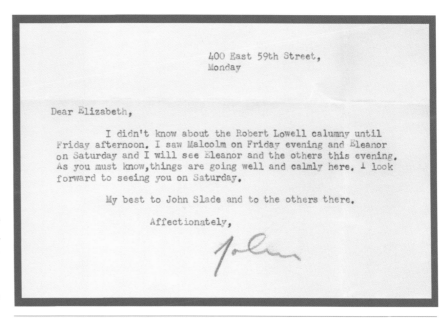

John Cheever was another Yaddo writer who championed Ames's leadership.

RFD Gaylordsville, Conn.,
March 14, 1949.

Dear Betty:

This morning I received a very nice letter from Eleanor Clark
and I am sending you a copy of it. Perhaps she has written you
separately. I think her letter should be copied for all the directors; and perhaps there are other letters that ought to be copied
for them at the same time, so that Bacon and others would have a
clearer picture of what happened. Also I think there might be something in the line of collecting testimonials or signatures that
Eleanor could do in NY. Her letter is especially good because she
is well known for her strong anti-Communist sentiments.

One unpleasant fact that stands out from her letter is that
the four guests are now talking. Pretty soon unless somebody talks
to them they will be talking to Hearst or Scripps-Howard reporters
and doing irreparable damage to a large part of the literary world.
Perhaps they should be reminded by a lawyer that there are libel
laws on the statute books; at any rate this is a subject you might
discuss with John.

What you say about Granville and Newton is partly right but
not altogether so. Lowell and Hardwick and Maisel are off on a tangent of their own and I'm sure that Granville knows that their charges
are preposterous. The fact has to be faced that in the long run the
situation looks pretty bleak. One good loud burst of laughter would
blow the smoke away, but these are times when people are afraid to
laugh. Meanwhile I hope there will be many more persons like Leonard
and Eleanor defending Yaddo's interests in New York. I've been writing as many letters as I have time to write, but that isn't very many.
Take care of yourself and I'll be seeing you soon in the city.

As ever,

Malcolm

P.S.—I'm enclosing a statement of my expenses at the directors'
meeting.—M.

politics   45 Astor Place
New York 3, N. Y.

*plase keep
in your file
for the present*

March 3, 1949.

Dear Mrs. Ames:

Thank you for your second note, saying that "because
of certain conditions at Yaddo, all guests are leaving on March
1," and inviting me to come up nevertheless, "if you do not
object to solitude."

Yesterday I had a long talk with Elizabeth Hardwick,
one of the March 1 walkers-out, and what she told me of the present
situation at Yaddo forces me to now decline your invitation. This
I do reluctantly, for I don't at all object to solitude, and I
had looked forward to two weeks' uninterrupted work on my book.

I agree with the position, and the action, taken by
the four guests who left March 1, of whom I know three personally.
Yaddo is supposed to be a refuge for writers and artists, not a
center for pro-Soviet propaganda. That a figure like Agnes
Smedley, whose lifelong activity has been as a fulltime journalistic
apologist for Communism and the Soviet Union, should make Yaddo
her headquarters for years, that she should — because of her
friendship with you — occupy a specially privileged and influential
status, and that, now that the whole scandal has come out in the
public, you should actually defend this transaction and should
insist that Smedley is just another of those nice old Jeffersonian
(or maybe agrarian?) democrats — all
this seems to me to indicate that, as Hardwick and her associates
charge, the Communists have had, and still do have, a strategic
behind-the-scenes position at Yaddo.

The objection, of course, is not to pro-Communist
writers and artists being invited to Yaddo, but to
persons like Smedley, who have no connection with cultural life
and activity, making Yaddo their base of operations. I know how
the Communists work, and I know that once they get the kind of
hold they apparently have over your administration, they will use
it ruthlessly to reward the faithful and knife the heterodox.
The details Hardwick told me confirm this generalization.

Yaddo has been perverted from the intentions of its
founders, and until this mess is cleaned up, I don't want to have
anything to do with it. So I must, regretfully believe me, my dear
Mrs. Ames, decline your invitation.

Sincerely,

Dwight Macdonald

P.S. I'm sending Elizabeth Hardwick a copy of this letter, to use
as she thinks best.

Editor: Dwight Macdonald   Business Managers: Judy Miller, Nancy Macdonald

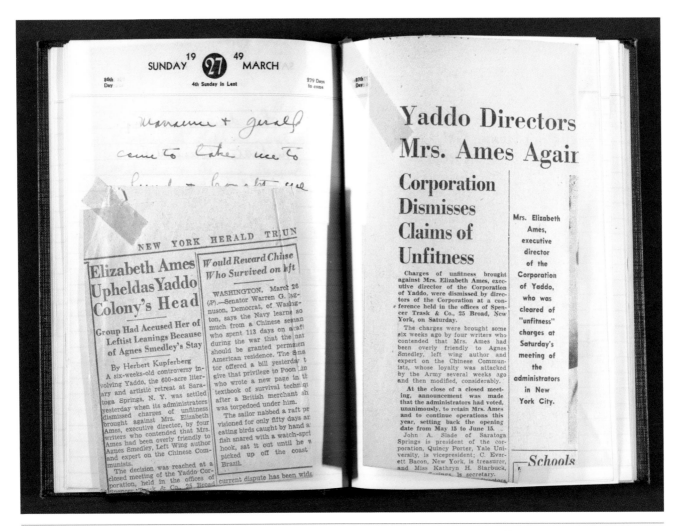

Yaddo's board vindicated Ames on March 26, 1949. She marked the date in her appointment book with news clippings that cleared her name.

cal intrigues preposterous, offered to testify against Lowell and his supporters—a move Yaddo president John Slade sagaciously declined.[32] Smedley was so amazed that Maisel, whom she described as Ames's "pet darling," had attacked Ames that she wondered whether he might work for the FBI.

On March 26, in a Manhattan office building, Yaddo's board members categorically rejected as unsupported by any evidence the charges made by Lowell, Hardwick, and Maisel (O'Connor had dropped off by this time). While they deliberated, Smedley and Lowell both participated in a conference at the nearby Waldorf-Astoria intended to encourage a more conciliatory posture to-

ward the Soviet Union. According to Agnes, "Lowell was in the Writing panel. . . . He stood up first, spread his legs wide as if he were going to pee, announced: 'I'm Robert Lowell the poet and I'm a Catholic', and proceeded to verbally abuse the composer Dmitri Shostakovich."[33] Three days later, Lowell was arrested for stealing a roll of theater tickets and assaulting a police officer while visiting Allen Tate. Following his "attack of pathological enthusiasm," as Lowell termed the incident, he was committed to a private hospital in Massachusetts, where Tate described his friend as "very nearly psychotic."[34]

Smedley died one year later, to the frustration of conservatives who had

been chasing her nearly all her adult life. Amid charges that she had been "liquidated by the Cominform" (the Comintern's successor organization), the House Un-American Activities Committee held a posthumous hearing on Smedley's activities. Later, her books were burned by U.S. Information Agency libraries abroad. Those actions formed the basis for liberal charges of McCarthyism.

In the 1970s, Smedley reemerged as an unblemished heroine of the modern women's movement. Her early novel, *Daughter of Earth*, was reissued to critical acclaim. Restored relations with China returned Smedley's China books to print; film and television projects about Smedley's life, based on her image as a selfless feminist heroine, were also optioned. It was a great story. It was just not the whole story. Similarly, while this extraordinary woman did indeed provide exemplary service to both the Comintern and Soviet military intelligence in China, she was never an ordinary operative. Less than candid about her political associations, she did not direct her activities against the United States. She was a spy, but not a traitor.

When Yaddo's founders articulated their vision for the community, they expressed the desire that it prove "to be a source of fruitful help and inspiration to many, and especially to those who are gifted with creative power and who have had the impulse to use it for their fellow men."[35] In her steadfast commitment to struggles for human dignity and well as her literary output, Smedley exemplified ideals of which Yaddo might be proud.

[OPPOSITE] Adolf Dehn. *Applause*, 1928. Dehn created a series of satirical renderings of audiences.

8 / Writ in Water

The Rise and Fall of Literary Reputations

David Gates

Since Samuel Johnson (naturally) put it more elegantly than I could, why not just rip off his lead? "No place affords a more striking conviction of the vanity of human hopes, than a publick library." That sentence, which begins essay number 106 of *The Rambler*, rolls on for a few more blocks, but you can see where it's heading: the odds on a writer's work enduring are about the same as the odds on winning the lottery. Johnson wrote this in 1751, and it remained true right up until libraries started bringing in computers and chucking out the seldom-read books and periodicals, as Nicholson Baker sickeningly details in

his 2001 exposé *Double Fold*. In Johnson's day, at least you could find neglected books moldering in the stacks. Now, if you can't find a writer's name by using Google, where's the proof that writer ever lived? Obscurity has been downgraded to nonexistence.

One place you can still turn to for a hit of humility—if you're a Gloomy Gus who refuses to see the glass as one percent full—is the long list of those who, since 1926, have repaired to Yaddo, the working retreat for writers, composers, visual artists, and such, in Saratoga Springs, New York. All of them presumably cherished enough human hope to get them there in the first place, and by

the latest count, Yaddo residents have racked up 62 Pulitzers, 58 National Book Awards, 24 MacArthur Fellowships, and 106 Rome Prizes—this last averages out to more than one a year. But try Googling such names as Harry Granich, Norbert Gutherman, H.H. Hartiwitz, Dr. Elliott Hutchinson, Dr. E.E. Jacob, Sophie C. Johnson, Lawiette MacDuffie Knight. . . . Need we go through the whole alphabet? Keats wanted his epitaph to be "Here lies one whose name was writ in water"; these names seem never to have been writ in pixels. Google does recognize some other unfamiliar names—but sometimes only on Yaddo's own Web site. (If this piece should go

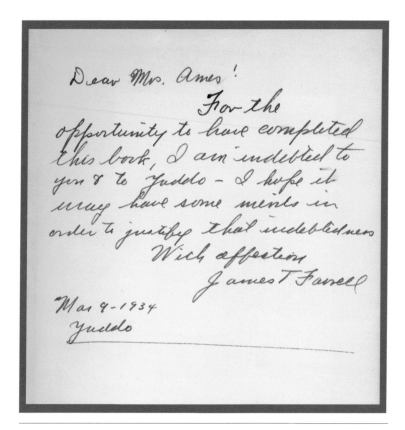

Dear Mrs. Ames!
For the opportunity to have completed this book, I am indebted to you & to Yaddo — I hope it may have some merits in order to justify that indebtedness
With affection
James T Farrell
Mar 9-1934
Yaddo

James T. Farrell and his wife, Dorothy, spent the year 1934 at Yaddo. Farrell completed *The Young Manhood of Studs Lonigan* while Dorothy worked as Ames's assistant. Farrell inscribed the novel to Ames with gratitude for her support.

up online, Granich, Gutherman, Hartiwitz, et al. will again spring into official existence, though we still may not know who they were or what they did.) This is not to say their work was not worth our attention, but how can it *get* our attention anymore?

Neglect has eroded other reputations less terminally. (It helps to have *had* a reputation.) Consider such writers as Jean Stafford and Katherine Anne Porter. Over the past few decades, their best-selling and critically revered books—in 1965, Porter's *Ship of Fools* even became a high-profile Hollywood film with a big-name cast including Vivien Leigh—have been fading from view, while the work of such coevals as Flannery O'Connor and Eudora Welty still thrives among young writers. Recently I mentioned Stafford's splendid story "Children Are Bored on Sunday" to a class of MFA fiction writers. Not

one had read it. Not one had heard of her. Possibly Stafford's and Porter's rich and leisurely prose, like that of Peter Taylor in his 1987 Pulitzer Prize–winning collection *A Summons to Memphis*, has become outmoded since the advent of Raymond Carver and Ann Beattie. At any rate, teachers seem to have stopped assigning their work, and word of mouth has fallen silent. Possibly one or more of them is due for posthumous rediscovery, like Richard Yates, Dawn Powell, and Patricia Highsmith—though you no longer hear as much about the latter two as you did five years ago. If it's not happening now for Donald Barthelme—who published 128 of his 145 stories in the *New Yorker*—it won't be for lack of advocates. And while John Cheever never vanished—and certainly not after *The Stories of John Cheever* (the big red one) came out in 1978—young writers seem to admire

him more year after year. The prospect of a more appreciative posterity may console the living—no names—who fall into neglect; so far, though, we haven't heard that Yates, Powell, and Highsmith are clinking glasses beyond the grave to celebrate their revivals.

And some writers whose names manage to survive nevertheless go largely unread. Once in a while someone will get a crush, passing or permanent, on Nelson Algren, James T. Farrell, Carson McCullers, Louis Zukofsky, Edward Dahlberg (who's lately been championed by the novelist Jonathan Lethem), or Harold Brodkey. (It seems only yesterday that Harold Bloom was calling Brodkey "an American Proust," and he was calling himself "someone who could be the rough equivalent of a Wordsworth or a Milton." And what's the title of his much-anticipated, perennially unpublished novel? Answer below.) James Baldwin is still taught in African American literature courses, and his story "Sonny's Blues" remains an anthology piece—but his best-selling 1962 novel *Another Country* has practically vanished. Sylvia Plath—and here's a shock—may still be a feminist martyr/heroine, but her reputation as a poet has been sinking for years, even as her husband Ted Hughes's has been rising. During their lifetimes, Robert Lowell's work overshadowed that of his friend Elizabeth Bishop—you know, that person to whom he dedicated "Skunk Hour"; today Bishop is increasingly read and admired, while Lowell seems more a representative figure of his time and less a model and an inspiration. (The title of Brodkey's novel, most of which probably never existed, is *Party of Animals*.)

The scholar Newton Arvin, the Americanist whose critical biography of Melville won the 1950 National Book Award, had a moment of posthumous celebrity in 2001, when *The Scarlet Pro-*

fessor, a biography by Barry Werth, told how homophobia and Arvin's own indiscretion—that he was required to *be* discreet is a blot on the time in which he lived—destroyed his career in a 1960 scandal. (Still, Arvin hasn't regained anything like his old readership.) Truman Capote, to whom Arvin was a mentor and a lover, also had a posthumous moment—as if he hadn't had enough moments when he was alive—thanks to Philip Seymour Hoffman's portrayal in Bennett Miller's 2005 film *Capote*. After the profound disappointment over Capote's posthumous *Answered Prayers*—his own *Party of Animals*—the film prompted some readers (I can't have been the only one) to rediscover *In Cold Blood*. Miller's film also gave the still-living but long-silent Harper Lee a moment; as always, it was smaller than Capote's.

Who'll be next? Right now, Saul Bellow, Nobel Prize and all, seems to be following Bernard Malamud (who'd been a Nobel contender) down the long road south, but give him—and Malamud—a few years, a twitch in the *zeitgeist*, and enough new readers stumbling onto that first sentence of *The Adventures of Augie March*. The onetime classicist Norman O. Brown, whose 1959 study *Life Against Death: The Psychoanalytic Meaning of History* was an unlikely favorite among the brainier participants in the 1960s counterculture, ought to be due for exhumation. Lionel Trilling, of all people, called the book "one of the most interesting and valuable works of our time." (Somebody ought to rediscover Trilling, too.) Neither Clifton Fadiman—longtime senior judge for the once-influential Book-of-the-Month Club, editor in chief of Simon and Schuster, and radio's number-one intellectual in the 1940s—nor Granville Hicks—the onetime Marxist critic who became an anticommunist, a HUAC

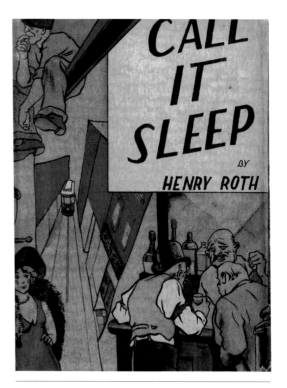

Henry Roth's novel *Call It Sleep* was an enormous success on its publication in 1934, as well as when it was reissued in paperback in 1964. However, Roth fell into obscurity when he did not produce another novel until 1994. Stuyvesant Van Veen, a guest in 1932, created the artwork for the book jacket.

> 61 Morton Street,
> New York City
> March 31, 1933
>
> Dear Mrs. Ames,
>
>   I should be very happy indeed to come to Yaddo. I am just finishing proof on a novel which Ballou is publishing early this fall. As soon as that is done, I shall probably start on a new novel, the ideas of which are already beginning to impede my reading the proof of the first one. The subject is to be proletarian. The scene strangely enough is Park Avenue, but a Park Avenue that very few people know--namely that portion of it that lies under and in the vicinity of the New York, New Haven and Hartford trestle at 120th Street. The characters will be drawn from the vanishing Irish, the wavering Jews and the gathering masses of Porto Ricans and Cubans who have been settling there. The plot will probably depend on how I can manipulate 300 pages of notes without having to discard a page.
>
>   Undoubtedly you will advise me as to letters of recommendation and the like should you care to have me come. Thanking you, I am,
>
>   Yours sincerely,
>
>   Henry Roth
>   Henry Roth

In 1933 Henry Roth wrote Elizabeth Ames describing the next novel he wished to write.

witness, and a *Saturday Review* contributing editor—seems likely to be a hot item again, but who would have predicted the recent vogue for John Clare?

A lucky few actually make their comeback while they are still around to enjoy it, or at least to experience it. It happened for Henry Roth—twice, in fact. His 1934 novel *Call It Sleep* got decent reviews, but its publisher soon went under because of the depression. When it reappeared as a paperback in 1964, it sold a million copies. Meanwhile, Roth was in the middle of his six decades of rural reclusiveness and near-total literary silence. Then, in 1994 and 1995, he published a pair of well-received—and much wondered-at—novels, *Mercy of a Rude Stream*, volumes one and two. And then, also in 1995, he died. J. D. Salinger (same rustication, but only four decades of silence so far) might still have time to publish that 15,000-page novel he had damn well better have been working on all these years, but even his most loyal admirers gave up hope long ago. Paula Fox's 1970 novel *Desperate Characters*—which Irving Howe ranked with *Billy Budd* and *The Great Gatsby* and which became a film starring Shirley MacLaine—went out of print until 1999. It then reappeared with an introduction by Jonathan Franzen, who said it was better than anything by Bellow, Philip Roth, or John Updike. Marilynne Robinson's first novel, the 1980 *Housekeeping*, was a Pulitzer Prize finalist, but she didn't publish another novel until *Gilead* in 2004—and this time it won.

But attention must be paid to those writers who could hardly get arrested while they were alive, whose neglect now seems permanent, and whose stories and achievements are well worth remembering. One figure who's at least dimly remembered is Agnes Smedley, a long-lived feminist, journalist, and novelist who did jail time in 1918 for agita-

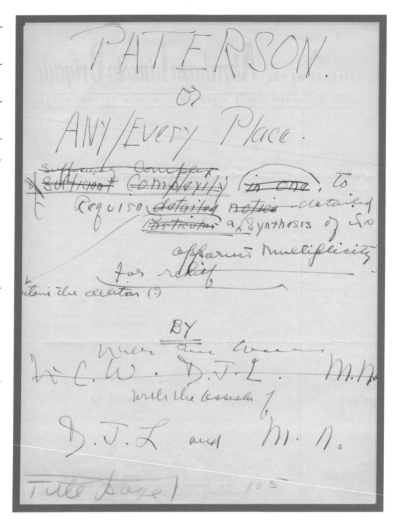

William Carlos Williams, a guest in 1950, had included the letters of poet Marcia Nardi without attribution in book 2 of his modernist masterpiece, *Paterson*. Here the title page of the manuscript suggests that he originally planned on noting her contribution with her initials, M. N.

tion against British rule in India—and was also charged with disseminating information about birth control. She began publishing before 1920; spent years in China, where she sided with the Communist revolutionaries and hung out with Mao Zedong (a spelling she would not have recognized). When she died in 1950, her ashes ended up in Beijing's National Revolutionary Martyrs Memorial park. In the 1970s, she was rediscovered by feminists, and in 1987 the Feminist Press reprinted her 1929 roman à clef *Daughter of Earth*, which the *Nation* had called "America's first feminist-proletarian novel." Kenneth Fearing, a

poet who helped found the *Partisan Review* and whose work appeared in the *New Yorker*, had his 1946 noir novel *The Big Clock* adapted for film. Twice, in fact: in 1937 with Ray Milland and Charles Laughton, and in 1987 (as *No Way Out*) with Kevin Costner and Gene Hackman. Shouldn't posterity give him a tumble?

What about the poet Marcia Nardi, born Lillian Massell? William Carlos Williams appropriated portions of her letters, without her permission and attributed to "Cress," in book 2 of his epic poem *Paterson*, where they make up a substantial part of the text. When does she get *her* props? Her contribution is

WILLIAM CARLOS WILLIAMS
9 RIDGE ROAD
RUTHERFORD, N. J.   Oct. 24, 1951

My dear Elizabeth Ames:

          This is a barefaced imposition, I swore to
myself that I would not bother you again with mention of
applicants for the privileges of Yaddo and yet here I
am at it once more. But this is positively the last time
I shall do it for at least a year. I would not do it
now were it not a special case.

          Marcia Nardi is a difficult woman, an insigni-
ficant little woman of forty perhaps, foolish, frightened
but gifted, who has somehow existed among the unfortunate
beaten wastrels of Greenwich Village and the Bowery in
New York. Yet, believe it or not, she is gentle and
though erratic very intelligent. She has had a hell of a
life - much of it her own fault.

          . And yet I have a soft spot for her in my heart.
I have helped her as I could, gotten her benefits of
various sorts and achieved publication of some of her
work that has won praise abroad.

          Now this unfortunate person, unprepossessing,
friendless is at me again. I should be angry at her but
I can't. She is too much like a part of me that is
unattractive, even debased even, but innocent, I give
you my word it is guiltless as I believe this woman is
guiltless. She badly needs help, she is not a parasite
but one for whom we must all share the guilt - that such
people exist in the world.

          That's no reason why YOU should help her aside
from the fact that she is talented. But I cannot pass
up her plea. I send it on to you. Do what you can with it.
I acknowledge that this emotional introduction does
attempt to prejudge the case and influence you perhaps
unjustifoably in the woman's favor. I acknowledge it.
Yaddo would be a godsend to her.

                    Sincerely yours

                    W. C. Williams

                    William Carlos Williams

Marcia Nardi turned to Williams for a letter of recommendation to accompany her 1951 application to Yaddo. Despite Williams's disparaging letter, written to Ames on October 24, 1951, Nardi was eventually invited to Yaddo, first in 1953 and again in 1956.

Guests in 1953. *Top row*: Edgar Acker, Clay Putnam, Thomas McMahon, Isabel Bolton, Tobias Schneebaum, Helen Auger, Clifford Wright, Sari Dienes, Keith Botsford, Laura Douglas. *Bottom row*: Marcia Nardi, Babette Deutsch, Margaret Marshall, Theresa Sherman, Avrahm Yarmolinsky, Jeanne Wacker, Roger Shattuck.

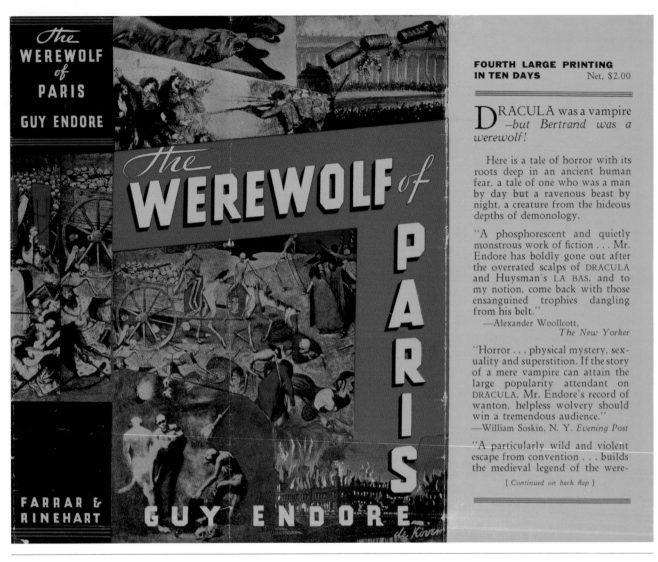

Guy Endore, a guest in 1932, spent his stay working on a popular novel, *The Werewolf of Paris*, published in 1933. Endore hoped the horror novel would pay back the advance on his earlier book, *Sword of God*, an account of the life of Jeanne d'Arc, which had not been earned out.

no secret—the correspondence between her and Williams was published in 1998—and Williams encouraged her to publish the one book of her poems that has ever appeared, but only a specialist would recognize her name. In fact it looks like Williams himself is becoming a back number. In the 1970s, certain revisionists held that Pound, Williams, and Charles Olson were the big three of modern American poetry. You seldom hear that anymore (Frost, Eliot, and Stevens might be closer to the conventional wisdom), but if Williams's reputation should rise again, maybe Nardi will fi-

nally get her fifteen minutes. And let us give a nod in passing to Guy Endore. In 1933 he published *The Sword of God*, then the definitive biography of Joan of Arc and—according to Amazon—still available in paperback. But he's best known for the novel he published that year, *The Werewolf of Paris*, the *Dracula* of lycanthropy. He ended up in Hollywood as a screenwriter, a target of HUAC, and a proud blacklistee, who resumed writing under the name Harry Relis. He got an Oscar nomination for the 1945 *Story of G.I. Joe*, and—far more important these days—cowrote Tod

Browning's 1936 cult film *The Devil Doll*. In contrast to Nardi, Endore is at the extreme high end of the neglected—if you can call someone neglected who has at least half a dozen books listed on Amazon. And like Fox and Dahlberg, he has a champion: Jamaica Kincaid, who wrote an introduction to the reissue of *Babouk*, his 1934 novel about a Caribbean slave rebellion.

Guy Endore may never make the canon, but he had a far-more-than-respectable career, and far greater worldly success than most writers ever achieve. So did Smedley, Fearing, and

June 6, 1934

Mrs. Elizabeth Ames,
Yaddo,
Saratoga Springs, N.Y.

Dear Elizabeth:

Did I or did I not send you a letter from the train while I was on my way out here? I know that I intended to. Henrietta, the baby and myself are very pleased with Hollywood. I, for one, would have liked to have spent some time at Yaddo again. I'm afraid that pleasure is now rather out and I shall have nothing but the memory of the good times I spent there.

The last I heard, George Milburn had received a Guggenheim and was off with Vivian to Oklahoma. He did not answer my letter nor did he meet me at an appointment we had in New York City. If you hear from him will you send him my congratulations and apprise him of my whereabouts and discover for me when he is going away to Europe (or wherever he is going) and how long he intends to stay?

The difficulty I had with my slave novel seems finally to have been settled. Vanguard will do the book. Expect a copy from me hot off the press sometime this fall. There is some talk, too, of its being done as a play for production next season.

One of my chief delights in Hollywood, aside from the climate and vegetation, is the fact that it will give me an opportunity to rest up from the harrassing business of hack-writing in New York and catch up, too, with my innumerable debts. Have no idea how long I shall stay here - possibly years.

How is your sister? How is Brownie, Mary, George, and the rest? Are you having a big season? I should love to know what writers and artists have come out to Yaddo this summer. Henrietta and Marcia wish to be remembered to you and all of us send our best regards to Miss Pardee and Mr. Peabody. Please let us hear from you.

Sincerely,

GE:ws
My home address: 1319 N. June Street, Hollywood.

Faced with continuing financial struggles and trouble finding a publisher for the politically charged *Babouk*, Endore moved himself and his family to Hollywood, where he began a screenwriting career at Paramount Pictures. Endore became a successful screenwriter, receiving an Oscar nomination for his 1945 screenplay *The Story of G.I. Joe*. During the McCarthy era he was blacklisted but continued to write for film under the name Harry Relis.

how many more, just in the past century? A hundred? A thousand? At the rate we're going, there will be at least as many more in the century that's beginning. And look back at the people Johnson wrote about in his ten-volume *Lives of the Poets*—not just Pope and Milton, but Thomas Yalden, Richard Duke, George Stepney, Samuel Garth, and Gilbert West. Most of these names survive only in connection with Johnson's. They ought to be remembered, all of them: not just to pull down our vanity, but because they worked, they hoped and despaired, they felt the same exaltation at the end of a good writing day and suffered the same sense of failure that every writer with any sense must endure. ("What an artist does, is fail," Donald Barthelme wrote. "Fail again," Samuel Beckett wrote. "Fail better.") Living and dead, they're our fellow travelers to the Big Neglect—when some fool pushes a button, or, at the very latest, when the sun goes out at last.

9 / Crème de la Crème

HIGHBROWS, LOWBROWS, VORACIOUS OMNIVORES, HIGH, LOW, AND HI-LO

Marcelle Clements

PRESTIGE HAS seldom been the artist's friend. Whether present or absent, it is more likely to create conflict and ambivalence than to motivate. Yet Yaddo is so often said to be prestigious that some may suspect it to be a kind of self-conscious Mount Parnassus, a wooded paradise for the arts where Orpheus smugly strums his lyre, the muses hang from trees, and postmodern poets pluck Pulitzers off low-lying branches while famous painters frolic and mate. Whether in praise or insult, descriptions of Yaddo often include any number of euphemisms for privilege: elite, exclusive, distinguished, and, my personal fa-

vorite, la crème de la crème. In John Cheever's words, "The 40[0] or so acres on which the studios and principal buildings of Yaddo stand have seen more distinguished activity in the arts than any other piece of ground in the English-speaking community or perhaps in the entire world."[1]

Offended by this effluvium of elitism and crème—or perhaps merely fatigued or bored by the burden of the past— some would surely translate *prestigious* into snobbish, stodgy, and boring. But they would be wrong. The truth is that all sorts of artists make their way to Yaddo, and always have. Of the more than six thousand guests, as they are

called, who have been admitted, some are fancy, but many are plain, and many more are blessedly off the charts. Or, in another of John Cheever's formulations—less well-known but more precise than the one above—Yaddo has always drawn "all kinds—lushes down on their luck, men and women at the top of their powers, nervous breakdowns, thieves, geniuses, cranky noblemen, and poets who ate their peas off a knife."[2]

It's the roll call of names, I believe. Some trick of the mind concatenates our appetite for celebrity with the luster of those names, causing us to squeeze into a single image a century's worth of guests in real encounters. As if in a perennial tableau vivant set against the backdrop of the mansion and the innumerable pine trees, ageless luminaries eternally romp: Leonard Bernstein is forever raising his glass to Hannah Arendt while Philip Guston looks on; James Baldwin and Carson McCullers talk shop; Virgil Thomson plays poker with Henri Cartier-Bresson; Robert Lowell cheats on Jean Stafford with Elizabeth Hardwick (et al.); Clyfford Still is on a bender; Truman Capote exasperates Katherine Anne Porter; Philip Roth, reclining on a velvet-covered divan, dreams of breasts.

It's a pleasant daydream—artists have it too. It's fun to sleep in *their* beds, work at *their* desks, yet dangerous: do we really want to compare ourselves to Guston, Still, or Roth every time we go to work? But it serves the purpose of actualizing, if only in fantasy, what many of us unconsciously seek in art: all the artists are beautiful and free from want; their suffering is picturesque; their mental health problems are fascinating; and the sexual stuff is, let's face it, incredibly entertaining. And, of course, they bestow the gift of art to a waiting, adoring audience. As for remuneration, no problem: nectar is always free of charge.

The trickiest proposition implicit in such idealizations is that glory is the stuff of art-making, rather than, say, work, craft, emotion, memory, drive, luck, flow, trial and error—to say nothing of undignified ambition. But then fuzzy logic often accompanies the concept of artistic achievement, and therefore the very idea of a creative community, be it an authentic avant-garde, an old guard, a new wave, a bohemia, the academy, or, for that matter, the entire so-called art world, or any of the other slippery concepts that, together, vaguely add up to our idea of who populates the arts. For real-life artists, these are not considerations. On the contrary, they come to Yaddo to simplify their situa-

tion and escape their career. They are not embracing but fleeing obsession with prestige, hierarchy, competition, and the politics of the arts. Those who succeed will tell you that Yaddo is not only a place where they get a huge amount of work done but also a transformative experience. Hence, the often repeated superstitious statement—"Yaddo is magic." Admittedly, the escape is inherently incomplete—insofar as all art expresses and sustains endlessly unfolding cultural attitudes about power, money, and envy, including the artist's. But the real magic of Yaddo is that when it all goes well, this endless unfolding reverts to being a side show, rather than the main event. Here's the source of the magic: even in our psychotically anxious (read: competitive, consumerist—whatever makes you most anxious) society, it is possible to be reminded that art is above all an artifact of the play of one human being's imagination.

THE YADDO EFFECT

There is a phenomenon I have noticed at Yaddo that I've come to think of as the "Yaddo effect." It is as difficult to describe as any of the other conditions we term magic—love, for example, with which it has a great deal in common. It doesn't happen to everyone and it doesn't happen all the time. But it's been documented by the letters, journals, and, of course, work of the Yaddo guests often enough that we can be sure it's real.

When an exquisite combination of factors is in place, a sort of transformative dynamic pulls all the artists into a distinctive state of altered consciousness. Some conditions are built into the Yaddo program: the place, the tradition, the minimizing of all external stimulation, the remoteness, the silence. You also have to have a bit of luck—the right

Philip Roth, a guest several times between 1964 and 1972, dedicated his 1972 book, *The Breast*, to Elizabeth Ames and Yaddo, describing them as "the best friends a writer could have." Roth inscribed this edition of his 1969 bestseller, *Portnoy's Complaint,* to the Yaddo library.

project, the right group, the right weather . . . who knows, exactly? But if you are lucky, these elements seem to combine synergistically to allow for some form of what psychoanalysts call regression in service of the ego.

A surge in creativity is only one aspect of this childlike state. Symptoms of the Yaddo effect often include outsized hunger, energy, passion of every kind, regret, and randiness. During the day, the intensity of the work stirs up archaic memories; in the evening, even casual social situations cause transference phenomena to bloom. At dinner, there are brilliant conversations, as well as plenty of silly ones. In the exotic safety of Yaddo, curiosity ceases to be blunted by the wear and tear of routine, and it's possible to reconnect with one's interest in one's own perceptions. "Lifting a corner of the heavy curtain of habit (stupefying habit which conceals from us almost the whole universe)," Proust writes in *The Fugitive*, "makes us observe our own most trivial actions with a lucid exaltation which makes that intense minute worth more than the sum-total of the preceding days."[3] And the less one needs to protect one's work from one's life, the more one is likely to lift a corner of the heavy curtain of habit, and the more interesting and vivid life becomes.

And when things aren't going well? Well, then Yaddo is hell, of course. Among the more social, factions are intense and belligerent, cabals solidify, nasty gossip travels fast, and paranoia reigns. If your own work isn't going well, it's tiresome to be polite to the others. You feel antisocial, dissociated, and exasperated. But every week some guests leave and new ones arrive; the weather evolves, as does the foliage. One day as you're in your studio trying to work (after all, there's nowhere else to go, nothing else to do, and a limit to how much you can sleep), you realize that what you thought was a dead end was, on the contrary, a well-camouflaged breakthrough. You find you can finish a week's work in an afternoon. At the end of the day, on the way to the dining room, you realize how much you're looking forward to dinner.

Not the least astonishing aspect of the Yaddo effect is that the lion lies down with the lamb. The truth is that the lion who is just starting a novel feels just as vulnerable as the lamb. Think of it as a peaceable kingdom, where young, old, famous, obscure, hip, and dowdy mingle and bond, where the austere and rigorous creator consorts with the hyperemotional artiste, where the retro-Byronic lies down (or at least sits down, but occasionally lies down, too) with the postmodern. When it's a good group, and it's a good moment, and everything is just right, the outside world's hierarchy is, as a matter of course, turned topsy-turvy. One often notices odd couples deep in conversation on the terrace after dinner—a well-established painter and a young poet still in graduate school, an edgy writer-performer and a neoromantic composer. Then, what's really interesting is that one ceases to notice.

BIG BUCKS, HIGH CULTURE

The writer and teacher Robert Towers, longtime and much-beloved Yaddo board director, used to say that "Mac-Dowell is Henry David Thoreau and Yaddo is Henry James." How can we account, in the outside world, the supposedly real world, for the inevitable linking of Yaddo with elitism? Why, for example, does the MacDowell Colony's reputation retain class neutrality—from a distance, at least—and Yaddo's does not? After the illustrious names (since, after all, MacDowell has its own illustrious roster, and, in fact, many artists attend both colonies), it's the place itself that has helped build for Yaddo such a chic reputation—the vast, beautiful estate in Saratoga Springs.

Never mind that it is architecturally dubious (to be charitable), the grand and ponderous fifty-five-room mansion contributes copiously to the Yaddo myth—and it always did, even in the leanest years when the roof leaked and the rugs were threadbare. For the artists these remnants of nineteenth-century high style are a source of unending humor and pleasure: Any number of them will have borrowed money for the train ride to Yaddo, but there will be hand-rolled butter balls on the table.

On the one hand Yaddo is a Gilded Age aesthete's fantasy of an exalted refuge, founded on a reverence for art and a deeply romantic, idealized view of the artist. On the other, in the time between Katrina Trask's founding vision and Yaddo's opening its doors in 1926, there was World War I, the Russian Revolution, the collapse of the European social order, the rise of modernity and of modernism, flux and fragmentation. Neither art nor artists would ever be thought of in the same way again. Yaddo, however, with its fancy Mount Parnassus–style guest list, its Tudor-style mansion replete with shameless allusion to feudal and bourgeois structures, its formal rose garden adjoining a great lawn leading down to a fountain at the center of which a cherub forever teases two water nymphs, Yaddo was set to go and, as hardy and incongruous in the real circumstances of producing art in the twentieth and twenty-first centuries as the butter balls, its reputation would somehow always be marinated in the aura of high art.

AN ABRIDGED HISTORY OF HIGH AND LOW OUTSIDE YADDO

Since no one really seems to understand post–World War I cultural history, it is futile to try to state with any certainty when it became impossible to distinguish between high and low art, or even to define art. What is clear is that the putative problem of high and low art did not start recently, and Yaddo and other contemporary arts institutions are merely the latest nexi of the projections and disputes that it so easily provokes. As soon as one caveman or -woman scribbled a sketch of a mastodon on the wall, it is likely that another caveperson declared it to be trash. But the argument evolved very slowly at first, when Plato codified what was beautiful by uniting it with the good and the useful. In the sixteenth century, as if the world had just woken up with a start, the Enlightenment philosophers decided to argue with him and started to speak of the *je ne sais quoi* (their phrase!) that differentiates the banal from the great, and the great from the sublime. By 1757, in the essay "On Taste," which was published in the *Encyclopédie*, Montesquieu proposes that beauty is far from universal, but that what gives us pleasure is in part based on "biases and prejudices"—that class, custom, and background create taste. He also specifically evokes the high-low problem, by speaking of the pleasure we draw from the naïf, which, he points out, "is the style which is hardest to grasp—the reason being that it is precisely between the noble and the low, but is so close to the low that it is difficult to always stay alongside of it without falling into it."[4]

This anxiety about "falling into" lowness seems to have waxed and waned in the following few centuries according to a complex formula of economic and political conditions, and so did its populist counterpoise: fear and/or contempt for intellectualism. By the end of the nineteenth century, this schism was institutionalized on both sides of the Atlantic with what has been called the *sacralization* of art, the blooming of philanthropy, the establishment of high art meccas such as symphony halls and museums.[5]

The words "highbrow" and "lowbrow" were coined in the late nineteenth century and are thought to have been inspired by the science of phrenology—the study of the shape of the skull and its purported relationship to intelligence and criminality. But the use of these two terms as pejoratives proliferated in that same fateful period at the beginning of the twentieth century—the interregnum between Katrina's vision and Yaddo's opening, when a passionate argument about the merits of high culture exploded in Britain. A third and even more appalling category was discovered when the BBC began its programming in 1922. According to *Punch*, "The BBC claims to have discovered a new type, 'the middlebrow.' It consists of people who are hoping that some day they will get used to the stuff they ought to like."[6]

By 1927, D. H. Lawrence was declaring, "I can't stand high-browish . . . people any more,"[7] while Leonard Woolf was writing "Hunting the Highbrow," an account of the persecution and a defense of an endangered animal, which he declared to be not one but several distinct species:

1. *Altifrons altifrontissimus*, the original, primitive and real highbrow or intellectual who . . . prefers the appeal of his intellect rather than that solely to his senses.

2. *Altifrons aestheticus* var. *severus*, the man who only likes what is best in literature, art, and music. . . .

3. *Altifrons frankauensis*, the man who is not entertained and uplifted by the novels [of popular authors].

4. *Pseudoaltifrons intellectualis*, the man who only likes what nobody else can understand.

5. *Pseudaltifrons aestheticus*, the man who, in literature, art, and music, only likes the latest thing or the oldest thing or the thing which the majority dislikes.[8]

The noble *Altifrons altifrontissimus* Virginia Woolf, meanwhile, plunged into the melee with both fists, with the surprising—and prophetic—argument that high-, middle-, and lowbrow should be separated from high, middle, and low class, that there could be such a thing as "a democratic highbrow."[9] Soon, there was no one left without an opinion about the merits and dangers of high- and lowbrowism, both of which were termed arrogant, dangerous, and tyrannical. Within a few years, the highbrow/lowbrow debate had expanded to the middlebrow forums—newspapers and magazines—where, for the next several decades, any number of people would analyze, report on, and ridicule supporters of the other faction. Highbrows got the worst of it:

The British crime writer and journalist Edgar Wallace: "A highbrow is a man who has found something more interesting than women."[10]

The American scholar Brander Matthews: "A highbrow is a person educated beyond his intelligence."[11]

The novelist A. P. Herbert: "A highbrow is the kind of person who looks at a sausage and thinks of Picasso."[12]

On the Continent, anything as genteel as the high- and lowbrowism debate was dispensed with, and the big guns were aimed directly at the question of high art as a fortress of privilege. In Paris, Dada segued into surrealism, and artists met in cafés to make communal drawings and experiment with automatic writing. André Breton soon published his manifesto in which he praised "pure psychic automatism," as well as "the absence of all control exercised by reason."

In 1936, Walter Benjamin, in *The Work of Art in the Age of Mechanical Reproduction*, posited that mass reproduction would destroy the "aura" of a work of art and "brush aside a number of outmoded concepts, such as creativity and genius, eternal value and mystery."[13] The Frankfurt School was revving up to go.

Nonetheless, in the United States, where a tenacious tradition of pragmatism and of valuing common sense over intellect was not to be dispensed with by anything as frivolous as the games of the Dadaists or the cerebrations of the fellows in Frankfurt, the high-low debate still raged on. And while the debate itself may have been a high-class European invention, it soon enough became a red, white, and blue commodity in the business of American culture. In 1949, Russell Lynes's essay "Highbrow, Lowbrow, Middlebrow,"[14] which set forth the rules of highbrow behavior and consumer preferences in *Harper's* magazine, garnered instant notoriety. *Life* magazine promptly published a chart and, from coast to coast, low- and middle-brow Americans of every class and stripe now had access to the code, if they wanted it.

All unreconstructed *Altifrons altifrontissimi*—highbrows, intellectuals, academics, and critics still out in the wild—now took cover. The rest is not history, since no one to date has written a cogent account of the convulsion of Western thought in the twentieth century, the splintering of culture, or the resulting explosion of form in the arts. One would have to put together more ideas that any one human being can encompass (who can even do the reading?): modernism, aesthetic modernism, aesthetic realism, Freudian psychoanalysis, Ultraísmo Marxism, Freudo-Marxism, art nouveau, art deco, cubism, the Jazz Age, New Criticism, abstraction, modern dance, socialist realism, Kleinian psychoanalysis, Bauhaus, existentialism, reception theory, the Harlem Renaissance, the Beats, linguistics, semiotics, suburbia, object relations, television, youth culture, structuralism, poststructuralism, abstract expressionism, pop art, op art, conceptual art, Fluxus, deconstruction, cultural theory, critical theory, feminist theory, queer theory, EST, postmodernism, Southern Agrarians, confessional poetry, language poetry, multimedia art, *Understanding Media*, media studies, "Turn on, tune in, drop out," Lacanian thought, minimalism, happenings, performance art, video art, the New Journalism, the New York School [painting], the New York School [criticism], realism, neorealism, Classical Realism, Magic Realism, hyperrealism, hypermodernism, Mad Ave, neoclassical music, atonality, serialism, indeterminism, electronic music, musique concrète, aleatory music, trance music, postmodern music, neoromantic music, New Complexity, jazz, blues, R&B, rock 'n' roll, the British invasion, punk, postpunk, heavy metal, psychedelic rock, psychedelic art, camp, kitsch, New Wave [music], New Wave [novels], New Wave [film], cinema verité, *The Anxiety of Influence*, niche marketing, hip hop, sampling, rap, street art, technomusic, house music, microhouse music, minimal technomusic, the Internet, *The Closing of the American Mind*, *The Opening of the American Mind*, *critique génétique*, postcolonialism, visual culture, and globalization.

As the twentieth century progressed, the arguments within and about art were becoming increasingly factionalized and incomprehensible. Few voices called for broadening the scope of the conversation about art—so few that the exceptions remain distinct and memorable. The great art historian Meyer Schapiro comes to mind, as well as his declaration that "Our concern with the work of art, however touched by vanity or greed, is an homage beyond self-interest." He told the Art Dealers Association of America when accepting an award in 1973: "Through it [art] we surmount, if only at rare moments, the limitations of our striving, possessive selves and, as an old poet says, 'into glory peep.'" For some these were comforting thoughts to remember in the 1980s, when the words "art" and "market" became nearly inseparable companions.

As for the twenty-first century, no one even seems to have any new and interesting big categories yet. Web 2.0 (defined, by Wikipedia, as "a perceived second generation of Web-based communities and hosted services—such as social-networking sites, wikis, and folksonomies—which aim to facilitate creativity, collaboration, and sharing between [sic] users")? Is that the best we can do? Perhaps. This democratization of creativity would certainly fulfill both Walter Benjamin's prediction about the outmoded artist as hero and, incidentally, the early to mid-twentieth-century highbrow's worst fears. But if we have learned anything since the turn of the century when the Dadaists began to make fools of themselves (and, at their best, of the rest of us as well), it is that it's an error to declare anything dumb (in public) until we've seen what it leads to.

THE RISE OF THE VORACIOUS OMNIVORE

It was around the turn of the millennium that the fusillade of big ideas died away, and in the ensuing silence, synthesis began to seem suspect. Perhaps the arguments of the 1960s and 1970s had exhausted all the combatants? Perhaps the entire culture was sinking under the weight of political and economic contradictions too overwhelming to process? Suddenly a show at the Museum of Modern Art entitled *High and Low: Modern Art and Popular Culture* drew an extraordinary number of jeers. With the advantage of nearly twenty years' hindsight, the very vehemence of the attack seems odd unless one is prepared to connect it to a general exasperation with the endless battles around any and all Big Ideas. If there was anything everyone agreed about, it was that such ruminations were the realm of the press, which was now seen as a déclassé and untrustworthy source of tastemaking that everyone on all sides (including within) agreed to despise. As can now be seen by anyone calmly perusing its still impressive companion volume, the MoMA show attempted to provide evidence of correspondences between high art and popular culture, rather than to lob yet another manifesto into the tired discourse. But the concepts of high and low had been overmasticated in the previous hundred years.[15] As if filled with empty calories, any such categories were deemed fit only for the lite cuisine of the mind. Hi-Lo.

Nowadays, no one in their right mind presumes to speak of art in monolithic categories, though, of course, there are crazy die-hards in every camp. Some snobs still consider "low" forms to be a serious threat. Other snobs still speak sneeringly of "high" art. But none of the texts that could support their positions has maintained its vitality. Even Dwight Macdonald's legendary and deliciously ferocious essay, "Masscult and Midcult," now seems more picturesque than convincing.[16] Essentially, the argument became too simple, too dualistic to compete with the loud cacophony of complexity.

Myriad wounded curators and theoreticians limped off the battlefield, and rights to the domain of taste then quietly reverted to the sociologists—those for whom categories are not threats but bread and butter, and who are not afraid to speak their minds, because they have evidence to back up their ideas (or so they hope). These scholars and researchers turned away from the endless and unquantifiable perplexities of art and instead set to examining the behavior of the audience. Especially influential in the late twentieth century was Pierre Bourdieu, the French theorist who returned to Montesquieu's project of making distinctions in what causes taste, writing of how members of an audience are prepared by social origin and early environment to accumulate "cultural capital" in the form of art.[17]

In American journals, Bourdieu's ideas were greeted with an interest that has since been sustained by an impressive bouquet of theorists. But a brand new set of observations also emerged in the late 1980s, based on the minute study of census reports and records kept by cultural institutions. Several re-searchers began to describe heretofore unnoticed patterns of audience behavior that were encapsulated in 1992, when the sociologist Richard A. Peterson coined the term *omnivorous* to describe "the many high-status persons [who] are far from being snobs and are eclectic . . . in their tastes." By 1996, in an article entitled "Changing Highbrow Taste: From Snob to Omnivore," Richard A. Peterson and Roger M. Kern wrote that "a historical shift from highbrow snob to omnivore is taking place."[18]

According to this view, "dominant-status groups" have traditionally defined popular culture as brutish and despicable—all the better to keep it from acquiring influence counter to their interests. More recently, however, the strategy has changed to "gentrifying" aspects of popular culture and incorporating them into the dominant status culture. Sort of like slum neighborhoods, you might say, in a booming real estate market.

Peterson then refined the omnivore concept, by pointing out some omnivores are not content to abandon the world of snobbish, high-class art for one or two trysts with low-life popular culture—but, instead, systematically sample many genres that would once have been termed low. These, he called voracious omnivores. Peterson's appellation was seized on with gusto by researchers on both sides of the ocean. As it turns out, there were voracious omnivores in Spain too, and in France and England, and even in Israel.

You could use the voracious omnivore concept to explain why entire genres can have aesthetic mobility, bobbing up and down as social status markers in the murky sea of culture. Comic books and graffiti, for example, are often cited. In music, the influence of deep-pocketed voracious omnivores (and their children) has been decisive. Bebop jazz hurtled from saloon to salon within a couple of decades, as did the blues. Rap, on the other hand, seems universally attractive to young omnivores but is almost always deemed repellent or incomprehensible by even the most carnivorous of their omnivorous parents. Cinema has always been a crossover art in Western Europe, but in the United States commercial priorities kept high and low carefully segregated until recently.[19] Nowadays, your average voracious omnivore film buff thinks nothing of sampling from high and low and everything in between on an ongoing basis and, faced with a choice between a Godard retrospective and *Ocean's Thirteen*, will experience a paroxysm of indecision.

That there may be more to all this than mere pragmatic questions of dominance, status, and cultural capital is something that seems not to occur to the sociologists. So the task of teasing out the role of cross-pollination in the arts remains formidable and nearly intact. Luckily, whether anyone is going to satisfactorily explain it or not, artists continue to mix and match elements of disparate subcultures and time zones. They are armed with more or less talent, more or less craft, more or less vision, but, essentially, the notion of creative cross-pollination may be seen as a good outcome: the consequence of complexity is the embrace of plurality. (Or it may be seen as a bad outcome, but where does that get us?)

Sociologist Herbert Gans identified an even more perverse phenomenon— the high-cultural equivalent of what marketers call "repositioning." "Cultural elevations happen regularly to folk and popular artists—Winslow Homer, Edgar Allan Poe—once the folk have dropped them," he writes, to explain Norman Rockwell's recent *succès d'estime* among the cognoscenti.[20]

Finally, many people of the sort who would once have been called highbrows have deserted their own institutions, as if disgusted that they have found popular support. I first noticed this phenomenon in 1977 with the fantastically successful opening of the Centre Georges Pompidou in Paris. Many French intellectuals withdrew, appalled, when the hordes invaded the art world. Beaubourg's escalators, which zigzag up and down the outside of the building, were blamed for attracting the sort of tourist who could just as easily have ridden up and down the elevator in the Eiffel Tower. "Vertical penetration!" was the horrified cry of those who suspected the tourists were riding up and down the side of the building without ever entering the galleries to look at the art. Soon, in all the world's major cities, the so-called blockbuster show came to be seen as indispensable to a museum's survival.

Culture had become all about "fluidity" and "blurring."[21] The highbrow could no longer be hunted—it had become extinct. Granted, this brief and abridged history does not come with a neat ending (it doesn't have a neat beginning either). It only appears here to help the reader understand everything that Yaddo has *not* been, and to gauge the soundness of Katrina Trask's idea: Yaddo was created by nineteenth-century aesthetes, but it has somehow managed to survive the death of aesthetics. The fact is that artists in residence at Yaddo, especially those susceptible to the Yaddo effect, had to be, like the members of all the other bohemias, early adopters of the carnivorous omnivore approach.

YADDO, HIGH AND LOW

As yet another surrealist downed yet another absinthe in Paris, and Leonard Woolf persuaded Virginia not to send yet another letter to the editor complaining because a reviewer had accused her of

being a highbrow, Elizabeth Ames was overseeing the folding of the linen at Yaddo.

The business of running Yaddo has always had more to do with logistics than with big ideas about art. Now and then there is a flurry of argument about what sort of artists should be admitted, and the minutes of the meetings of the Corporation of Yaddo contain traces of an occasional spirited argument about whether filmmakers should be included (yes, they have been), choreographers (yes), jazz musicians (still being argued), video artists (yes), writers for television (no). But, for the most part, all decisions are made on a case-by-case basis by the artists' panels. "Nothing matters except for the work itself," is the byword. No one notices anymore that the origin of such a statement is buried in the ideological cataclysms of the twentieth century and the New Criticism, but at any rate, all this time it has continued to provide artists serving on the panels with seven-league boots in which to stride over the isms, the politicking, the contradictions, the whole paralyzing mess.

Do individual biases creep into the panels' deliberations? Yes, of course, but less than one might imagine. As we have seen, the Yaddo effect democratizes social connections among artists. They meet at Yaddo, forget their differences, become fast friends, and invite one another to serve on panels.

Nevertheless, Yaddo is a working artists' colony, not a utopia. As arts institutions go, Yaddo has been more open than most, in many ways, welcoming women, gays, people of color, people of unpopular politics. But there are limits, and not everyone is judged worthy to share the benefits of the Yaddo effect. Sometimes it isn't the guest's work that is objectionable, but his or her sense of decorum. When James Baldwin left Yaddo, Elizabeth Ames wrote a note for

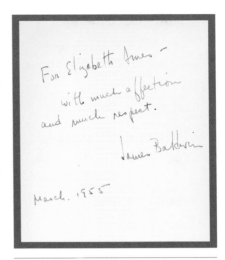

James Baldwin, a guest in 1955, inscribed *Go Tell It on the Mountain* to Elizabeth Ames. He applied for a second residency in 1959 and was declined.

the file, expressing her hope he would not be reinvited. How much this may have had to do with Baldwin's drinking and how much with his style of romancing is anyone's guess, but Baldwin's extraordinarily warm dedications of his books to "Dear Mrs. Ames" are poignant clues to how much he would have wished to return.

THE CASE OF APPLICANT MARIO F. PUZO

The 1950s and 1960s were especially problematic for those wishing to maintain tidy boundaries between high and popular culture, and anyone curious about such matters will not be disappointed by the records found in the Yaddo archives. Here we can see how individuals grappled with these problems and in what language they articulated their thoughts. Many still held unshaken convictions about what was high, noble, real art, but a new need for discretion was taken for granted. The working metaphor was purity—pure art was unsullied while popular art was corrupt, polluted. Of course, the judges didn't use words such as *corrupt*

Yaddo

SARATOGA SPRINGS
NEW YORK

novel not rec'd
as of 9/10/57

23 August 1957

Report for Committee on Admissions

I   Name and Address:

Mario F. Puzo

2745 Sampson Avenue, Bronx 65, New York   SY 2-0882

II   Brief Biographical Notes: (To include such information as the applicant wishes to submit at his or her discretion, place and date of birth, education, special training, etc.)

DOB: NYC   15 Oct 1920

Studied writing at CCNY, Columbia Univ and New School for Social Research

III   Plans for work which would be done at Yaddo:

Novel on Italian immigrant family and first generation Americans

External and internal effects, family stresses.   Not just a broad novel

but trying for depth.   Book has been contracted for by Random House

Use other side of sheet if necessary

Mario Puzo applied to Yaddo in 1957 to work on an early novel, *The Fortunate Pilgrim*.

IV Professional achievements: (Published work including date and name of publisher; exhibits; gallery associations; performance of compositions; fellowships and awards, etc.)

Novel published in Feb 1955 by Random House Title "The Dark Arena".

Short stories in American Vanguard, New Voices, Pulse

Copy of Novel will be sent under separate cover.

V References: Mention names and addresses of sponsors who have agreed to make detailed and informative statements upon request.

Mr. Hiram Haydn, Editor in Chief, Random House, NYC NY

Mr. Norman Wasserman 8 Bank Street, New York City, NY

Mr. Charles Glicksberg, New School For Social Research, West 12 St NYC

VI Please indicate during which period you would prefer to visit Yaddo:

May and June
Would prefer the month of   July and August
February and could make it in   Between September and May
March. However not possible   X
for me to leave my job any other time.

Please mail this report as soon as possible to:

Mrs. Elizabeth Ames, Executive Director
Yaddo
Saratoga Springs, New York.

Yaddo

SARATOGA SPRINGS
NEW YORK

5 September 1957

Dear Mr. Glicksberg:

Mario F. Puzo
.... , who is asking for residence
at Yaddo, has listed you as a sponsor.

Please answer the following questions. (Use both sides of this sheet, if necessary.) Any
information you give us we will, of course, consider absolutely confidential.

1. In your opinion is this person self-sufficient and adaptable enough to be able to work
well and to live harmoniously with others? This question, always important, becomes
increasingly so in the fall and winter months when the groups are sometimes very small.

2. What is your opinion of the work this person has done and now proposes to do?

Please sign, date and return this as soon as possible to:

> Mrs. Elizabeth Ames, Executive Director
> Yaddo
> Saratoga Springs, New York

Let me first explain how well I know Mr. Puzo. I have known him for
approximately the past ten years. As a professor of creative writing, I have
been familiar with his creative work from the time he first started his
writing career. In fact, I believe I published his first short story, "The
Last Christmas," in the 1950 AMERICAN VANGUARD, which I edited. When he
worked under my direction, I watched the gradual evolution of the manuscript,
in its various stages of revision, that was finally published by Random House
as THE DARK ARENA. In 1953 or 1954, when I was the Director of the Fiction
Writers Conference in Vermont, I recommended him for a scholarship. I mention
these personal details in order to make it clear that I have a fairly intimate
knowledge of Mr. Puzo as a writer and as a man.

Though he has had to produce his work under severe economic hardships,
he has never become embittered. Compassionate in all his dealings with people,
he is the soul of gentleness, and it is this quality of compassion that pervades
his work in fiction. I have been told by others that in order to support his
family he has had to hold down two jobs at the same time, working at least sixteen
hours a day. Despite this heavy burden, he does not complain. His one desire
at present is to ahead with his writing, to fulfill himself creatively. If he
could be given a fellowship at Yaddo for a year or six months, I am confident
he would carry his project for a second novel through to completion.

I have no hesitation in recommending Mr. Puzo most highly. A gracious
and understanding person, he is able to get along with all sorts of people.
What is more important, he is a conscientious worker. A writer of genuine
talent, he deserves all the encouragement and support you can give him.

Puzo's writing professor Charles Glicksberg and others provided enthusiastic letters of support.

<u>Mario Puzo</u> - for a February (2nd choice March) 1958 visit. His novel,
        THE DARK ARENA enclosed.
                                        9/16/57

    M. D. Z.

            We have only one letter of recommendation here, and that is
    from Hiram Haydn, who is the applicant's publisher at Random House,
    and we have not found very helpful these letters from editors or
    publishers who see the writer from a trade or business point of view.
    Mario F. Puzo seems to be, personally, a decent and serious man, and
    with a wife and four children he should be a responsible citizen.
    He has published one novel and some stories in sufficiently literary
    and independent magazines.
            The novel itself I have fairly well read through. It is another
    G. I. novel, of a kind of which there has been a surfeit in the
    last 10 or 15 years, using a vein of material which certainly has its
    limitations and which is running thinner and thinner all the time.
    Of this class it is definitely nowhere near the top. I see in it
    the usual elements of honesty, reportorial fidelity, real talk,
    a considerable grasp of reality, etc.; also the usual elements of
    ----ing, ----ing, and ----ing.   I find it increasingly hard to judge
    such work. I'm respectful of this book and also bored by it: its
    distinctly literary quality is very debatable, in fact I'd call it
    slight.
            I wish we could get better statements from sponsors. I would not
    be against giving Puzo the one month he asks for, in February or March.
    I'd call him a <u>low B</u> or <u>B minus</u> case. He <u>has</u> done some reputable
    publishing, has a reputable publisher, and may grow toward sounder
    work.
                                        M. D. Z.   9. 23. 1957
                                            (at Yaddo)

        Later note by M. D. Z.

                I think, in view of Granville Hicks's statement, that
        Mario Puzo can be given the four weeks he asks for. Richard Eberhart says he will
        report after he has received the novel, but I imagine his verdict will be fairly
        close to G. H.'s and mine. I don't really think that Puzo is anything of an artist,
        and that at best he will produce a kind of journalistic fiction, though Hiram
        Haydn has hopes for improvement in the next book. We still have only Haydn's
        letter of recommendation, and coming from the candidate's editor and publisher, it
        is not the kind of letter we ever find really reliable or helpful; moreover, we
        have very little idea about the personality. But I have a notion that Puzo will
        make a sufficiently agreeable guest, and he probably is a good worker; with a family
        of four children behind him, he ought to mean business. So unless more urgent
        claims come from better applicants, and if there is room for him, I think he
        can be given the one month he requests.
                                        M. D. Z. Oct. 8, 1957. Chicago.

The Yaddo admissions panel's response to Puzo's application was mixed, but he was invited for his first stay in 1958.

The novel itself I have fairly well read through. It is another G.I. novel, of a kind of which there has been a surfeit in the last 10 or 15 years. . . . Of this class it is definitely nowhere near the top. I see in it the usual elements of honesty, reportorial fidelity, real talk, a considerable grasp of reality, etc.; also the usual elements of—ing, —ing, and —ing. I find it increasingly hard to judge such work.

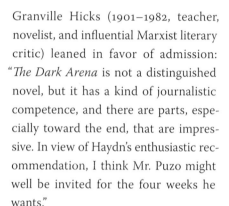

Granville Hicks (1901–1982, teacher, novelist, and influential Marxist literary critic) leaned in favor of admission: "*The Dark Arena* is not a distinguished novel, but it has a kind of journalistic competence, and there are parts, especially toward the end, that are impressive. In view of Haydn's enthusiastic recommendation, I think Mr. Puzo might well be invited for the four weeks he wants."

Another communication from Zabel follows:

I think, in view of Granville Hicks's statement, that Mario Puzo can be given the four weeks he asks for. Richard Eberhart says he will report after he has received the novel, but I imagine his verdict will be fairly close to G. H.'s and mine. I don't really think that Puzo is anything of an artist, and that at best he will produce a kind of journalistic fiction. . . . But I have a notion that Puzo will make a sufficiently agreeable guest, and he probably is a good worker; with a family of four children behind him, he ought to mean business. So unless more urgent claims come from better applicants, and if there is room for him, I think he can be given the one month he requests.

In 1966, with two novels published, Puzo applied for a third residency at Yaddo to work on a "novel about Mafia family" and was again invited.

or *unclean*, just as they didn't speak of "popular" or "high" art. Instead, they said "journalistic" or "polemical" versus "distinguished." "Competent" was faint and damning praise indeed.

In 1957, an application arrived at Yaddo from thirty-seven-year-old Mario F. Puzo, former G.I., son of a railroad trackman.[22] Under "Plans for work which would be done at Yaddo," he typed: "Novel on Italian immigrant family and first generation Americans External and internal effects, family stresses. Not just a broad novel but trying for depth. Book has been contracted for by Random House."

On the admissions panel, Morton D. Zabel (1901–1964, author, critic, editor of *Poetry*, scholar of nineteenth-century English and European literature, and lecturer at the University of Chicago) was not impressed by *The Dark Arena*, Puzo's first novel, about a disillusioned G.I., which had garnered mixed reviews. Zabel begins by dismissing the recommendation Puzo had received from Hiram Haydn, head of Random House:

We have not found very helpful these letters from editors or publishers who see the writer from a trade or business point of view. Mario F. Puzo seems to be, personally, a decent and serious man, and with a wife and four children he should be a responsible citizen. He has published one novel and some stories in sufficiently literary and independent magazines.

Dear Elizabeth,

Sorry I didn't get to see you before
I left and I was sorry I couldn't stay.
I was having a good time but for some reason
I wasn't working too well. Probably
because the older I get the more
Italian-peasant I get and so I can't be
happy unless I'm bossing a bunch of kids
around and hearing a lot of noise.

Thanks for having me up, I enjoyed
it and enjoyed meeting the usual wonderful
people that are always at YADDO

Mario Puzo

Puzo started on his Mafia novel, the manuscript that would become his best seller, *The Godfather,* on his third visit. But he found himself unable to work well and returned to New York City to complete the book.

Richard Eberhart (poet, 1904–2005, former tutor of the prince of Siam, teacher, and poet, who would earn a Pulitzer Prize in 1966) turned out to be more sanguine: "He is competent and interesting and I am glad to say yes to an invitation."

The novel that Puzo worked on at Yaddo, *The Fortunate Pilgrim*, earned a favorable—if patronizing—review in the *New York Times*. Under the headline "Pasta with Gusto," it was deemed "a small classic."[23]

His stay at Yaddo had also made him many friends. He even impressed Elizabeth Ames, and the next time he applied, in 1960—on the form his project was a novel "about a mafia family"—she

wrote the panelists: "He was a hardworking man and, in his kind of abrupt simplicity, he was agreeable and pleasant to have here. If you think he deserves it and if there is room—at the moment this is doubtful—I'd be glad to see him invited."

Morton Zabel yielded ever so slightly:

Apparently, he is moving into his own kind of subject matter now (Italian family life), and may produce better work than he has in the past. He is still fundamentally a *C* to *C plus* case in the Yaddo categories. *If* by some chance there is room enough for him for the *two week* visit he wants

in April 1960, I would not hold out against him; he could be allowed that fortnight's time. But only if there is room available and no better claims come up…. Far from urgent.

But Puzo was only granted ten days. He wrote Elizabeth Ames that "the arrangements I would have to make down here are so highly strategic that they are not worth bothering about unless the visit was at least two weeks."

When he reapplied for a month in 1966, Elizabeth Ames urged his admission:

A number of people here have, in the last year, spoken well of his second novel, THE FORTUNATE PILGRIM. I don't know if you have seen it? Harvey Swados, for one, said he thought it was an excellent book and was sorry it didn't receive more attention. His earlier 2 visits were short ones because he does miss his family. He was, then, a most appreciative and worth[y] guest and one very much enjoyed by others. Harvey Swados, for instance, never is here without asking if Mario Puzo has been back.

Zabel was warmer, and Hicks was willing to concur: "I am not full of enthusiasm for Mario Puzo's THE FORTUNATE PILGRIM, but it does have some good qualities, and I think he is a writer to be taken seriously. I think he should be invited for November if space is available."

Puzo went to Yaddo in January 1967 for the last time, but he departed early. He left a note for Elizabeth Ames:

Please excuse this abrupt leaving. I had thought my problem was an external one of finding time and place to work and so forth but I guess not since I'm not getting it done here (the writing).

The visit has been a great help. It made me think things out and so get a clear view of the position I'm in and its relation to what I'm trying to do. However there is no point in my staying when I know I won't get any work done.

When he got home, he wrote again:

Dear Elizabeth,

Sorry I didn't get to see you before I left and I was sorry I couldn't stay. I was having a good time but for some reason I wasn't working too well. Probably because the older I get the more Italian-peasant I get and so I can't be happy unless I'm bossing a bunch of kids around and hearing a lot of noise.

Thanks for having me up, I enjoyed it and enjoyed meeting the usual wonderful people that are always at YADDO.

The Godfather was published in 1969 and sold 21 million copies. The *New York Times* review was written by the sports writer Dick Schaap, who began by pointing out how much the protagonist had in common with that of *Portnoy's Complaint*, but then ended the comparison by pointing out that Portnoy was more artfully drawn.

Puzo's last communication in the file is a handwritten note, dated three years after his final visit, and accompanied by a check for $500. "Yaddo is one of my fondest memories and was a great help to me."

In the *New York Times*, his obituary mentions that he began *The Godfather* reluctantly:

His first two novels had received favorable reviews but had earned him a total of $6,500. . . . From the author's account, he had scant encouragement from publishers and received an advance of only $5,000. . . . The film outdid the book in popularity and in critical respect. When it opened in 1972, Vincent Canby, in his review in the New York Times, called it "one of the most brutal and moving chronicles of American life ever designed within the limits of popular entertainment."

Lest we too quickly erect our own barriers, however, between good guys and bad guys, and allow ourselves any easy conclusions about the arrogance of those who feel entitled to define the *je ne sais quoi* of great art, I feel compelled to mention that in 1968, under the headline "His Cardboard Lovers," Mario Puzo gave at least as good as he got, in his review of James Baldwin's *Tell Me How Long the Train's Been Gone*—in the *New York Times* (where it hurt). Baldwin, he opined, was "not a true or 'born' novelist": "A propaganda novel may be socially valuable ('Grapes of Wrath,' 'Gentlemen's Agreement'), but it is not art."[24]

At Yaddo as the twentieth century wore on, it became increasingly difficult to dismiss an applicant with the disdainful declaration that he is "not anything of an artist." What constitutes great art at last became too complex a question to grapple with, and those who had to judge other artists would be reduced to knowing what they liked, and standing by it.

It is poignant in some ways, when one imagines how many artists in the past have been to Yaddo aspiring to be "great"—by which they meant, without a doubt, great in the framework of high art—how much was sacrificed for that greatness, which once seemed to so many to be irreducible, inarguable, a pure value. Some failed, as did Mario Puzo with *The Godfather*, by creating a cultural icon, but without artistic respectability (which, paradoxically, the film gained—but then Mario Puzo's work did not have the elements that

would have enabled him to profit from the omnivores' attention, and Francis Ford Coppola's did). Others, on the contrary, like Leonard Bernstein, Truman Capote, or Patricia Highsmith, managed to escape (though not unscathed) from the immediate vicinity of the proverbial (never seen but much believed in) ivory tower, to gain popular appeal.

But all this is the stuff of reputation, posterity, p.r.—what artists yearn to escape when they arrive at Yaddo for their stipulated stay. When time is precious, process is all. "Ars longa, vita brevis," as they say. Though, come to think of it, the point I'm making is that both life and art are increasingly compressed, and feel more and more *brevis* these days. Perhaps Chaucer is more pertinent here: "The lyf so short, the craft so long to lerne."

THE SNOBBISH AND THE SUBLIME

Somehow surviving all the storms mentioned above as if lashed to the mast, the terms "popular culture" and "high culture" have remained in use, but the purity of their old, clean conflict is irretrievably compromised. For many artists now, categories like high and low are irrelevant or, even more remarkably, the boundaries between high and low have become mere playthings, the subject of complicity between creator and audience. A political engagement—explicit or not—is often an aspect of these creations, albeit a nondenominational one, because they evoke a vision of a peaceable kingdom in the "real" world. And one can only hope that the new, more generous artistic subcultures that may spring up as a result will also benefit from something like the Yaddo effect.

The objects of snobbism constantly evolve, but our search for the sublime

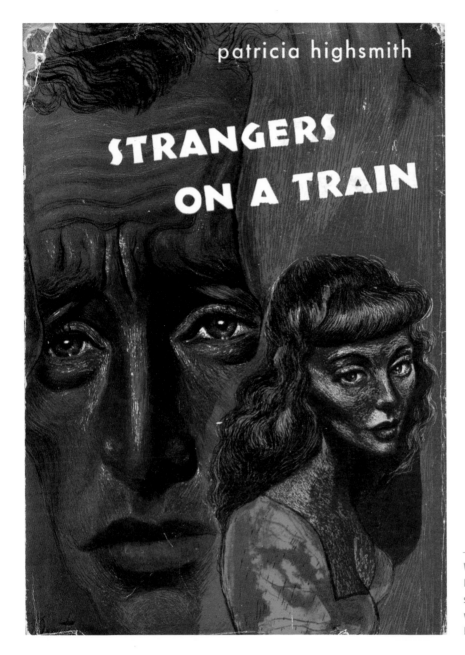

patricia highsmith

STRANGERS ON A TRAIN

Writer Patricia Highsmith was recommended to Yaddo by her friend Truman Capote. In the summer of 1948, she completed work on the novel *Strangers on a Train,* which would become the basis of the 1951 Alfred Hitchcock film of the same name.

continues. Although the Yaddo effect remains very difficult to describe and document, glimpses of the Yaddo magic appear in hundreds of letters and journal entries. Among the many pleasures of perusing the Yaddo Records now at The New York Public Library is encountering evidence of its existence right from Yaddo's inception. This seems especially valuable now that the first generations of artists are no longer alive. For those of us left behind in this very complicated era—less lyrical, perhaps more exciting, but much more anxiety

provoking—it is often more comfortable to bandy about terms like *elitist* and to promote or sneer at prestige than to convey how vulnerable artists really can be, how much in need they are of protection, and how wonderfully and powerfully they thrive when they feel safe, at least for a time.

While we await a new and better future, sure to be kinder to art and to artists, and no matter what is happening in the world in the meanwhile, Yaddo, fortunately, remains steadfastly what it has always been—an eccentric concatena-

tion of philanthropy, good will, idealism, tradition, fantasy, and nimble logistics. Once the confusions among wealth (or the illusion of it), prestige, and high culture are dispelled, Yaddo returns to something like its real status: an enchanting place for many of those who have experienced it but in every other way merely a real-life site, perpetually in need of funds for leaky roofs, where twice a year artists' panels gather for the formidable task of sifting through applications. Those who are accepted are just that—the accepted, not the elite.

Mansion staircase with stained-glass window.

Note on the Trasks and the Founding of Yaddo

Micki McGee

Spencer Trask photographed his children at play. *Left to right:* Spencer Jr. seated on the donkey; Allena Pardee, the children's nanny; the family dog, Duke; cousin Acosta Nichols on the bicycle; Christina Trask supporting the bike; and an unidentified girl on horseback.

Tennis on the lawn was another summer activity in the Trasks' early days at Yaddo.

IMAGINED AS a place of retreat—of "Rest and Refreshment"—for artists of all types, Yaddo originally served as an escape for Spencer and Katrina Trask themselves, as they struggled to come to terms with the loss of their first son, who died in the spring of 1880 before reaching his fifth birthday. The following summer, the Trasks rented a ramshackle mansion on the outskirts of Saratoga Springs, New York, a popular resort for Wall Street's wealthy weekenders. Before the family had secured the title to the property, Katrina Trask reported that their surviving child, four-year-old Christina, named the estate out of her dislike for the darkness that had descended on the family with the death of

Portrait of the Trask Family, ca. 1886. *Left to right:* Christina Trask, Spencer Trask Jr., Katrina Trask, Spencer Trask, and the family dog, Duke.

her brother. "Call it Yaddo, Mamma," she is reported to have said. "It makes poetry—Yaddo, shadow, shadow—Yaddo . . . Yaddo sounds like shadow but it's not going to be shadow."[1]

The Trasks renovated the estate and enjoyed six idyllic summers at Yaddo, hosting family and friends for tennis matches on the expansive lawns, pony rides on the estate's trails, and elaborate pageants and masques. The couple's second son, Spencer Jr., was born in the spring of 1884. Spencer Trask took up photography and recorded scenes of their life together. Life was abundant for the Trasks, and all seemed without shadow until March 1888, when a hun-

dred-year nor'easter—the Great White Hurricane of 1888—blew across the Atlantic seaboard, leaving forty-foot snow drifts in its wake and hundreds dead. At home in the family's Brooklyn Heights townhouse, Katrina contracted diphtheria.[2] When it seemed as though the thirty-five-year-old would not survive, her physician allowed the children to visit her bedside to say their last goodbyes. Almost unimaginably Katrina recovered, but both children were stricken and died by mid-April. At the urging of friends and family, Katrina published *The Chronicles of Yaddo*, a small printed book commemorating her lost children and their happier days at Yaddo. The fol-

Yaddo's first mansion, a Queen Anne–style structure, was photographed by Spencer Trask in 1887.

In the spring of 1891, the Yaddo mansion burned to the ground. Spencer Trask was bedridden in Brooklyn with pneumonia, but he dispatched a photographer to shoot the ruins so plans for rebuilding could begin immediately.

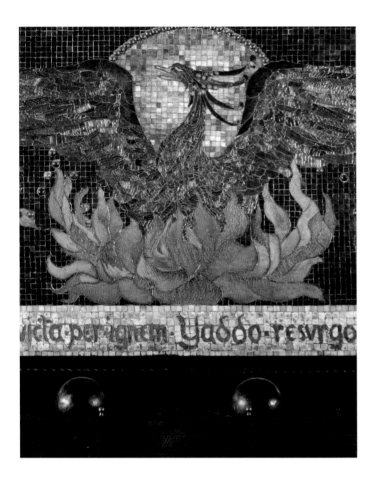

The fireplace mantel in the Great Hall includes an 1893 mosaic by Louis Comfort Tiffany depicting a phoenix rising, with the words *"Flammis invicta per ignem Yaddo resurgo ad pacem"*: Unconquered by flame, I, Yaddo, am reborn for peace.

lowing year, the Trasks conceived their fourth and last child, a daughter, Katrina, who died within two weeks of her birth.

If the loss of four children had not been enough to level the Trasks, in the spring of 1891, while Spencer Trask was seriously ill with pneumonia at their Brooklyn home, Katrina Trask received word that the old Queen Anne–style mansion at Yaddo had burned to the ground. Fearful that news of the calamity would worsen his condition, Katrina and family friend George Foster Peabody debated whether to tell Trask, but eventually they did. To their relief, Spencer rallied and instructed that a photographer be dispatched immediately to survey and photograph the damage so that he could begin plans for rebuilding.[3] The Trasks retained William Halsey Wood to design a fifty-five–room mansion that was completed in 1893 and continues to house many of Yaddo's guests. Louis Comfort Tiffany was commissioned to create stained-glass windows and a fireplace mantel mosaic depicting a phoenix rising from the ashes, with the inscription *"Flammis invicta per ignem Yaddo resurgo ad pacem"*: Unconquered by flame, I, Yaddo, am reborn for peace.

Left without biological heirs and with an acute awareness of the uncertainties of procreativity, the Trasks turned their attention to more durable creative enterprises. Katrina continued her writing in earnest, publishing dozens of books of plays and verse, including *Christalan*, a book-length poem of medieval chivalry, and *Under King Constantine*, an Arthurian tale dedicated to her husband.[4] The summer salons resumed, and the Trasks hosted numerous artists and writers, among them clergyman and poet Henry van Dyke, educator and African American leader Booker T. Washington, as well as portrait painters Eastman Johnson, John Singer Sargent, and Arthur de Ferraris. Spencer played

New York February 1900

To the Trustees of Pine Garde
        Dear Sirs

                We propose to lean to you
by Will the Estate of Yaddo, together
with the Residuary Estate of Spencer
Trask & Katrina Trask, Subject only
to a life use thereof of Some one person
in Case we may hereafter designate
Such one — Yaddo we are glad to
believe has come to be a Source
of fruitful help & inspiration
to many, and especially to those
Gifted with Creative power & who have
had the impulse to use it for their
fellow men —

In February 1900, Spencer Trask established a trust called Pine Garde to ensure that his and Katrina Trask's vision for Yaddo would be realized.

Eastman Johnson. *Portrait of Katrina Trask*, 1887.

a central role in the founding of the National Arts Club in New York City, as well as in countless Saratoga Springs cultural and civic enterprises. Trask's motto, one that he is said to have carried on a torn shred of paper in his wallet throughout his life, was: "For a Man's Life Consisteth Not in the Abundance of the Things Which He Possesseth."[5]

The question of exactly what to do with the abundance of things that they did possess weighed on the couple until the summer of 1899, when Katrina was seized by inspiration. As she and Spencer strolled through the lush woods of the estate, Katrina reported that she "felt an unseen hand laid upon me, an unheard voice calling to me."[6] The vision for the estate's future was suddenly revealed:

> Yaddo is not to be an institution, a school, a charity: it is to be, always, a place of inspiration, a delightful, hospitable home where guests may come and find welcome. Here will be a perpetual series of house-parties—of literary men, literary women and other artists. Those who are city-weary, who are thirsting for the country and for beauty, who are hemmed in by circumstance and have no opportunity to make for themselves an harmonious environment, shall seek it here. At Yaddo they will find the inspiration they need: some of them will see the Muses—some of them will drink of the Fountain of Hippocrene, and all of them will find the Sacred Fire and light their torches at its flame.

She turned to her startled husband and said, "Look, Spencer, they are walking in the woods, wandering in the garden, sitting under the pine trees—men and women—creating, creating, creating!"[7]

Revitalized by their new vision for Yaddo, the couple set about preparing

Eastman Johnson preparing his study of Katrina in 1877 for the larger portrait. *Left to right*: Man thought to be George Foster Peabody, Katrina Trask, Eastman Johnson.

Yaddo's mansion, designed by William Halsey Wood, was completed in 1893. It is located on the site of the estate's first mansion, which was destroyed by fire in 1891.

the estate for its future purpose, improving the grounds with a formal rose garden that would later inspire the poetry of Marya Zaturenska (resident at Yaddo three times in the early 1930s), Sylvia Plath (a guest in 1959), and Musa McKim (at Yaddo in 1969).[8] Within a year the Trasks had incorporated Pine Garde, a trust to hold their vision of Yaddo in confidence until their deaths, when their plans for the artists' retreat would come to fruition. They would acquire additional properties: in the center of Lake George, forty miles to the north of the Saratoga Springs estate, they joined together three small islands to form a camp called Triuna, where they could retreat from the active social life that had come to characterize Yaddo; and on the shore of Lake George they founded Wiawaka with land deeded to Katrina by George Foster Peabody. Wiawaka served as a summer resort for working women in need of a respite from the city, and in the summer of 1908,

perhaps in a trial run for Yaddo's future purpose, Spencer Trask arranged for the camp to host a group of students from the Art Students League of New York, including, according to the local newspaper, a promising young art student, Miss Georgia O'Keeffe.[9]

In a stroke of painful irony, the entrepreneur who had made his fortune in the expansion of America's railroads would have two fateful encounters with rail cars. In June 1909, a collision between a streetcar and an automobile in which he rode resulted in the loss of his left eye. Then, on the morning of December 31 of the same year, as Trask was en route to New York City to participate in a meeting regarding the preservation of the water resources of Saratoga Springs, his private railroad car was struck by a freight train outside New York near Croton, killing the sixty-five-year-old instantly.

Having buried four children and her husband, Katrina would face yet further

challenges. As the speculative capitalism of the period produced both exuberant bubbles and desperate panics, the Trasks' economic fortunes had waxed and waned over the years. At the time of Spencer's death, the couple's fortune had not yet recovered from the Panic of 1907. To conserve the assets needed to realize their vision for Yaddo, Katrina Trask closed the mansion and moved into a small house on the property, where she continued writing plays and editorials on the importance of women's suffrage and the need for world peace. Her longtime admirer, and Spencer Trask's business partner for a quarter century, George Foster Peabody, remained a close and influential friend. On February 6, 1921, the two married. Within a year, on January 8, 1922, Katrina Trask, who had been plagued by heart disease for more than two decades, passed away, leaving Peabody to implement the Trasks' vision for Yaddo.

Yaddo Timeline, 1874–1980

Still photograph from performance of *Twelfth Night: Yaddo: Arrival of the Hostess*, 1899.

1874 NOVEMBER 12: Spencer Trask (b. 1844) and Kate (Katrina) Nichols (b. 1853) wed.

1875 DECEMBER 19: The Trasks' first child, Alanson, is born.

1877 MAY 25: The Trasks' second child, Christina, is born.

1880 APRIL 23: Alanson Trask dies before reaching his fifth birthday.
DECEMBER 17: With financial support from Spencer Trask, Thomas Edison establishes the Edison Illuminating Company. The company creates the first electrical generating stations in New York City, becomes the model for electrification, and is later renamed Consolidated Edison.

1881 MAY 2: George Foster Peabody (b. 1852) becomes a partner in the new investment firm of Spencer Trask & Company.
SUMMER: The Trasks rent a ramshackle old mansion on the outskirts of Saratoga Springs, New York. Later that year they purchase the estate, which their daughter, Christina, names "Yaddo."

1884 MARCH 24: The Trasks' third child, Spencer Jr., is born.

1888 MARCH 12: In the midst of the Great Blizzard of 1888, Katrina Trask falls ill with diphtheria, but unexpectedly recovers. Her two children—Christina and Spencer Jr.—contract the disease and die on April 15 and 18 respectively.
DECEMBER: Katrina Trask publishes *The Chronicles of Yaddo* in a limited edition for family and friends.

1889 AUGUST 29: Katrina Trask's fourth and last child, baby Katrina, dies twelve days after birth.

1891 MARCH 9: Yaddo's first mansion burns to the ground.

1892 Katrina publishes *Under King Constantine* under a pseudonym.

1893 SPRING: Yaddo's new mansion, designed by William Halsey Wood, is completed.

1896 Spencer Trask plays a key role in the refinancing of the *New York Times*.

1899 Katrina and Spencer Trask plan for the use of Yaddo after their deaths. Spencer creates the Yaddo Rose Garden as a gift to Katrina.

1900 The Trasks incorporate Pine Garde as a trust to ensure that their plans for Yaddo are implemented after their deaths.

1902 George Foster Peabody, Spencer's business partner, deeds a Lake George estate, Wiawaka, to Katrina Trask for the creation of a summer refuge for working women.

1906 Spencer Trask purchases three islands in Lake George and connects them to create

Triuna, a refuge for the Trasks from the increasing social obligations at Yaddo.

1907 The Trasks' wealth is significantly impacted by the Panic of 1907, when the U.S. stock market lost fifty percent of its value.

1909 JUNE 20: Spencer Trask is injured in a streetcar collision. DECEMBER 31: Spencer Trask dies in a train crash in Croton-on-Hudson, New York, on New Year's Eve as he is traveling to New York City.

1913 Katrina Trask's pacifist play, *In the Vanguard*, is published and goes through eight editions, performed by women's groups and church groups. Despite the efforts of pacifists such as Trask, World War I erupts the following year.

1921 FEBRUARY 6: Katrina Trask and George Foster Peabody marry.

1922 JANUARY 8: Katrina Trask dies.

1923 Elizabeth Ames comes to Yaddo to visit her sister, Marjorie Knappen Waite, who is working closely with George Foster Peabody. Peabody appoints Ames executive director of Yaddo.

1924 Ames begins seeking advice on guests from influential American writers, editors, publishers, artists, composers, and educators.

1926 JUNE 6: The *New York Times* hails Yaddo as "a new and unique experiment which has no exact parallel in the world of the fine arts." JUNE 7: First guests arrive—an international group of Polish, Jewish, French, English, and American writers and artists—with women and men equally represented. The first guests include poet Louise

Louis Lozowick. *Farm House* (thought to be North Farm at Yaddo), ca. 1929. Lozowick, a Precisionist printmaker, was a guest in 1929 and 1930.

Bogan, playwright Thomas H. Dickinson, and composers Louise and Tadeusz Jarecki.

1927 New studios for artists are built south of the existing barns. The guests in the second season include painter Marion Greenwood and writer James Rorty.

1928 Elizabeth Ames continues reaching out to influential American writers and editors, including Van Wyck Brooks, Alfred Kreymborg, Lewis Mumford, and the Van Dorens—Carl, Irita, and Mark—to develop Yaddo's guest lists. Literary critic Newton Arvin arrives as a guest, along with printmaker Hugh Botts, editor Clifton Fadiman, poet Stanley Kunitz, and others.

1929 Writers John Metcalfe, Lola Ridge, Evelyn Scott, Gerald Sykes, and Eda Lou Walton; photographer Ralph Steiner; and printmaker Louis Lozowick are among the guests.

1930 Guests include critic Newton Arvin; composers Paul Bowles and Aaron Copland; novelists Leonard Ehrlich, Albert Halper, and Irving Stone; and poets Lola Ridge and Genevieve Taggard. Copland, in conversation with guest Theodore Chanler, conceives the idea for the Yaddo music festivals.

1931 During the summer season, thirty-three artists, composers, and writers are hosted, including writers Louis Adamic, Horace Gregory, Sidney Hook, Evelyn Scott, Diana and Lionel Trilling, and Marya Zaturenska; composer Marc Blitzstein; and visual artist Nicolai Cikovsky.

1932 APRIL 30–MAY 1: Yaddo hosts its first Festival of Contemporary American Music, organized by Aaron Copland. MAY 14–24: Yaddo convenes a literary conference that inspires Malcolm Cowley's first book, *Exile's Return*.

Philip Reisman. *The Meeting*, 1930. Reisman wrote to Elizabeth Ames on May 14, 1934: "The air here is full of deep distrust and unrest. There are fascist meetings in Union Square and I fear the worst will soon be with us in an undisguised form. I fervently hope that I may be wrong."

Yaddo executive director Elizabeth Ames, composer Aaron Copland, literary critic Newton Arvin, and others, 1930.

Guests in 1931. *Back row*: Alexander Byer, Lionel Trilling, Sidney Hook, John Metcalfe, Marc Blitzstein, Max Lerner, B. B. Haggin. *Front row*: Horace Gregory, Oakley Johnson, Charlotte Wilder, Marya Zaturenska, Evelyn Scott.

Artist Philip Reisman; poet Marya Zaturenska; her husband, critic Horace Gregory; Patricia Shannon; Reisman's wife, painter and illustrator Penina Kishore (*seated*) in 1933.

SUMMER: Guests include writers Newton Arvin, Malcolm Cowley, Guy Endore, Waldo Frank, and Josephine Herbst, and painter Marion Greenwood.

AUGUST 12: Newton Arvin weds Mary Garrison at Yaddo.

1933 In the midst of the Great Depression, Yaddo adapts to the economic crisis. The dairy farm on the estate closes, ending the era of self-sufficiency for the estate. For guests, lunch boxes are adopted in lieu of a seated lunch in the interests of economy. An old farmhouse, North Farm, is renovated to house additional guests. The Lake George estate of Triuna houses several writers and their families.

SEPTEMBER 30–OCTOBER 1: Second Festival of Contemporary American Music takes place, again organized by Copland.

1934 Guests include writers Louis Adamic, John Cheever, James T. Farrell, Horace Gregory, Muriel Rukeyser, and Marya Zaturenska; composer Dante Fiorillo; and visual artists Ilya Bolotowsky, Louis Hechenbleikner, and Clyfford Still.

1935 Triuna is officially included in Yaddo's operations. In Saratoga Springs, many guests from prior years return, including Arvin, Farrell, and Zaturenska. In a report to Yaddo's directors, Elizabeth Ames notes that fewer painters are applying to Yaddo because of their temporary employment on Works Progress Administration commissions: "The world of writers is, for the time being, undergoing profound changes and yields Yaddo, therefore, fewer important workers. In time, all of this will change, of course, and writers and painters will

Jean Liberté at easel, 1933. Liberté was a guest again in 1934, 1935, and 1942 and had a distinguished career, showing his paintings at the Corcoran Gallery of Art, the Museum of Modern Art, and the Whitney Museum of American Art.

again be considered by us in greater numbers."

JUNE 27–AUGUST 26: An "Arts in the Theatre" summer educational program is directed by playwright Thomas H. Dickinson at Triuna.

1936 SEPTEMBER 11–13: The third music festival is held under the direction of a committee including John Duke, Ralph Kirkpatrick, Otto Luening, and Quincy Porter. The festival is renamed the Music Period as older classical pieces are performed.

1937 JULY: As a result of the continuing financial uncertainty of the Depression, Yaddo opens late, on July 25, and a short season is run. One composer and his wife and two children were put up at North Farm. Writers John Cheever, Leonard Ehrlich, Daniel Fuchs, Josephine Herbst, and Wallace Stegner are among the summer guests. Two composers and their families, a total of eight persons, are housed at Triuna.

SEPTEMBER 4–19: The fourth music festival takes place. A music-recording machine was purchased and is used to document the performances.

Guests in 1933 with Rose Garden pergola in background. *Top row*: James T. Farrell, unidentified man, unidentified woman, unidentified man, Penina Kishore, Jean Liberté, Leo Fischer. *In front*: Harry Slochower, John Metcalfe.

Guests in 1933. *Back row*: John Metcalfe (*seated*), Richard Donovan (*standing*), Sylvia Lowenthal, Harry Slochower, Morris Cohn, Jean Liberté, Elizabeth Ames, Alexander Byer. *Middle row*: Leo Fischer, Louis Adamic, Louis Corey, Penina Kishore, Horace Gregory, Evelyn Scott, Clara Stillman, Jacob Getlar Smith. *Front row*: Philip Reisman, unidentified man, Marya Zaturenska (*far right*).

1938 During the winter months, four writers—John Cheever, Loyd Collins Jr., Leonard Ehrlich, and Daniel Fuchs—stay on at Yaddo. MARCH 4: Philanthropist and Yaddo president George Foster Peabody dies in Warm Springs, Georgia, at age eighty-five. SUMMER: Writers Kenneth Fearing and Henry Roth are new guests, along with returning guests Cheever, Ehrlich, Rukeyser, Stegner, and Morton Dauwen Zabel. Composer Quincy Porter and his wife are invited to take over Triuna for the summer, covering the cost of food and service to reduce Yaddo's expenses. SEPTEMBER 10–11: The fifth music festival takes place.

1939 SUMMER: The Mansion, North Farm, and East House operate for guests from mid-June, and six refugees from Germany and Austria are hosted. First-time guests include composer David Diamond, writers Jerre Mangione and Delmore Schwartz, and painter Frederico Castellon. Yaddo's artists and writers, many of whom are actively involved in anti-fascist politics, are stunned by the August 28 Hitler-Stalin Pact, which crushes hopes that Soviet communism will be a force against fascism. Within a week, World War II begins. A planned music festival is cancelled because of financial concerns.

1940 Triuna Island is sold for $20,000 to support ongoing expenses of hosting artists and writers. Furnishings from Triuna are brought to Yaddo to replenish those in the mansion. Among the new summer guests are writers Granville Hicks and Katherine Anne Porter. Returning guests include Arvin, Castellon, Cheever, Greenwood, among others. SEPTEMBER 7–8: The sixth music festival takes place.

1941 Yaddo's board of directors votes to admit African American writers. There are three resignations from the board during this period, two of which may be related to this decision.

In the late 1930s, writer John Cheever served as Yaddo's boatman, ferrying guests to the Triuna camp on Lake George. *Left to right*: unidentified man, Elizabeth Ames, Ames's dog Brownie, Cheever, unidentified man and woman.

Guests in 1938. *Back row*: Hubert Skidmore, Kenneth Fearing, Fred R. Miller, unidentified man, Wallace Stegner, unidentified man, Joseph Vogel, Charles Naginsky, Henry Roth. *Front row*: Leonard Ehrlich, Muriel Parker, Marjorie Peabody Waite, Mary Barnard, Rebecca Pitts, Muriel Rukeyser, Edna Guck, unidentified woman, Margaret Helene, Elizabeth Ames, Mrs. Willard Thorp, Susie Fuchs, Daniel Fuchs, Willard Thorp.

Guests in 1942. *Standing*: Newton Arvin, Nicholas Marsicano, Nathan Asch, Philip Rahv, Michael Seide, Karol Rathaus, Carson McCullers, Malcolm Cowley, unidentified man, Langston Hughes, Kenneth Fearing, unidentified man, Leonard Ehrlich, Jean Liberté. *Seated*: Mrs. Asch, Frances Mingorancz, Merle Marsicano, Katherine Anne Porter, Helena Kuo, Juan Mingorancz, Nathalie Rahv, Elizabeth Ames.

SUMMER: New guests at Yaddo include writers Carson McCullers and Eudora Welty, who will complete her first collection of short stories, *A Curtain of Green*, while living at North Farm.

1942 In a report to Yaddo's board, Ames reports: "The vote of the Directors to admit Negroes, properly qualified, to Yaddo puts Yaddo in the good society of those who are fighting against racial discrimination." As a result, Yaddo hosts two African American artists, poet Langston Hughes and composer R. Nathaniel Dett. Other new guests include Alfred Kazin, Weldon Kees, and Philip Rahv.

1943 As a consequence of the war, Yaddo reduces the number of guests hosted. Among the new guests are Agnes Smedley, returned from China where she had reported on the rise of the Chinese Communist party, and Danish writer Karin Michaëlis, who had fled the Nazi occupation of her country. Langston Hughes

and Carson McCullers are among the returning guests.

1944 Yaddo's mansion remains closed, and many fewer guests are hosted because of reduced resources. Writers Eleanor Clark, Helen S. Fisher, Carson McCullers, Katherine Anne Porter, and Agnes Smedley are the sole guests.

OCTOBER 25: J. Edgar Hoover initiates an investigation of Agnes Smedley's political activities.

DECEMBER 6: Yaddo's second president, Marjorie Peabody Waite, dies after a long period of invalidism.

1945 As the war continues, Yaddo hosts a small group, including Japanese American émigrés Eitarō Ishigaki and his wife Ayako Ishigaki, who wrote under the pseudonym Haru Mitsuo.

1946 With World War II over, Yaddo places notices in the *New York Times*, the *New Republic*, and the *Nation* alerting artists and writers that full operations will resume. That summer, forty guests work at Yaddo. First-time

guests include writers Truman Capote, Horace R. Cayton, Jean Garrigue, and Edgar Snow; composer Ulysses Kay; photographer Henri Cartier-Bresson; and painter Minna Citron. Returning guests include Arvin, Cowley, Kazin, Mangione, and Smedley. *Life* profiles the estate's activities.

SEPTEMBER 13–15: The seventh music festival is held.

1947 New guests at Yaddo include writers Robert Lowell, Edward Maisel, and Theodore Roethke, and composer Otto Luening, along with many returning guests from the previous summer.

1948 **MARCH 9:** Smedley leaves Yaddo after a confrontation with Ames over her political organizing work.

SUMMER: New guests at Yaddo include writers Elizabeth Hardwick, Patricia Highsmith, Chester Himes, and Flannery O'Connor, and painter Clifford Wright. Returning guests include Lowell and Maisel.

1949 **FEBRUARY 11:** A *New York Times* article implicates Agnes Smedley in a spy ring.

FEBRUARY 14: FBI agents interview two Yaddo guests, Hardwick and Maisel.

FEBRUARY 17: FBI agents interview Elizabeth Ames.

FEBRUARY 20: A secret meeting of Robert Lowell and three other Yaddo guests with members of Yaddo's board foments concerns about Ames's leadership.

FEBRUARY 26: A larger group of Yaddo's board members convenes to consider Lowell's charges against Ames.

MARCH 26: Yaddo's board meets in New York City and

votes to continue Elizabeth Ames's directorship.

APRIL 30: Yaddo's board approves the sale of the North Farm property to Skidmore College.

SEPTEMBER 16–18: The eighth music festival is held.

1950 New guests include poets Jane Mayhall, Howard Nemerov, May Swenson, and William Carlos Williams, and painter Beauford Delaney. Returning guests include Elizabeth Bishop, John Cheever, and Alfred Kazin.

1951 In a summer that marks its twenty-fifth year of supporting creative workers, Yaddo hosts some sixty-one guests, more than half of whom are first-time guests.

1952 New guests include philosopher Hannah Arendt, novelist Saul Bellow, and printmaker Antonio Frasconi. Returning guests include Kenneth Fearing, Alfred Kazin, and Morton D. Zabel.

SEPTEMBER 12–14: The ninth and final music festival takes place.

1953 New guests include poet Marcia Nardi, while returning guests include poet Babette Deutsch, writer and archivist Avrahm Yarmolinsky, and writers Malcolm Cowley and Josephine Herbst.

1954 First-time guests include painters Pat Adams, Rosemarie Beck, and Vincent Longo; photographer and film curator Jay Leyda; and literary critic Van Wyck Brooks.

1955 First-time guests include writers Alston Anderson, James Baldwin, Hortense Calisher, Dawn Powell, and Mona Van Duyn, along with painters Milton and Sally Avery.

1956 Art critic Hilton Kramer is among the new guests this

Guests in 1947. *Standing*: Harvey C. Webster, J. F. Powers, Betty Wahl Powers, Robert Friend, Henri Cartier-Bresson, Edward McGehee, Wallace Fowlie, John Malcolm Brinnin. *Seated*: Horace Cayton, Bucklin Moon, Joseph Lasker, Clarisse Blazek, William Barrett, Agnes Hart, Eli Cartier-Bresson, Michael Seide, Katherine Shattuck, O'Connor Barrett.

Guests in 1947. *Top row*: Arna Bontemps, Katherine Shattuck, Michael Seide, unidentified man, Charles Seide, Owen Dodson, Eleanor Goff, Seymour Krim, Joseph Lasker, Alexei Haieff, Theodore Roethke, Betty Wahl Powers, O'Connor Barrett. *Bottom row*: Ruth Domino, Clarisse Blazek, Charles Neider, Steve Raffo, Ulysses Kay, J. F. Powers, Elizabeth Ames, Marguerite Young, Robert Lowell, Horace Cayton.

Guests in 1953. *Top row*: Avrahm Yarmolinsky, Albert Herzing, Simon Moselsio, Herta Moselsio, Claude Clark, Milton Klonsky, Saul Bellow, Elizabeth Sparhawk-Jones, Babette Deutsch, Frederick Sternfield, Margaret Lowery, Clifford Wright, Ben Weber, Theresa Sherman. *Bottom row*: Mary Doyle Curran, Martin Nelson, Esther Rolick, Paolo Milano, Josephine Herbst, Vladimir Talberg, Dorothy Van Ghent.

Guests in 1954. *Standing*: Harvey Webster, Jay Leyda, Vincent Longo, Clifford Wright, Anthony Ostroff, Van Wyck Brooks, Stanford Whitmore, Parker Tyler, Dan Curley, Herta Moselio, Simon Moselsio, Bruno Brauskopf. *Seated*: Gladys LaFlamme, Si-lan Chen, Olive Brazzi, Pat Adams, Gladys Brooks, Aileen Ward, Simmons Persons.

Guests in 1958. *Standing*: John Malcolm Brinnin, Jane Cooper, Robert Mezey, R. V. Cassill, Lou "Bink" Noll, Roger Crossgrove, Steven Marcus, Louis Schanker, Perrin Lowrey, Rosemarie Beck, Chou Wen-chung, Donald Jenni, Meyer Schapiro. *Seated*: Gerald Sykes, Buffie Johnson, Hunter Johnson, Etta Blum, Emily Hargraves, Charles Bell, Marianne Ehrlich, Lillian Schapiro. *Seated on floor*: Robert Garis, Dan Curley, Charles Shapiro, Hyde Solomon, Lawrence Osgood.

Guests in 1960. *Back row*: Thomas Vance, Bink Noll, Robert Towers, Theodore Holmes, Jack Gottlieb, Burrill Phillips, Ned Rorem, Richard Schickel, Jarvis Thurston, David Bazelon, Robert Rieff, Helena Frost, Carl Herman Voss, Jane Mayhall. *Front row*: Wen-chung Chou, Leon Hartl, James Phillips, Jean Garrigue, Inga Hayes, Maxwell Gordon.

season, while returning guests include John Cheever, Malcolm Cowley, and Marcia Nardi.

1957 MAY 23: Yaddo president John Slade reports that the proposed extension of Interstate 87, the Adirondack Northway, will cut through the Rose Garden, which had long been open to the public. Painter Nell Blaine and writer Curtis Harnack are among the new guests this summer. Harnack will later become Yaddo's second director.

1958 Writers Bernard Malamud, Dorothy Parker, and Mario Puzo, along with art historian Meyer Schapiro, are among the first-time guests.

1959 MAY 20: Elizabeth Ames receives the National Institute of Arts and Letters Award for Distinguished Service to the Arts. First-time guests include poets Ted Hughes and Sylvia Plath, and composer Ned Rorem.

SEPTEMBER 20: Plans for building a swimming pool on the estate are discussed at Yaddo's board meeting.

1960 New York State takes possession of the eastern segment of Yaddo's lands to extend I-87, but the highway is diverted slightly farther east than originally planned in order to preserve the Rose Garden. Residents include first-time guest Robert Towers and returning guests Cheever, Deutsch, Harnack, Kramer, Mayhall, Powell, Puzo, and Yarmolinsky.

1961 New guests include philosopher Norman O. Brown and poet Galway Kinnell. At the urging of avid swimmer John Cheever, plans for a swimming pool are approved by the board.

MAY 18: Newton Arvin resigns from the board after he is prosecuted on pornography charges in Massachusetts.

1962 SEPTEMBER 22: Vandalism is on the rise in the Rose Garden, which is open to the public. The bronze sundial that was in the garden for sixty-two years is stolen.

1963 New guests include visual artist George Biddle and writer Alison Lurie.

1964 Writers Harold Brodkey, Philip Roth, and May Sarton, and writer and artist/illustrator Jules Feiffer, are among the new guests this year.

1965 FEBRUARY 27: The minutes of the Yaddo planning committee meeting question whether Yaddo remains important for artists in this period of greater prosperity: "The young artist is much better off and perhaps reluctant to leave his family and studio as well as his market." Poets Isabella Gardner, Donald Hall, and Louis Zukovsky are among the new guests.

1966 Returning guests include Beck, Cowley, Lurie, Rorem, and Philip Roth.

1967 First-time guests include Janet Frame and Paule Marshall.

1968 Writers William Gass and Romulus Linney are among the first-time guests.

1969 After more than four decades as Yaddo's director, Elizabeth Ames steps down. Writer Grace Paley and painter Philip Guston are first-time guests. Yaddo files for private foundation status, and a decree is issued giving the organization not-for-profit foundation status retroactive to 1927.

Guests in 1968. *Top row*: John Unterecker, Marvin Brown, George Essayian, Konstantinos Lardas, Doe Lindell, James Clay, Romulus Linney, Richard Wilson, Diane Churchill, Ernst Hacker, Donald Petersen. *Front row*: Marlene Sellers, Harold Blumenfeld, Phyllis Rose Thompson, Ann Cameron.

Guests in 1969. *Top row*: Robert Phelps, Maud Morgan, George Essayian, Raja Rao, Edith Konecky, Michel Fougères, Diana Kurz, Zelda Popkin, Louis Sheaffer, Philip Guston, Nancy Potter, Musa McKim Guston, William Gass, Ruth Anderson. *Bottom row*: Wook-Kyung Choi, Warren Slesinger, Peter Viereck, Irwin Bazelon, Cecile Bazelon.

Guests in 1973. *Back row*: Ruth Herschberger, Kay Burford, John Dilg, Glen Krause, Byron Burford, Etta Blum, Susan Crile, Jules Feiffer. *Middle row*: Margaret McBride, June Kessler, Jerome Gray, Marion Fishman, Andrea Karchmer, Claude Brown. *Front row*: Chinary Ung, Irina Kirk, Tomaž Šalamun, Grace Schulman, Carl Rakoh, Henry Mollicone.

Guests in 1975. *Back row*: Peter Klappert, Daniel Fuchs, Allan Gurganus, M. D. Elevitch, Roger Rath, Sally Appleton. *Front row*: John Haffenden, Maureen McCabe, Sister Bernetta Quinn, Anne Tabachnick, Edwin Honig, Altoon Sultan, Julie Gross, Tillie Olsen, David McKain, Jillian Denby.

1970 JANUARY 1: Longtime board member Granville Hicks serves as an interim director for one year.

SUMMER: New guests this year include visual artists Susan Crile and Mary Frank, along with composer David Del Tredici and writer Kenneth Burke.

1971 FEBRUARY 1: Writer Curtis Harnack is appointed Yaddo's second executive director.

SUMMER: Painter Jules Olitski and poet Jean Valentine are among the first-time guests. Yaddo files for and receives public foundation status.

1972 New guests include visual artist Haim Steinbach and writers Laura Furman and Mark Strand.

1973 Painter Helen Frankenthaler and writer Louise Meriweather are among the new guests this year.

1974 New guests this year include artist Anne Truitt, who will later serve as an acting executive director of Yaddo, and writer Richard Yates.

1975 First-time guests include writers Allan Gurganus, Denise Levertov, Bharati Mukherjee, and Tillie Olsen.

1976 New guests include writers Joseph Caldwell, Hayden Carruth, and Nora Sayre.

1977 MARCH 28: Elizabeth Ames dies at age ninety-two, having lived at Yaddo for fifty-four years. Jerre Mangione, a former director of the Federal Writers Project and a longtime Yaddo member, serves as acting director for eight months. New guests include writers Richard Price and Richard Seltzer.

1978 To support continued operations and strengthen the organization's endowment, Yaddo's directors vote to

Artist studio.

sell the Lower Manhattan office building that had once housed Spencer Trask's offices; occupancy rates had declined since the World Trade Center opened its doors to tenants in 1970. Visual artist Jacques Hnizdovsky and photographer Ruth Orkin are among the new guests this year.

1979 Yaddo receives its federal not-for-profit corporation status as a 501(c)3 cultural institution. Visual artists Harmony Hammond and Martin Puryear and writer Paul Auster are among the first-time guests.

1980–present Yaddo continues hosting artists, writers, composers, filmmakers, and other creative workers, but these pages of the community's archives are not yet public.

ACKNOWLEDGMENTS

Y*ADDO: MAKING AMERICAN CULTURE* contends that creative projects are always joint ventures, calling on the hands, hearts, and minds of countless individuals. It is my pleasure to thank some of the many people who have made this volume, and the exhibitions that it accompanies, possible.

My deepest gratitude goes to the leadership of Yaddo, who entrusted me with the remarkable story of Yaddo's first century. Elaina Richardson, president of Yaddo, has been a champion of the project at every level of its development and is someone whom I feel privileged to think of as both a colleague and a friend. Yaddo board members Susan Brynteson, Linda Collins, and Margo Viscusi worked for years, and with three previous leaders of Yaddo—Curtis Harnack, Myra Sklarew, and Michael Sundell—to ensure the preservation and placement of the Yaddo archive. The Morris and Alma Schapiro Fund supported the transfer of the archives, which made all that followed possible. Peter Kayafas and Jaime Wolfe have shepherded the project through many corridors with grace and an unwavering joie de vivre. Susan Brynteson also conceived and spearheaded a project to coordinate partnering exhibitions at a host of libraries and archives nationwide. Without the talents, energy, and efforts of these leaders, only a small circle of individuals would ever have learned of the treasures in the Yaddo Records or of its remarkable contributions to twentieth-century American culture.

The directors and membership of The Corporation of Yaddo have welcomed me into their worlds, opening paths into American cultural history that might otherwise have been neglected. Pat Towers, Patricia Volk, Joe Caldwell, Peter Cameron, Jonathan Sandlofer, A. M. Homes, James Sienna and Katia Santibañez, Shay Youngblood, and Gardiner McFall have offered their support and enthusiasm. Peter Gould, Yaddo's board chair, has been an unwavering supporter, and never hesitated to take on the fund development challenges that such a project entailed. Jane A. Wait and Pat Adams each opened their home and files to me, sharing rare letters, photographs, and recollections.

Yaddo's skilled and devoted staff, past and present, including Vince Passaro, Lynn Farenell, Candace Wait, Linda Bottiglieri, Patricia Sopp, Jenny Godlewski, Sue Gersin, Cathy Clarke, and Dana McClure each provided invaluable support for this complex and multifaceted project. Don Farmer and Lindia Douglas guided me through basements, closets, and garages where many of the Yaddo materials are stored. Lesley Leduc is owed a very special thanks for working to identify mysterious faces in yellowing photographs, answering hundreds of questions regarding Yaddo's guests and history, and coordinating several rounds of photography at

Yaddo. Joanne Heyman steered this project between the NYPL's lions, and continued to provide support and encouragement long after her work had taken her elsewhere. Retired Yaddo staff members John Nelson and Rosemary Misurelli agreed to interviews that helped to shape my understanding of Yaddo's daily operations in the mid-twentieth century.

At The New York Public Library, Paul LeClerc, the Library's president, and David S. Ferriero, the Andrew W. Mellon Director of The New York Public Libraries, embraced this project from the outset. Heike Kordish, former director of the Humanities and Social Sciences Library, welcomed me as a guest curator. William Stingone, assistant director for Manuscripts and Archives, and his staff in the Manuscripts and Archives Division, offered the Yaddo exhibition research team the assistance and quality of service for which they are renowned among researchers and scholars from around the world. Manuscript specialists Thomas Lannon and Laura Ruttum were consistently warm, welcoming, and enthusiastic about the project, and technical assistant Nasima Hasnat worked tirelessly to provide our research team with requested materials.

Susan Rabbiner, the library's assistant director for exhibitions, and her team have made the preparation for the Yaddo exhibition one of my most memorable professional experiences. Research coordinator Jeanne Bornstein organized countless visits for me throughout the library's many divisions and stayed the course as assistant research coordinators Meg Maher, Kenneth Benson, and Kailen Rogers each in turn worked on various aspects of the project. Registrar Jean Mihich and her associate Caryn Gedell, along with exhibitions conservator Myriam de Arteni, have embraced the challenges associated with a project of this scope and scale, and safeguarded the treasures in our exhibition. Exhibition designer Roger Westerman, of Roger Westerman Design, and the library's installation coordinator, Andrew Pastore, generously shared their experience working in Gottesman Hall, and helped to steer us past the space's challenges. Graphic and Web designer Dmitry Krasny and his firm, Deka Design, came on board far into our process, providing new insights and inspiration as we moved the project toward completion. The NYPL's director of publications, Karen Van Westering, guided the book-production process, and Barbara Bergeron edited texts for the exhibition.

Curators across the Research Libraries have offered their advice and support. At the Humanities and Social Sciences Library, Roberta Waddell, former curator of prints in the Miriam and Ira D. Wallach Division of Art, Prints and Photographs, and her staff, especially Margaret Glover, were a rich source of insight into the Yaddo visual artists whose works are held by the Print Collection. Stephen C. Pinson, the Robert B. Menschel Curator of Photography, and his colleague David Lowe pulled countless photographs of Yaddo artists and writers for our consideration. Michael Terry, chief librarian of the Dorot Jewish Division, shared his materials on early twentieth-century novelist Henry Roth. Elizabeth Diefendorf, the former Frederick Phineas & Sandra Priest Rose Chief Librarian of the General Research Division, provided insights on twentieth-century authors at Yaddo. Edward Kasinec, curator of the Slavic and East European Collections, along with his associates Robert H. Davis and Tatyana Salman, advised us on the many Eastern European artists and writers included in the exhibition. Isaac Gewirtz, curator of the Henry W. and Albert A. Berg Collection of English and American Literature, took time from his own exhibition preparation to review lists of Yaddo authors and writers represented in the Berg Collection, and Stephen Crook and Philip Milito opened those drawers to this researcher. Paul Holdengräber provided moral support, good humor, and excellence in public programming.

Joshua M. Greenberg, the library's first director of digital strategy and scholarship, and his team of digital designers and programmers, including Barbara R. Taranto, Jennifer Anderson, Michelle Misner, Lee Horowitz, and metadata specialist Janet Murray, joined forces with the Yaddo project research team to develop a groundbreaking digital-scholarship component. Valdis Krebs provided crucial consultation on social network mapping.

At The New York Public Library for the Performing Arts, Jacqueline Z. Davis, the Barbara G. and Lawrence A. Fleischman Executive Director for the Performing Arts, welcomed the Yaddo research team. Sara Velez, curator of the Rodgers & Hammerstein Archives of Recorded Sound, and her predecessor, Donald A. Mc-Cormick, were eager and enthusiastic about possibilities for including recorded sound in the exhibition. George E. Boziwick, chief of the Music Division, advised our research team on how to access his collection's relevant treasures. David Callahan, director of the Donnell Media Center, proposed a full-scale film program to accompany the exhibition, highlighting the contributions of Yaddo's artists to both mainstream Hollywood cinema and American independent and experimental filmmaking. At the Schomburg Center for Research in Black Culture, Diana Lachatanere, assistant director for collections and services; Mary Yearwood, curator of the Photographs and Prints Division; and Sharon M. Howard, head of public service, Jean Blackwell Hutson General Research and Reference Division, were kind enough to meet with us in the earliest stages of the project, and Tammi Lawson opened the Art and Artifacts Division to our research team.

From outside the NYPL's halls and Yaddo's circles there are also many individuals to thank. Jennifer Crewe, editorial director at Columbia University Press, has been an enthusiast regarding this project since she first encountered the book proposal. Her team at Columbia has been extraordinarily helpful, in particular Lisa Hamm and Joseph J. Erdos, who managed myriad changes with grace and aplomb. I am deeply grateful for their patience and flexibility as we managed competing exhibition and book-production schedules. Nancy Kuhl, associate curator, Collection of American Literature, Beinecke Rare Book and Manuscript Library at Yale University, provided extraordinary assistance in allowing me access to the William Carlos Williams manuscripts in the final days before these papers were moved offsite for cataloging. We are immensely grateful to Adam D. Weinberg, Alice Pratt Brown Director of the Whitney Museum of American Art; Donna De Salvo, associate director for programs and curator; and Dana Miller, associate curator of the permanent collection, whose willingness with the loan of a key work by Clyfford Still contributed greatly to our ability to convey the little-known story of Yaddo's contribution to visual arts in America. Danielle Jackson at Magnum Photos helped us identify Henri Cartier-Bresson photographs for the exhibition. halley k. harrisburg, director of Michael Rosenfeld Gallery, assisted in locating a Beauford Delaney artwork for the exhibition. Musa Mayer generously loaned rare photographs of Philip Guston at Yaddo. Paul Elie shared insights from his work on Flannery O'Connor and information about many on Yaddo's guest rosters.

Without a team of research assistants on this project, the work would not have been possible in the short period available to us. I have been fortunate to have a committed research team that included Stephanie Grace and William J. Levay, who worked independently and inventively on the numerous tasks that this venture required. François Alacoque provided creative support, research advice, and countless hours of counsel. Former New York University colleagues George Yudice, Harvey Molotch, Robin Nagle, Laurel George, and Bruce Altshuler sent me some of their best and brightest as part of the original archive research crew. Eileen O'Connor and Meghan Falvey were two among them whose research "finds" continue to illuminate the project. Fordham University graduate student Robert Martin was an enthusiastic and keenly-focused researcher for the database that informs every aspect of the exhibition. And Matthew S. Santirocco, the Sheryl Kushner Dean of the College of Arts and Sciences at New York University, has been a steadfast supporter, working to develop a series of symposia and other events to accompany the exhibition. New colleagues at Fordham University, including Mark Massa, S.J.; Angela O'Donnell; Eileen Burchell; Doyle McCarthy; and James Fisher, have been generous with their help, and Fordham's Francis and Ann Curran Center for American Catholic Studies will generously support public programming to accompany the exhibition. Tracy Cole and her colleagues at Baker Hostetler provided the counsel that made this multiorganizational project possible.

Special thanks go to Kevin Kimberlin of Spencer Trask & Co. for supporting the research that made this project possible. Funders for the exhibition include: The Morris and Alma Schapiro Fund; Mary H. White and J. Christopher Flowers; the New York Council for the Humanities; the New York State Council on the Arts; Gladys Krieble Delmas Foundation; George Rickey Foundation, Inc.; Harold Reed; Allan Gurganus; Peter C. Gould; Anthony and Margo Viscusi; Susan Brynteson; Nancy Sullivan; Bruce and Ellen Cohen; Rick Moody; Barbara Toll; Rackstraw Downes; Matthew Stover; Van der Veer Varner; Gardner McFall and Peter Olberg; Joseph Caldwell; John Ashbery; Geoffrey Movius; Patricia Volk; and two anonymous donors.

The essayists for the volume, who are listed in the table of contents and so are not reiterated here, worked on a tight schedule for honoraria that were academic at best, and they produced remarkable contributions to the scholarship on Yaddo. They are owed a round of applause, as well as perhaps a round of another sort. Karl E. Willers deserves special thanks for having originally encouraged me to take on this project. My friends Chris Ford and Jolieange Wright took part in brainstorming the earliest themes for both the exhibition and book, while Carolyn Sakai and Allison Barlow offered ongoing advice. Richard K. Parker, associate professor emeritus, Lockhaven University of Pennsylvania, has generously shared his time and his knowledge of Yaddo's history and led me to many treasures that were unmapped. He, along with Anna McCarthy and Hillel Schwartz, read drafts of the introductory essay for this volume, and their insights greatly improved the outcome.

NOTES

Materials from the Yaddo Records, housed in The New York Public Library's Manuscripts and Archives Division, are cited below by box and (where available) file number. So, for example, Yaddo Records, Box 271, File 30 is given as YR 271.30. Where files were named but not numbered, the file name is given. Researchers interested in consulting any of the materials from the Yaddo Records should be sure to check the citation against the collection guide—available online through the Manuscripts and Archives Division Web site (http://www.nypl.org/mss)—and to contact division staff (http://www.nypl.org/mssref) in advance of their visit.

1 / CREATIVE POWER

Epigraphs: Katrina Trask, *Yaddo* (Saratoga Springs, N.Y.: privately printed, 1923), p. 93. *NB*: Between 1882 and 1891, Katrina Trask kept a record of her family's life at Yaddo. In December 1888 the Trasks published or more properly printed a small numbered edition of *The Chronicles of Yaddo*, which eulogized her children Christina and Spencer Jr., who had died earlier that year. In 1893, most copies of this edition were destroyed in a fire. However, in 1923, on instructions left by Katrina at her death, her longtime assistant Allena Pardee prepared and printed a posthumous edition of a more extensive series of Trask's recollections of the 1882 to 1891 period. Although Katrina's introduction in the posthumous volume refers to the book variously as *The Chronicles of Yaddo* and *The Story of Yaddo*, the title page lists the book simply as *Yaddo*. Recent research, as, for example, Ben Alexander, "The Lowell Affair," *New England Quarterly* 80, no. 4 (December 2007), refers to the 1923 book as *The Chronicles of Yaddo*, but to distinguish the expansive reconstructed "chronicles" of 1923 from the 1888 eulogy, I refer to the 1888 publication as *The Chronicles of Yaddo*, and the 1923 book as *Yaddo*.

Letter to the Trustees of Pine Garde, February 1900, YR 197.6.

1. Technically, of course, it was Spencer Trask, rather than Katrina Trask, who saw his efforts rewarded by the marketplace. As members of the nineteenth century's upper class, the Trasks had a typically gendered division of labor that called for men to work in the commercial arena while women were sequestered in the intimate arena of the home and feminized world of "culture."
2. Lawrence W. Levine, *Highbrow/Lowbrow: The Emergence of Cultural Hierarchy in America* (Cambridge, Mass.: Harvard University Press, 1988).
3. For the clearest discussion of this notion, see Lewis Hyde, *The Gift: Imagination and the Erotic Life of Property* (New York: Vintage, 1983).
4. Susan E. Tifft and Alex S. Jones, *The Trust: The Private and Powerful Family Behind the New York Times* (Boston: Little, Brown, 1999), p. 35.
5. See "Note on the Trasks and the Founding of Yaddo," in this volume for aspects of this story.
6. The relative value of $15 million at the turn of the twentieth century to the current value can be calculated using factors derived from several different measures. At the

low end of valuation, the Consumer Price Index would estimate the value of $15 million at the turn of the twentieth century at $382 million. At the higher end, the relative share of Gross Domestic Product would put the value at $1.1 billion. See http://www .measuringofworth.com (accessed March 20, 2008).

7. See Richard Rorty, *Contingency, Irony, and Solidarity* (Cambridge: Cambridge University Press, 1989) for a well-articulated case for the artist as the agent of social change. Interestingly, it is a little-known fact that James Rorty, the philosopher's father and a novelist, was a guest at Yaddo in 1927. One wonders to what extent the familial memory of Yaddo figured in the younger Rorty's formulations of the role of artists.

8. Levine, *Highbrow/Lowbrow*, pp. 83–167. See also Toby Miller, *The Well-Tempered Self: Citizenship, Culture, and the Post-Modern Subject* (Baltimore: Johns Hopkins University Press, 1993).

9. The idea of sequestering oneself from the labors of daily life to take up what is characterized as the more important work of creating lasting art has deep roots in Western culture. Philosopher Hannah Arendt, herself a Yaddo guest in 1952, explored the idea of art as a separate sphere of work in her 1958 book *The Human Condition* (Chicago: University of Chicago Press). She noted that as far back as classical Greece, there was an expectation that artists, architects, writers, and other professionals would insulate their practices from pecuniary concerns and the labors of daily life. Arendt points out that the words "work" and "labor," although used almost interchangeably in our culture, are etymologically distinct and retain distinctive usages despite the modern tendency to blur them. Greek distinguishes between *ponein* and *ergazesthai*, Latin between *laborare* and *facere* or *fabricari*, French between *travailler* and *oeuvrer*, and German between *arbeiten* and *werken* (pp. 80–81). The word "labor," Arendt points out, when used as a noun, never designates the finished product, the result of the laboring. In every European language, it is associated with the physical exertion of childbirth. Quite the opposite is the case for the word "work." Work is used to describe both the process of producing something and the product produced. And, Arendt notes, "it is also interesting that the nouns 'work,' *oeuvre*, *Werke*, show an increasing tendency to be used for works of art in all three languages" (pp. 81–82). Labor—exertion in an effort to sustain one's life or produce biological progeny—was ranked second to the great works that would endure, thereby defying mortality. To insulate one's activities from this degraded status, ancient physicians, navigators, and architects (among others) engaged in an "art of earning money" (or *technē mistharnētikē*) as a practice separate and distinct from their professional work. Arendt writes: "This additional art is by no means understood as the element of labor in the otherwise free arts, but on the contrary, the one art through which the 'artist,' the professional worker, as we would say, keeps himself free from the necessity to labor" (p. 128). As with Richard Rorty's familial association with Yaddo, one must wonder to what extent Arendt's 1952 visit may have influenced her idea of art making as work that is necessarily set apart from other kinds of labor.

10. See, for example, Bob Colacello, *Studios by the Sea: Artists of Long Island's East End* (New York: Abrams, 2002); Nancy E. Green, *Byrdcliffe: An American Arts and Crafts Colony* (Ithaca, N.Y.: Cornell University Press, 2004); Helen A. Harrison and Constance Ayers Denne, *Hamptons Bohemia: Two Centuries of Artists and Writers on the Beach* (San Francisco: Chronicle, 2002); Loretta Hoagland, *Lawrence Park: Bronxville's Turn-of-the-Century Art Colony* (Bronxville, N.Y.: Lawrence Park Hilltop Association, 1992); Michael Jacobs, *The Good and Simple Life: Artist Colonies in Europe and America* (Oxford: Phaidon, 1985); Richard Kostelanetz, *Soho: The Rise and Fall of an Artists' Colony* (New York: Routledge, 2003); Susan G. Larkin, *The Cos Cob Art Colony: Impressionists on the Connecticut Shore* (New York: National Academy of Design; New Haven: Yale University Press, 2001); Dorothy Gees Secker and Ronald A. Kuchta, *Provincetown Painters, 1890's–1970's* (Syracuse, N.Y.: Visual Artis Publications, 1977); Steve Shipp, *American Art Colonies, 1850–1930: A Historical Guide to America's Original Art Colonies and Their Artists* (Westport, Conn.: Greenwood Press, 1996); Patricia Brecht, *Woodstock, an American Art Colony, 1902–1977* (Poughkeepsie, N.Y.:

Vassar College Art Gallery, 1977); and Carter Wiseman, *A Place for the Arts: The Mac-Dowell Colony, 1907–2007* (Peterborough, N.H.: MacDowell Colony, 2006).

11. Katrina Trask's epiphany regarding Yaddo's purpose: "At Yaddo they will find the inspiration they need: some of them will see the Muses—some of them will drink of the Fountain of Hippocrene, and all of them will find the Sacred Fire and light their torches at its flame." Trask, *Yaddo*, p. 193.

12. "Milestones," *Time*, May 17, 1926, http://www.time.com/time/magazine/article/0,9171,769372-1,00.html (accessed January 10, 2008).

13. "Recommendations, 1928," March 7, 1928, YR 311.

14. Lewis Mumford to Elizabeth Ames, April 21, 1928, YR 270.32.

15. Mark Van Doren to Elizabeth Ames, January 18, 1928, YR 221.32. Alfred Kazin to Elizabeth Ames, February 3, 1955, promised gift of The Corporation of Yaddo to The New York Public Library currently held at Yaddo. These literary networks and legacy are mapped in the exhibition and on the accompanying Web component on the Library's Web site, http://exhibitions.nypl.org/yaddo.

16. Irita Van Doren to Elizabeth Ames, January 28, 1936, YR 238.2.

17. Malcolm Cowley's recollection *Six Decades at Yaddo* (Saratoga Springs, N.Y.: Corporation of Yaddo, 1986) commemorated sixty years of operations. His support of Agnes Smedley's application is documented in Ruth Price, *The Lives of Agnes Smedley* (New York: Oxford University Press, 2005), p. 363. Cowley's support of Capote is documented in the admissions committee notes regarding his application, YR 234.4.

18. Diana Trilling, *The Beginning of the Journey: The Marriage of Diana and Lionel Trilling* (New York: Harcourt Brace, 1993), p. 178.

19. Yaddo's guest records suggest that in the community's earliest days some artists were accompanied by their non-artist spouses, and that plans to host families with children were considered. By the late 1930s these rules were adjusted, with husbands, wives, and children no longer included in invitations.

20. Reinhold Niebuhr to Elizabeth Ames, March 9, 1937, YR 271.30.

21. Robinson Jeffers to Elizabeth Ames, January 22, 1926, and Arthur Miller to Elizabeth Ames, March 2, 1961, YR 269.26.

22. Jerre Mangione, *An Ethnic at Large: A Memoir of America in the Thirties and Forties* (New York: Putnam, 1978), p. 254.

23. Mario Puzo to Elizabeth Ames, no date, but following a 1967 visit, YR 277.15.

24. In 1933, Ames reported to her board of directors:

> Yaddo, ever realistic in the midst of its idealism, (for what are ideals but the energy with which realistic action is generated?) at once addressed itself to a sterner task than it had known—a stern task because its responsibilities to its chosen work were becoming greater as its own resources were being cut down. To entertain at one time twenty guests (which represented an almost 50% increase) many simplicities and economies were called for. For example, a buffet breakfast, which saved labor for tasks elsewhere, was served. A studio lunch box with the same savings in view took the place of lunch in the dining room. It was during this period . . . that I went one day to the North Farm House to see what I could visualize there. . . . Here was Yaddo's chance for an all year service. . . . Now on this wintry morning six are living there. (Executive Director's Report, 1933, YR 344)

Once the lean years of the Depression had passed, Yaddo again provided full house-keeping service to guests, as they do today.

25. Ben Alexander, "The Lowell Affair," *New England Quarterly* 80, no. 4 (December 2007), pp. 556–557, notes Marya Zaturenska's concern over whether Ames would extend her stay. The correspondence of writer Evelyn Scott to Ames suggests a similar anxiety. Scott and her husband, the novelist John Metcalfe, had been guests several times from 1931 through 1933. Scott wrote to Ames on September 11, 1933:

> If it is wrong of me to wonder what has given you such a strong impression of my possible need of change, I think it is natural that I should wonder—and especially if

my manner with the group is responsible. I can't think of anything definite except my retirement last night, which came as a result of having my feelings hurt by your repeated remark that I could 'withdraw' if I didn't like the cold. (YR 269.10).

26. Executive Director's Report, 1939–1940, YR 346.14.

27. Letters from Arvin to Capote, recently acquired by The New York Public Library's Manuscripts and Archives Division and not yet catalogued, underscore the significance of the relationship.

28. Elinor Langer, *Josephine Herbst* (Boston: Little, Brown, 1984), pp. 126–130.

29. Ibid., p. 278.

30. Virginia Spencer Carr, *The Lonely Hunter: A Biography of Carson McCullers* (New York: Doubleday, 1975), p. 156.

31. Katherine Anne Porter to Elizabeth Ames, March 29, 1943, YR 276.14.

32. Mark Granovetter, "The Strength of Weak Ties," *American Journal of Sociology*, 78, no. 6 (May 1973), pp. 1360–1380.

33. Porter discusses her support for Welty in a letter to Elizabeth Ames, April 22, 1943, YR 276.14. In that letter, she explains why she withdrew her offer to write a foreword for Michael Seide's short story collection *The Common Thread* (New York: Harcourt, 1944), deeming the project too commercial.

34. Correspondence regarding Dante Fiorillo is scattered throughout the Yaddo Records, as many people were concerned for his well being. See, for example, Elizabeth Ames to Alexander Byer, October 4, 1933, YR 207.49; Hannah Moriarta, Secretary of the Musicians' Emergency Aid of New York to Mrs. John Carroll Ames (Elizabeth Ames), October 24, 1933, YR 344: File name, General Correspondence; and the multiple letters between Ames and Marion Sheffield, YR 219.33.

35. Langer, *Josephine Herbst*, pp. 322, 328.

36. Paul Elie, *The Life You Save May Be Your Own: An American Pilgrimage* (New York: Farrar, Straus and Giroux, 2003), p. 173.

37. Executive Director's Report 1931, "Yaddo in 1931 and Otherwise," YR 343.

38. Clyfford Still to Elizabeth Ames, September 17, 1934, YR 289.13. Still is referring to composer Dante Fiorillo, novelist James T. "Jimmy" Farrell, composer Berenice R. Morris, writer Richard B. Morris, and composer Roy Harris—fellow guests in 1934.

39. Howard S. Becker, *Art Worlds* (Berkeley: University of California Press, 1982).

40. These recordings are held at The New York Public Library for the Performing Arts.

41. Since, as is oft-repeated, the word utopia derives from the Greek *u-topas*, not + a place. Writer Louis Adamic, a Yaddo guest in 1931 and 1933, wrote a controversial article in which he described apocryphal dinner table debates during the 1933 season: Louis Adamic, "Ingrates at Yaddo," *Esquire*, July 1938, pp. 75, 180–184.

42. Dorothy Norman to Elizabeth Ames, January 4, 1942, YR 269.29.

43. Morton D. Zabel to Elizabeth Ames, February 6, 1960, p. 5, "Admissions, Guest List, 1960," YR 321.

44. Admission Committee notes, YR 254.1.

45. Executive Director's Report, 1941, YR 346.14.

46. Elizabeth Ames to Morton D. Zabel, April 10, 1959, held by The Corporation of Yaddo, promised gift to The New York Public Library. Other progressive organizations attempting to integrate in the 1940s faced similar "town and gown" community relationship challenges. See, for example, Martin Duberman's account of the 1944 integration of Black Mountain College in *Black Mountain: An Exploration in Community* (New York: Norton, 1993; New York: Dutton, 1972), pp. 172–232.

47. Herbert Block (a.k.a. Herblock) coined the term "McCarthyism" in a political cartoon in the *Washington Post*, March 29, 1950.

48. Transcript of Special Meeting of the Yaddo Board of Directors, February 26, 1949, YR 385.3.

49. Alexander, "The Lowell Affair," pp. 585–587.

50. Christine Stansell, *American Moderns: Bohemian New York and the Creation of a New Century* (New York: Holt, 2000).

51. See, for example, Patricia Hill Collins, "Black Feminist Epistemology," in Collins, *Black Feminist Thought: Knowledge, Consciousness, and the Politics of Empowerment* (New York: Routledge, 2000), pp. 251–272.

52. Sociologist Howard Becker made a similar observation in his 1984 *Art Worlds*, when he noted that any given work of art requires the labor of, at a minimum, dozens of individuals. In his "Heart of Darkness: A Journey into the Dark Matter of the Art World," in John R. Hall, Blake Stimson, and Lisa Tamaris Becker, eds., *Visual Worlds* (New York: Routledge, 2005), pp. 126–138, artist and critic Gregory Sholette has proposed that we think of the creative work of the many artists whose works go relatively unrecognized as essential to the making of the so-called "successes" or "masterpieces." Sholette proposes an analogy to the dark matter hypothesized by physicists. Just as the invisible "dark matter" unaccounted for in our perceptions of the world makes all other matter possible, so the underappreciated work of hobbyists and aspiring artists contributes to what we think of as the works of genius.

53. See, for example, Frances Stonor Saunders, *The Cultural Cold War: The CIA and the World of Arts and Letters* (New York: New Press, 2001), originally published as *Who Paid the Piper? The CIA and the Cultural Cold War* (London: Granta Books, 1999). See also Allan Sekula, "The Traffic in Photographs," *Art Journal* 41, no. 1 (Spring 1981), pp. 15–25; Greg Barnhisel, "Perspectives USA and the Cultural Cold War: Modernism in Service of the State," *ModernismModernity* 14, no. 4 (November 2007), pp. 729–754; Michael L. Krenn, *Fall-Out Shelters for the Human Spirit: American Art and the Cold War* (Chapel Hill, N.C.: University of North Carolina Press, 2005).

54. Elizabeth Murrie O'Neill, *The Last Word: Letters Between Marcia Nardi and William Carlos Williams* (Iowa City: University of Iowa Press, 1994).

55. William Carlos Williams to Elizabeth Ames, October 24, 1951, YR 271.9.

56. Helen Hennessy Vendler, *The Given and the Made: Strategies of Poetic Redefinition* (Cambridge, Mass.: Harvard University Press, 1995).

57. William Butler Yeats, *Yeats's Poetry, Drama, and Prose*, selected and edited by James Pethica (New York: Norton, 2000), pp. 107–108. "The intellect of life is forced to choose / Perfection of the life, or of the work / And if it take the second must refuse / A heavenly mansion, raging in the dark."

58. Van Wyck Brooks, "On Creating a Usable Past," *Dial* 64 (1918), pp. 337–341.

59. Van Wyck Brooks, *Letters and Leadership* (New York: B. W. Huebsch, 1918), pp. 62–63.

60. Ibid., p. 63.

61. Robert M. Coates, "The Art Galleries: Abroad and at Home," *New Yorker* 22 (March 30, 1946), p. 83. There is some debate as to whether Coates coined the term in America. See Helen A. Harrison, "Arthur G. Dove and the Origins of Abstract Expressionism," *American Art* 12, no. 1 (Spring 1998), pp. 66–83. But there is little doubt that in his role as the *New Yorker*'s art critic, he popularized the term. For an example of Meyer Schapiro's socially engaged art theory, see Meyer Schapiro, *Worldview in Painting—Art and Society, Selected Papers* (New York: George Braziller, 1999).

62. For her part, Ames had received the National Academy of Arts and Letters Distinguished Service Award in 1959 ("Yaddo Director to Get Art Institute's Award," *New York Times*, May 6, 1959, p. 8). Ames was succeeded by Granville Hicks, who served as acting executive director from 1970 to 1971, when Curtis Harnack accepted leadership of the organization. Harnack served as executive director from February 1971 through July 1987. Writer Jerre Mangione (1977–1978) and sculptor and writer Anne Truitt (April–December 1984) each served as acting directors during two sabbaticals taken by Harnack. Poet Myra Sklarew was executive director from July 1987 through September 1991. In 1992 Michael Sundell assumed the leadership of Yaddo as president of the corporation effective through December 2000. Elaina Richardson is currently the president of Yaddo.

63. Many of Ames's letters to artists during the 1930s conclude with this paragraph warning them that Yaddo eschewed propaganda. See, for example, Ames's letters in the guest files of Albert Halper (YR 212.9), Tess Slesinger (YR 219.46), and Benjamin Ginzburg (YR 211.37).

1. YR 205.44.
2. Barry Werth, *The Scarlet Professor: Newton Arvin, A Literary Life Shattered by Scandal* (New York: Nan A. Talese, 2001), p. 45.
3. Ibid., p. 76.
4. Ibid., p. 36.
5. Ibid.
6. Ibid., p. 41.
7. Ibid., p. 58.
8. YR 205.44.
9. Werth, *The Scarlet Professor*, p. 56.
10. YR 205.44.
11. Ibid.
12. Ibid.
13. Werth, *The Scarlet Professor*, pp. 76–77.
14. Ibid., p. 78.
15. Ibid., p. 81.
16. Ibid.
17. Ibid., p. 92.
18. Ibid., p. 93.
19. See Ruth Price's essay on Agnes Smedley at Yaddo.
20. Werth, *The Scarlet Professor*, p. 152.
21. Ibid., p. 98.
22. Ibid., p. 100.
23. Ibid., p. 101.
24. Ibid., p. 102.
25. Ibid., p. 149.
26. "*Life* visits Yaddo," *Life*, July 15, 1946, pp. 110–113.
27. YR 225.
28. Katrina Trask, *Yaddo* (Saratoga Springs, N.Y.: private printing, 1923).
29. Ian Hamilton, *Robert Lowell: A Biography* (New York: Random House, 1982), p. 148.
30. Paul Mariani, *Lost Puritan: A Life of Robert Lowell* (New York: Norton, 1994), p. 171.
31. Werth, *The Scarlet Professor*, p. 115.
32. Ibid., p. 136.
33. YR 385.3.
34. YR 385.2.
35. YR 385.3.
36. Werth, *The Scarlet Professor*, p. 115.
37. Ibid., p. 116.
38. Ibid., p. 128.
39. Ibid., p. 130.
40. Ibid.
41. Ibid., p. 141.
42. YR 225.
43. Werth, *The Scarlet Professor*, p. 165.
44. Ibid., p. 201.
45. Ibid., p. 218.
46. Ibid., p. 196.
47. Ibid., p. 225.
48. YR 225.23.
49. Werth, *The Scarlet Professor*, p. 228.
50. YR 225.23.
51. YR 225.
52. YR 225.23.
53. Blake Bailey, "John Cheever's 'Hollywood Problem,'" *Harvard Review* 30 (Spring 2006), pp. 94–103, 202.

54. Werth, *The Scarlet Professor*, p. 294.

55. Ibid., p. 298.

3 / THE TRAILBLAZER

1. Miriam Beard, "Yaddo's Gates Open to the Talented," *New York Times*, June 6, 1926, p. SM9.

2. Aaron Copland and Vivian Perlis, *Copland: 1900–1942* (New York: St. Martin's, 1984), p. 184.

3. Minutes of the Meeting of the Yaddo Board of Directors, TCK date, YR 343.

4. Copland and Perlis, *Copland*, p. 178.

5. Howard Pollack, *Aaron Copland: The Life and Work of an Uncommon Man* (New York: Holt, 1999), p. 158.

6. "Composers Assail Critics at Yaddo," *New York Times*, May 2, 1932, p. 13.

7. Olin Downes, "American Composers and Critics," *New York Times*, May 8, 1932, p. X6.

8. H. Howard Taubman, "Saratoga's Fortnight of Music," *New York Times*, September 12, 1937, p. X5.

9. Rudy Shackelford, "The Yaddo Festivals of American Music, 1932–1952," *Perspectives of New Music* 17, no. 1 (1978): 123.

4 / IN GOOD COMPANY

Epigraph: Beauford Delaney to Elizabeth Ames, September 16, 1951, YR 241.26.

1. Martin Puryear's comments here and throughout this essay are from an extended phone interview with the artist at his home and studio in the Hudson Valley, north of New York City. The conversation took place on January 30, 2008. Very special thanks to both Martin Puryear and Mary Frank for generously taking time to speak with the author about their residencies at Yaddo. While personal and unique, their comments also concisely communicate general aspects of the Yaddo experience that resonate with the generations of recollections preserved within the Yaddo Records. Much credit must be given to Micki McGee for helping to identify many specific sources from within the extensive Yaddo Records that enriched the text, and thanks especially to Elaina Richardson for so skillfully helping to integrate those sources within this essay.

2. Mary Frank's comments here and elsewhere in this text are from a face-to-face interview with the artist at an exhibition of her recent work at the D. C. Moore Gallery in New York City. The dialogue took place on January 26, 2008.

3. Marion Greenwood to Elizabeth Ames, June 25, 1940, YR 211.59.

4. Kenneth Emerson, "An Interview with Alfred Leslie," in *Committed to Artists and the Creative Process* (Saratoga Springs, N.Y.: Corporation of Yaddo, 2006), p. 13.

7 / THE LONGEST STAY

1. Ruth Price, *The Lives of Agnes Smedley* (New York: Oxford University Press, 2005).

2. For example, see Janice and Stephen MacKinnon, *Agnes Smedley: The Life and Times of an American Radical* (Berkeley: University of California Press, 1988).

3. Ruth Price, "Agnes Smedley and Her Biography of Zhu De," *Beijing Review* 31, no. 36 (September 5–11, 1988), pp. 32–35.

4. Ruth Price, "Naming Smedley's Name," *History News Network*, 2005; Ruth Price,

"Agnes Smedley, An Example to Whose Cause," *Chronicle of Higher Education* (July 29, 2005), pp. B9–10.

5. Price, *The Lives of Agnes Smedley*, p. 71.

6. Ibid., pp. 152–161.

7. Ibid., p. 364.

8. Ibid., pp. 210–211.

9. Ibid., p. 364.

10. Ibid., p. 366.

11. "Soul Marching On," *Time*, November 7, 1932, http://www.time.com/time/magazine/article/0,9171,744713,00.html (accessed March 20, 2008).

12. Price, *The Lives of Agnes Smedley*, p. 370.

13. Ibid.

14. Ibid., p. 371.

15. Special Meeting of the Directors of the Corporation of Yaddo, February 26, 1949, p. 39, "The Lowell Affair," YR 385.

16. Price, *The Lives of Agnes Smedley*, p. 375.

17. Ibid., p. 378.

18. Ibid., p. 379.

19. Ibid., p. 384.

20. Special Meeting of the Directors, p. 25.

21. Price, *The Lives of Agnes Smedley*, p. 386.

22. Ibid.

23. Ibid., p. 394.

24. Ibid., p. 403.

25. Special Meeting of the Directors, p. 15; Ruth Price, *The Lives of Agnes Smedley*, p. 402.

26. Special Meeting of the Directors, p. 16.

27. Ibid., p. 40.

28. Ibid., p. 27.

29. Malcolm Cowley to Betty Elizabeth Ames, March 11, 1949, YR 385.

30. Katherine Anne Porter to John Slade, March 25, 1949, YR 385.

31. Open letter from Harvey Breit, John Cheever, Eleanor Clark, Alfred Kazin, and Kappo Phelan, March 21, 1949, YR 385.

32. Agnes Smedley to Toni Willison, May 2, 1949, Lois Snow Papers, University of Missouri, Kansas City.

33. Ibid.

34. Ben Alexander, "The Lowell Affair," *New England Quarterly* 80, no. 4 (December 2007), p. 584.

35. Spencer Trask in a letter to the Trustees of Pine Garde, February 1900, p. 1, YR 197.

9 / CRÈME DE LA CRÈME

1. John Cheever, Comments on the directorship of Elizabeth Ames made to the Board of the Corporation of Yaddo, September 7, 1968, YR 356.

2. John Cheever, quoted in Jean Nathan, "Yaddo," *New York Times*, September 19, 1993, Section 9, p. 1.

3. Marcel Proust, *In Search of Lost Time*, vol. 5, *The Captive, The Fugitive*, trans. C. K. S. Moncrieff and Terence Kilmartin, rev. D. J. Enright (New York: Modern Library, 1993), pp. 732–733.

4. Montesquieu (Charles-Louis de Secondat), *Essai sur le goût dans les choses de la nature et de l'art, ou réflexions sur les causes du plaisir qu'excitent en nous les ouvrages d'esprit et les productions des beaux arts* (1757), (Paris: Édition Le Bigre Frères, 1834). French text available at La bibliothèque electronique de Lisieux, http://www.bmlisieux.com/curiosa/essaigou.htm.

5. Lawrence W. Levine, *Highbrow/Lowbrow: The Emergence of Cultural Hierarchy in America* (Cambridge, Mass.: Harvard University Press, 1988), pp. 85–168. See also

Paul Dimaggio, "Cultural Entrepreneurship in Nineteenth-century Boston: The Creation of an Organizational Base for High Culture in America," *Media, Culture, and Society* 4 (1982), p. 303.

6. Michael H. Whitworth, *Virginia Woolf* (New York: Oxford University Press, 2005), p. 83.

7. D. H. Lawrence, *The Letters of D. H. Lawrence*, vol. 5, *March 1924–March 1927*, eds. James T. Boulton and Lindeth Vasey (Cambridge: Cambridge University Press, 1991), p. 61.

8. Leonard Woolf, "Hunting the Highbrow." *Cambridge Quarterly* 24, no. 1 (1995), p. 80.

9. Melba Cuddy-Keane, *Virginia Woolf, the Intellectual and the Public Sphere* (Cambridge: Cambridge University Press, 2003), p. 18.

10. Russell Lynes, *The Tastemakers* (New York: Harper, 1954), p. 311.

11. Ibid., pp. 311–312.

12. Ibid., p. 312.

13. Walter Benjamin, "The Work of Art in the Age of Mechanical Reproduction," in *Illuminations: Essays and Reflections*, ed. Hannah Arendt, trans. Harry Zohn (New York: Harcourt, Brace & World, 1968), p. 218.

14. Russell Lynes, "Highbrow, Lowbrow, Middlebrow," *Harper's*, February 1949, p. 19.

15. Kirk Varnedoe and Adam Gopnik, *High and Low: Modern Art and Popular Culture* (New York: Museum of Modern Art, 1990).

16. Dwight Macdonald. "Masscult and Midcult," in *Against the American Grain* (New York: Random House, 1962).

17. Pierre Bourdieu, *Distinction: A Social Critique of the Judgment of Taste*, trans. Richard Nice (Cambridge, Mass.: Harvard University Press, 2007).

18. Richard A. Peterson and Roger M. Kern, "Changing Highbrow Taste: From Snob to Omnivore," *American Sociological Review* 61, no. 5 (1996), p. 900.

19. Rob King, "Made for the Masses with an Appeal to the Classes: The Triangle Film Corporation and the Failure of Highbrow Film Culture," *Cinema Journal* 44, no. 2 (2005), p. 3.

20. Herbert J. Gans, "Can Rockwell Survive Cultural Elevation," *Chronicle of Higher Education* 46, no. 33 (April 21, 2000), pp. B–8, 2p, 1c.

21. Michael Kammen, *American Culture, American Tastes: Social Change and the 20th Century* (New York: Knopf, 1999).

22. Material related to Mario Puzo is from the Yaddo Records, YR 277.15, unless otherwise noted.

23. David Boroff, "Pasta with Gusto: The Fortunate Pilgrim by Mario Puzo," *New York Times Book Review*, January 31, 1965.

24. Mario Puzo, "Tell Me How Long the Train's Been Gone," *New York Times Book Review*, June 23, 1968, http://www.nytimes.com/books/98/03/29/specials/baldwin-tell.html (accessed March 4, 2008).

NOTE ON THE TRASKS AND THE FOUNDING OF YADDO

1. Katrina Trask, *Yaddo* (Saratoga Springs, N.Y.: privately printed, 1923), p. 15. See also the *New York Times*, November 12, 1898, p. SM9.

2. Trask, *Yaddo*, p. 180.

3. Ibid., p. 18.

4. After Spencer Trask's death, she turned her attention to questions of social and political policies: *In the Vanguard* (New York: Macmillan, 1913), an antiwar play performed by women's clubs and church groups as World War I loomed, and *The Mighty and the Lowly* (New York: Macmillan, 1915), a sermon in which she denounced the spread of Christian socialism and advocated that love was the only answer to social inequality.

5. Marjorie Peabody Waite, with illustrations by Penina Kishore, *Yaddo: Yesterday and Today* (Albany, N.Y.: Argus Press, 1933), p. 52.

6. Trask, *Yaddo*, p. 193.

7. Ibid., pp. 192–194.

8. Marya Zaturenska, "The Rose Garden at Yaddo," in *Threshold and Hearth* (New York: Macmillan, 1934), p. 5; Sylvia Plath, "Private Ground," in *Collected Poems*, ed. Ted Hughes (New York: Harper & Row, 1981), p. 130; and Musa McKim, "What the Public Sees," in *Alone with the Moon: Selected Writings of Musa McKim* (Great Barrington, Mass.: Figures, 1994), p. 99. Zaturenska's correspondence and the manuscript page for her Yaddo rose garden poem are filed with the papers of her husband, Horace Gregory, YR 250.14.

9. "Spencer Trask Has Young Artist Guests," *Daily Saratogian*, June 4, 1908, p. 3.

Contributors

MARCELLE CLEMENTS's most recent book is the novel *Midsummer*. Her articles and essays on the arts, culture, and politics have appeared in many national publications. She is a Collegiate Professor in the College of Arts and Sciences at New York University.

DAVID GATES's first novel, *Jernigan* (1991), was a finalist for the Pulitzer Prize. His second novel, *Preston Falls* (1998), and a short-story collection, *The Wonders of the Invisible World* (1999), were finalists for the National Book Critics Circle Award. He has published short stories in the *New Yorker, Esquire, GQ, Ploughshares, Agni, Grand Street*, and *TriQuarterly*. He was a longtime writer for the arts section at *Newsweek* magazine. He teaches in the M.F.A. writing programs at Bennington College and the New School.

ALLAN GURGANUS is a novelist and short story writer. His 1989 debut novel, *Oldest Living Confederate Widow Tells All*, was a *New York Times* best seller and winner of the Sue Kaufman Prize from the American Academy of Arts and Letters. His other novels include *White People* (1990; Los Angeles Times Book Prize) and *The Practical Heart* (1993; Lambda Literary Award). Gurganus's short fiction has been honored in *The Best American Short Stories, New Stories of the South*, and *The O. Henry Prize Stories*. Gurganus lives in his native North Carolina.

MICKI MCGEE, who curated the exhibition "Yaddo: Making American Culture" for The New York Public Library, recently joined the faculty of sociology and anthropology at Fordham University, where she teaches the sociology of culture. The author of *Self-Help, Inc.: Makeover Culture in American Life* (2005), she holds a Ph.D. from the Graduate Center of the City University of New York and an M.F.A. from the University of California, San Diego; and is a former fellow of the Independent Study Program at the Whitney Museum of American Art. Her articles and essays have been published by *The Nation, Afterimage, Art & Text*, the *Chronicle of Higher Education, High Performance*, and *Social Text*, as well as by the Centre Georges Pompidou and the New Museum of Contemporary Art.

TIM PAGE won the Pulitzer Prize for criticism in 1997 for his writing about music in the *Washington Post*. From 1981 to 1992 he was the host of a program on WNYC-FM in New York, where he presented hundreds of radio premieres by contemporary composers. His books include *Tim Page on Music* (2002); *Dawn Powell: A Biography* (1999); and *The Glenn Gould Reader* (1984). He is currently a professor of music and journalism at the University of Southern California.

RUTH PRICE is the author of *The Lives of Agnes Smedley* (2005), the authoritative biography of one of America's lesser-known literary figures. Her prose has appeared in the *Chicago Tribune*, the *Beijing Review*, and the *Chronicle of Higher Education*. A lapsed professor of English, Price writes on women's and social justice issues and has published several works of genre fiction. She is currently at work on a mystery novel set in Oaxaca.

HELEN VENDLER is the A. Kingsley Porter University Professor at Harvard University. Vendler has written books on William Shakespeare, Wallace Stevens, John Keats, and Seamus Heaney, among many other works, including *Our Secret Discipline: Yeats and Lyric Form* (2007). Vendler did not major in English as an undergraduate but earned her degree in chemistry. She was awarded a Fulbright Fellowship for mathematics before earning her Ph.D. in English and American Literature from Harvard University.

BARRY WERTH is the author of *The Scarlet Professor* (2001), a biography of literary critic Newton Arvin, which was a finalist for the National Book Critics Circle Award. The book inspired the PBS documentary *The Great Pink Scare* by filmmakers Tug Yourgrau and Dan Miller. Werth is also the author of *The Billion-Dollar Molecule* (1994), *Damages* (1998), *31 Days* (2006), and the forthcoming *Dinner at Delmonico's*, which chronicles the rapid rise in popularity of Darwinism during the Gilded Age. He lives in Northampton, Massachusetts.

KARL EMIL WILLERS, a scholar of American and European art since 1800, has held directorial and curatorial positions at the Newport Art Museum; the Dorsky Museum of Art at the State University of New York at New Paltz; the Norton Museum of Art in West Palm Beach, Florida; and the downtown branch of the Whitney Museum of American Art. His recent writings include the essay "Drawing Out Ideas" in the book *Edge of the Sublime: Enamels by Jamie Bennett* (2008), an interview in the portfolio *Collector: The Collection of Elizabeth Brooke Blake* (2007), and the essay "Impressions (and Other Images of Memory)" in the catalogue *Rimer Cardillo* (2004).

ILLUSTRATIONS AND CREDITS

The Manuscripts and Archives Division, the Miriam and Ira D. Wallach Division of Art, Prints and Photographs, and the Dorot Jewish Division are collections of the Humanities and Social Sciences Library, The New York Public Library. Researchers interested in consulting any of the materials from the Yaddo Records (abbreviated as YR) should be sure to check the citation against the collection guide—available online through the Manuscripts and Archives Division Web site (http://www.nypl.org/mss)—and to contact division staff (http://www.nypl .org/mssref) in advance of their visit. Items from The New York Public Library's collections were photographed by Matt Flynn and Pete Riesett.

17, 127 Photographer unknown. Elizabeth Ames, Aaron Copland, Newton Arvin, and others, ca. 1930. Black-and-white photograph. 3 ½ × 2 ¾ in. Corporation of Yaddo.

18 Marion Greenwood. *Portrait of Newton Arvin*, 1932. Oil on canvas. 18 ½ × 14 ¼ in. Corporation of Yaddo.

19 Photographer unknown. Wedding photo of Newton Arvin and Mary Garrison, 1932. Black-and-white photograph. 5 × 7 in. Manuscripts and Archives Division, YR 456. Used with permission of Estate of Newton Arvin.

21 Elizabeth Ames. Executive Director's Report to the Board, 1941–1942, page 3 of 3. Manuscripts and Archives Division, YR 346.

22 Newton Arvin. Letter to Truman Capote discussing *Other Voices, Other Rooms*, n.d., probably 1947. Manuscripts and Archives Division, Capote 2004.37. Used with permission of Estate of Newton Arvin.

23–24 "*Life* Visits Yaddo," *Life*, July 15, 1946. Manuscripts and Archives Division, YR 390.

25 *Grecian Guild Pictorial*, May 1960. Manuscripts and Archives Division, International Gay Information Center Archive, Box 53.

— *Trim*, May 1960. Manuscripts and Archives Division, International Gay Information Center Archive, Box 113.

26 Elizabeth Ames. Carbon copy of letter to Alita Hodgkins, Arvin's parole officer, October 31, 1960. Manuscripts and Archives Division, YR 454.

27 Newton Arvin. Letter to Elizabeth Ames, November 15, 1960. Manuscripts and Archives Division, YR 454. Used with permission of Estate of Newton Arvin.

28 Alfred Kazin. Postcard to Elizabeth Ames, March 22, 1963. Corporation of Yaddo. Reproduced courtesy of the Wylie Agency, Inc.

29 The Tower Room today. © 2008 Brian Vanden Brink.

31 The Music Room today. © 2008 Brian Vanden Brink.

32 Photographer unknown. Group photograph at Triuna, 1931. Black-and-white photograph. 5 × 7 in. Manuscripts and Archives Division, YR 453.

— The Stone Tower today. © 2008 Brian Vanden Brink.

33 Aaron Copland. Letter to Elizabeth Ames, February 12, 1932. Manuscripts and Archives Division, YR 362. Reprinted by permission of the Aaron Copland Fund for Music, Inc., copyright owner.

34 Program, First Festival of Contemporary American Music, 1932. Manuscripts and Archives Division, YR 362.

35 H. B. Settle. Group photograph, Festival of Contemporary American Music, 1932. Black-and-white photograph. 5 × 7 in. Manuscripts and Archives Division, YR 386.

37 Nationwide News Service. Yaddo Music Festival committee, 1938. Black-and-white photograph. 8 × 10 in. Corporation of Yaddo.

38 Photographer unknown. Yaddo Music Group, 1949. Black-and-white photograph. 8 × 10 in. Manuscripts and Archives Division, YR 368.

39 Music Festival Program, Yaddo Music Group, 1952. Manuscripts and Archives Division, YR 367.

— H. B. Settle. Rehearsal for Music Festival, 1952. Black-and-white photograph. 8 × 10 in. Manuscripts and Archives Division, YR 368.

41 Louis Lozowick. *Roofs and Sky*. Works Progress Administration/Federal Art Project. Silkscreen, ca. 1939. 14 × 18 in. Miriam and Ira D. Wallach Division of Art, Prints and Photographs.

42 Louis Lozowick. Letter to Elizabeth Ames, November 2, 1930. Manuscripts and Archives Division, YR 215.

43 Hugh Pearce Botts. *Columbus Circle*, n.d. Aquatint, titled and signed "Botts" in pencil at bottom. 8 ⅞ × 9 ⅞ in. Miriam and Ira D. Wallach Division of Art, Prints and Photographs.

44 Nicolai Cikovsky, *Union Square*, 1934. Lithograph. 9 ⅜ × 12 ⅝ in. Miriam and Ira D. Wallach Division of Art, Prints and Photographs.

— Philip Reisman. *The South*, 1934. Etching and drypoint, signed lower right, inscribed "For Elizabeth Ames" center. 8 ¾ × 12 in. Corporation of Yaddo. © and reproduced courtesy of the Estate of Louise K. Reisman.

45 Ilya Bolotowsky. *Untitled*, 1937. Offset lithograph published by Squibb Galleries, printer, Cane Press. 12 × 9 3/16 in. Miriam and Ira D. Wallach Division of Art, Prints and Photographs. Art © Estate of Ilya Bolotowsky/Licensed by VAGA, New York, N.Y.

— Agnes Tait. *Front Street, New York*, 1936. Lithograph. 10 1/8 × 7 5/8 in. Miriam and Ira D. Wallach Division of Art, Prints and Photographs.

46 Ruth Gikow. *Flood*, ca. 1936. Works Progress Administration/Federal Art Project. Color silkscreen. 14 1/4 × 25 1/4 in. Miriam and Ira D. Wallach Division of Art, Prints and Photographs.

47 Minna Citron. *Men Seldom Make Passes*, 1946. Etching and engraving in color, signed in pencil lower right, titled lower center, ed. 50 lower left. 15 3/4 × 10 in. Miriam and Ira D. Wallach Division of Art, Prints and Photographs. Art © Estate of Minna Citron/Licensed by VAGA, New York, N.Y./Estate represented by the Susan Teller Gallery, New York, N.Y.

48 Nan Lurie. *Technological Improvements*, 1937. Lithograph. 17 5/8 × 11 7/8 in. Miriam and Ira D. Wallach Division of Art, Prints and Photographs.

49 Jacob Lawrence. *Confrontation at the Bridge*, 1975. Silkscreen, signed lower right, titled lower center, numbered 123/175 lower left. 19 1/2 × 26 in. Schomburg Center for Research in Black Culture, Art and Artifacts Division. © 2008 Jacob and Gwendolyn Lawrence Foundation, Seattle, Wash./Artist Rights Society (ARS), New York, N.Y.

50 Philip Guston. *Sea*, 1969. Lithograph. 31 3/8 × 40 3/4 in. Miriam and Ira D. Wallach Division of Art, Prints and Photographs. Estate of Philip Guston.

51 Mary Frank. *Man in the Water*, 1987. Color lithograph. 23 1/2 × 32 1/4 in. Miriam and Ira D. Wallach Division of Art, Prints and Photographs, Gift of Mrs. Lucien Goldschmidt. © Mary Frank. Courtesy DC Moore Gallery, New York, N.Y.

52 Martin Puryear. *Karintha*, 2000. Woodcut from *Cane* by Jean Toomer, San Francisco: Arion Press, 2000. Originally published by Boni and Liveright, 1923. Schomburg Center for Research in Black Culture, Manuscripts, Archives and Rare Books Division, G01.4. © and reproduced courtesy of Martin Puryear.

54 George Rickey. *Two Slender Lines Excentric*, 1977. Stainless steel. 23 × 15 ft. Art © Estate of George Rickey/Licensed by VAGA, New York, N.Y.

57, 129 Photographer unknown. Group on Lake George boat landing, ca. 1937. Black-and-white photograph. 3 1/2 × 5 in. Corporation of Yaddo.

58 Eastman Johnson. *Portrait of Christina Trask*, 1888. Oil on canvas. 69 × 35 1/4 in; *Portrait of Spencer Trask, Jr.*, 1888. Oil on canvas. 69 × 35 1/4 in. Corporation of Yaddo. Photographs by Emma Dodge Hanson.

— Photographer unknown. Yaddo guests, ca. 1926. Black-and-white photograph. 3 1/2 × 5 in. Manuscripts and Archives Division, YR 453.

59 Gustave Lorey. Group photograph, 1934. Black-and-white photograph. 8 × 10 in. Manuscripts and Archives Division, YR 457.

60 Photographer unknown. Group photograph, 1928. Black-and-white photograph. 8 × 10 in. Manuscripts and Archives Division, YR 456.

61 Truman Capote. *Other Voices, Other Rooms*, inscribed to Elizabeth Ames. Back cover of book jacket. New York: Random House, 1948. Corporation of Yaddo. "Book cover," copyright 1948. Used by permission of Random House.

— Ellen Lanyon. *Yaddo 1976*. Color photograph in mat with pen-and-ink drawing. 5 3/8 × 7 5/16 in. Corporation of Yaddo. Photographer unknown.

64 The Rose Garden today. © 2008 Brian Vanden Brink.

67 Archway and artists' studios today. © 2008 Brian Vanden Brink.

68–69 Clyfford Still. Letter to Elizabeth Ames, September 17, 1934. Manuscripts and Archives Division, YR 289.

70 Clyfford Still. *Untitled*, 1945. Oil on canvas. 42 1/8 × 33 1/8 in. Accession number 69.3. Courtesy Whitney Museum of American Art. © Estate of Clyfford Still.

71 Adolf Dehn. *Lunch at Yaddo*, 1955. Watercolor and ink on paper. 13 1/2 × 21 in. Corporation of Yaddo.

— Yaddo's dining table. © 2008 Brian Vanden Brink, *Architectural Digest*, © Condé Nast.

72–73 Tobias Schneebaum. Illustrations for Vance Nye Bourjaily, *The Girl in the Abstract Bed*. New York: Tiber Press, 1954. Numbered edition, 219/2000. Corporation of Yaddo.

74 Antonio Frasconi. Birth announcement, 1952. Woodcut. 18 ½ × 9 ½ in. Miriam and Ira D. Wallach Division of Art, Prints and Photographs. Art © Antonio Frasconi/Licensed by VAGA, New York, N.Y.

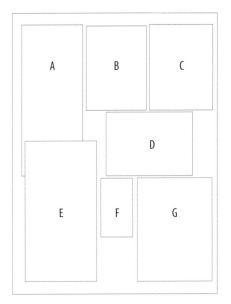

76–77 a. Rosemarie Beck. Holiday card (Yellow angel and pink musician), ca. 1950. Tempura on cardstock. 7 ¹³/₁₆ × 3 ¼ in. Gift of Pauline Hanson to The Corporation of Yaddo. Courtesy of the Rosemarie Beck Foundation.
b. Patricia Mangione. Dancing Star '74, 1974. Inscribed in ink "For Polly, with our warmest holiday wishes, love, Pat and Jerre." 8 ⅜ × 6 ⅛ in. Gift of Pauline Hanson to The Corporation of Yaddo.
c. Louis Hechenbleikner. Mother and child, 1941. Black-and-white engraving. 7 ¼ × 5 ⅝ in. Corporation of Yaddo.
d. George Biddle. "Chiapas." Black-and-white reproduction, signed and dated in ink, "George Biddle, III/19/62, Chiapas." 5 × 7 in. Gift of Pauline Hanson to The Corporation of Yaddo.
e. Rosemarie Beck. Holiday card (Angel Noel), ca. 1950. Tempura on cardstock. 7 ¼ × 3 ⅞ in. Gift of Pauline Hanson to The Corporation of Yaddo. Courtesy of the Rosemarie Beck Foundation.
f. Milton Avery. Holiday card (Dove and stars), 1957. Black-and-white reproduction. 6 × 4 in. Gift of Pauline Hanson to The Corporation of Yaddo. © 2008 Milton Avery Trust/Artists Rights Society (ARS), New York, N.Y.
g. Langston Hughes. "Christmas Cards," poem printed on card, sent to John and Caroline Slade, December 18, 1942. Inscribed in ink, "Happy Holidays to you!" and signed in ink, "Langston." 6 ⅛ × 4 ⅝ in. Gift of Michael and Bea Sweeney to The Corporation of Yaddo. Reprinted by permission of Harold Ober Associates, Inc.

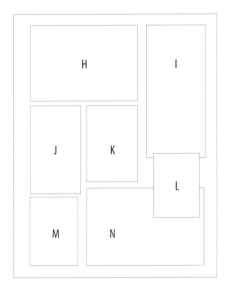

h. Milton Avery. Holiday card (Yaddo pool players), ca. 1950. Black-and-white reproduction. 4 ⁵/₁₆ × 6 ³/₁₆ in. Gift of Pauline Hanson to The Corporation of Yaddo. © 2008 Milton Avery Trust/Artists Rights Society (ARS), New York, N.Y.
i. Louis Hechenbleikner, Holiday card (mechanical man walking mechanical dog), ca. 1950. Color lithograph. 8 ¼ × 4 in. Gift of Pauline Hanson to The Corporation of Yaddo.
j. Hyde Solomon. Holiday card, ca. 1950. Watercolor on paper, inscribed on verso, "To Polly, A Merry Christmas and a happy new year and many thanks, Hyde." 6 × 3 ½ in. Gift of Pauline Hanson to The Corporation of Yaddo.
k. Minna Citron. Holiday greeting, ca. 1950. "Etching" noted in pencil on lower left, signed lower right, inscribed at bottom of sheet, "Xmas Greetings to you Polly and all of Yaddo." 9 ½ × 6 ⁹/₁₆ in. Gift of Pauline Hanson to The Corporation of Yaddo. Art © Estate of Minna Citron/Licensed by VAGA, New York, N.Y./ Estate represented by the Susan Teller Gallery, New York, N.Y.
l. Antonio Frasconi. "An Old Czech Carol with Woodcuts by Antonio Frasconi," ca. 1950. 18-page holiday booklet. 5 ¼ × 4 in. closed. Corporation of Yaddo. Art © Antonio Frasconi/Licensed by VAGA, New York, N.Y.
m. Vincent Longo. Blue geometric image, ca. 1950. 5 ⅞ × 3 ⅝ in. Gift of Pauline Hanson to The Corporation of Yaddo.
n. Nell Blaine. Merry Christmas (garden scene), 1957. Signed in ink "from Nellie" watercolor and ink on paper, 5 ½ × 8 ½ in. closed. Gift of Pauline Hanson to The Corporation of Yaddo.

79 Photographer unknown. Group photograph, 1943. Black-and-white photograph. 8 × 10 in. Manuscripts and Archives Division, YR 457.

80 Agnes Smedley. Letter to Elizabeth Ames, June 26, 1943. Manuscripts and Archives Division, YR 286. Reproduced by permission of Pollinger Limited and the Estate of Agnes Smedley.

81   Agnes Smedley. *Battle Hymn of China*. Book jacket, artwork by Jean Carlu. New York: Knopf, 1943. Collection of the editor. "Book cover," copyright 1943 and renewed 1971. Used by permission of Alfred A. Knopf, a division of Random House, Inc.

84   Elizabeth Ames. Appointment book, detail of entry for March 9, 1948. Manuscripts and Archives Division, YR 381.

85   Agnes Smedley. Letter to Elizabeth Ames, n.d., probably March 9, 1948. Manuscripts and Archives Division, YR 385. Reproduced by permission of Pollinger Limited and the Estate of Agnes Smedley.

86   Corporation of Yaddo. Transcript of a Special Meeting of the Yaddo Board of Directors, February 26, 1949, page 15 of 75. Manuscripts and Archives Division, YR 385.

—   Robert Lowell, Elizabeth Hardwick, Edward Maisel, and Flannery O'Connor. Statement to the Yaddo Board of Directors for use at their March 26, 1949, meeting. Manuscripts and Archives Division, YR 385.

88–89   Corporation of Yaddo. List of "Communists at Yaddo," 1949, 2 pages. Manuscripts and Archives Division, YR 385.

90   Harvey Breit, John Cheever, Eleanor Clark, Alfred Kazin, and Kappo Phelan. Statement to the Board of Directors of Yaddo in support of Elizabeth Ames, March 21, 1949, 2 pages. Manuscripts and Archives Division, YR 385.

91   Carson McCullers. Letter to Elizabeth Ames, 1949, page 1 of 2. Manuscripts and Archives Division, YR 385. Reproduced by permission of Pollinger Limited and the Estate of Carson McCullers.

—   John Cheever. Letter to Elizabeth Ames, 1949. Manuscripts and Archives Division, YR 385. Reproduced courtesy of the Wylie Agency, Inc.

92   Malcolm Cowley. Letter to Elizabeth Ames, March 14, 1948. Manuscripts and Archives Division, YR 385. © Estate of Malcolm Cowley.

—   Dwight Macdonald. Letter to Elizabeth Ames, March 3, 1949. Manuscripts and Archives Division, YR 385. © Yale University.

93   Elizabeth Ames. Appointment book, detail of entries for March 27–28, 1949, with news clippings. Manuscripts and Archives Division, YR 381.

95   Adolf Dehn. *Applause*, 1928. Lithograph, signed lower right, titled at center, numbered 13/30 lower left. 15 × 11 in. Miriam and Ira D. Wallach Division of Art, Prints and Photographs. © and reproduced courtesy of Virginia E. Dehn Living Trust.

96   James T. Farrell. *The Young Manhood of Studs Lonigan*, inscribed to Elizabeth Ames. New York: Vanguard Press, 1934. Corporation of Yaddo.

97   Henry Roth. *Call It Sleep*. New York: R. O. Ballou, 1934. Book jacket, artwork by Stuyvesant Van Veen. Dorot Jewish Division.

—   Henry Roth. Letter to Elizabeth Ames, March 31, 1933. Manuscripts and Archives Division, YR 376. Permission granted by Lawrence I. Fox, trustee of the Henry Roth Literary Properties Trust.

98   William Carlos Williams. Title page of manuscript for *Paterson*, book 2, 1948. Yale Collection of American Literature, Beinecke Rare Book and Manuscript Library: Za Williams 185. © 2008 by the Estates of Paul H. Williams and William Eric Williams. Used by permission of New Directions Publishing Corporation.

99   William Carlos Williams. Letter to Elizabeth Ames, October 24, 1951. Manuscripts and Archives Division, YR 271. © 2008 by the Estates of Paul H. Williams and William Eric Williams. Used by permission of New Directions Publishing Corporation.

—   Photographer unknown. Group photograph, 1953. Black-and-white photograph. 8 × 10 in. Manuscripts and Archives Division, YR 457.

100   Guy Endore. *The Werewolf of Paris*. Book jacket. New York: Farrar & Rinehart, 1933. Manuscripts and Archives Division, YR 210.

101   Guy Endore. Letter to Elizabeth Ames, June 6, 1934. Manuscripts and Archives Division, YR 210. Courtesy of Marcia Endore Goodman.

103   Nan Lurie. *Art Colony Preview*. Lithograph, n.d., signed lower right, titled

lower center. 16 × 23 in. Miriam and Ira D. Wallach Division of Art, Prints and Photographs.

104 Philip Roth. *Portnoy's Complaint*, inscribed for the Yaddo Library. New York: Random House, 1969. Corporation of Yaddo.

109 James Baldwin. *Go Tell It on the Mountain*, inscribed to Elizabeth Ames. New York: Knopf, 1953. Corporation of Yaddo.

110–111 Mario Puzo. Yaddo application, August 23, 1957, 2 pages. Manuscripts and Archives Division, YR 277. Reproduced by permission of Donadio & Olson, Inc.

112 Charles Glicksberg. Letter to Yaddo Admissions Committee, September 5, 1957. Manuscripts and Archives Division, YR 277.

113 Corporation of Yaddo. Admissions Committee Notes, September 16, 1957. Manuscripts and Archives Division, YR 277.

114 Mario Puzo. Yaddo application, 1966, page 1 of 2. Manuscripts and Archives Division, YR 277. Reproduced by permission of Donadio & Olson, Inc.

115 Mario Puzo. Letter to Elizabeth Ames, 1966. Manuscripts and Archives Division, YR 277. Reproduced by permission of Donadio & Olson, Inc.

117 Patricia Highsmith. *Strangers on a Train*, autographed author's copy. New York: Harper & Brothers, 1950. Corporation of Yaddo.

118 Mansion staircase with stained-glass window today. © 2008 Brian Vanden Brink.

119 Spencer Trask. Children, donkey, and pony: Acosta Nichols on bicycle leaning on Christina Trask, 1887. Black-and-white contact print from glass negative number 352. 5 × 7 in. Manuscripts and Archives Division, YR 520, restricted.

— Spencer Trask. Tennis on the lawn, 1884. Black-and-white photograph in album. 5 × 7 in. Manuscripts and Archives Division, YR, vol. 19.

— Photographer unknown. Portrait of the Trask Family, ca. 1886. Black-and-white photograph. 3 ½ × 2 ¾ in. Manuscripts and Archives Division, YR 457.

120 Spencer Trask. Mansion at Yaddo, 1887. Black-and-white photograph. 5 × 7 in. Manuscripts and Archives Division, YR, vol. 20.

— Photographer unknown. Ruins of the first Yaddo mansion, 1891. Black-and-white photograph in album. 5 × 7 in. Manuscripts and Archives Division, YR, vol. 18.

121 Mansion fireplace mantel today. © 2008 Brian Vanden Brink, *Architectural Digest*, © Condé Nast.

122 Spencer Trask. Letter to the Trustees of Pine Garde, February 1900, page 1 of 11. Manuscripts and Archives Division, YR 197.

123 Eastman Johnson. *Portrait of Katrina Trask*, 1887. Oil on canvas. 91 ½ × 65 ¼ in. Corporation of Yaddo. Photograph by Emma Dodge Hanson.

— Spencer Trask. Eastman Johnson making a study for portrait of Katrina, 1887. Black-and-white photograph. 5 × 7 in. Manuscripts and Archives Division, YR, vol. 18.

124 The Yaddo mansion today. © 2008 Brian Vanden Brink.

125 Photographer unknown. Still from performance of *Twelfth Night: Yaddo: Arrival of the Hostess*, 1899. Black-and-white photograph. 7 ¼ × 9 ¼ in. Corporation of Yaddo.

126 Louis Lozowick. *Farm House* (thought to be North Farm at Yaddo), ca. 1929. Lithograph. 11 ½ × 15 ¾ in. Corporation of Yaddo.

127 Philip Reisman. *The Meeting*, 1930. Etching, signed, titled, and numbered 31/100 in pencil on lower edge. 6 × 7 ⅞ in. Miriam and Ira D. Wallach Division of Art, Prints and Photographs. © and reproduced courtesy of the Estate of Louise K. Reisman.

— Photographer unknown. Group photograph, 1931. Black-and-white photograph. 5 × 7 in. Corporation of Yaddo.

— Photographer unknown. Philip Reisman, Marya Zaturenska, Horace Gregory, Patricia Shannon, and Penina Kishore, 1933. Black-and-white photograph on album sheet. 3 ½ × 2 ¾ in. Corporation of Yaddo. © and reproduced courtesy of the Estate of Louise K. Reisman.

128 Photographer unknown. Jean Liberté at easel, 1933. Black-and-white photograph.

3 ½ × 5 in. Manuscripts and Archives Division, YR 453. © and reproduced courtesy of the Estate of Louise K. Reisman.

— Photographer unknown. Group photograph with Rose Garden pergola in background, 1933. Black-and-white photograph. 3 ½ × 5 in. Manuscripts and Archives Division, YR 457.

— Gustave Lorey. Group photograph, 1933. Black-and-white photograph. 8 × 10 in. Manuscripts and Archives Division, YR 456.

129 H. B. Settle. Group photograph, 1938. Black-and-white photograph. 8 × 10 in. Manuscripts and Archives Division, YR 457.

130 Photographer unknown. Group photograph, 1942. Black-and-white photograph. 8 × 10 in. Manuscripts and Archives Division, YR 457.

131 Photographer unknown. Group photograph, 1947. Black-and-white photograph. 8 × 10 in. Manuscripts and Archives Division, YR 457.

— Photographer unknown. Group photograph, 1947. Black-and-white photograph. 8 × 10 in. Manuscripts and Archives Division, YR 457.

— Photographer unknown. Group photograph, 1953. Black-and-white photograph. 8 × 10 in. Manuscripts and Archives Division, YR 458.

132 Photographer unknown. Group photograph, 1954. Black-and-white photograph. 8 × 10 in. Manuscripts and Archives Division, YR 458.

— Photographer unknown. Group photograph, 1958. Black-and-white photograph. 8 × 10 in. Manuscripts and Archives Division, YR 458.

— Charles H. Hutchins. Group photograph, 1960. Black-and-white photograph. 8 × 10 in. Manuscripts and Archives Division, YR 458.

133 Photographer unknown. Group photograph, 1968. Black-and-white photograph. 8 × 10 in. Corporation of Yaddo.

— George Bolster. Group photograph, 1969. Black-and-white photograph. 8 × 10 in. Corporation of Yaddo.

134 Photographer unknown. Group photograph, 1973. Black-and-white photograph. 8 × 10 in. Corporation of Yaddo.

— Photographer unknown. Group photograph, 1975. Color photograph. 8 × 10 in. Corporation of Yaddo.

135 Artist studio today. © 2008 Brian Vanden Brink.

137 Louis Comfort Tiffany. *View of the Vermont Green Mountains Through the Yaddo Rose Garden Pergola*, ca. 1900. Stained-glass window. 43 ¾ × 33 ⅝ in. Corporation of Yaddo. Photograph by Emma Dodge Hanson.

Index